Bahá'í Children's Classes
and Retreats: Theme #3

The Báb:
Gate to Bahá'u'lláh

Dr. Randie S. Gottlieb

Published by
UnityWorks LLC

The Báb: Gate to Bahá'u'lláh
Teacher's Guide with Lesson Plans for Ages 8-12

ISBN 978-0-9828979-3-5

© 2011 UnityWorks LLC. Second printing 2012.

All rights reserved. No part of this book may be reproduced or transmitted in any form or by any means without prior written permission from the publisher.

UnityWorks hereby grants permission for one children's class teacher or Bahá'í school to copy student handouts as needed. Handouts are also available for downloading from: www.UnityWorksStore.com.

The small fee charged for our materials helps to cover printing costs, the development of new products, and the maintenance of our website to make these resources more widely available. If you find these items useful, please let others know about them. Thank you!

Available from: www.UnityWorksStore.com

Quotations from the Bahá'í writings reprinted with permission of the National Spiritual Assembly of the Bahá'ís of the United States and the Bahá'í Publishing Trust of Wilmette, IL.

Special thanks to my husband, Steven E. Gottlieb, M.D. for his support and editorial assistance.

Appreciation to Jordan Gottlieb for assistance with the cover design and pre-press work.

Cover illustration, Kamal Siegel

Clip art images taken or adapted from:
The Big Box of Art from www.Hemera.com

All websites and references listed are correct at the time of publication.

Published by UnityWorks, LLC
www.UnityWorksStore.com
Yakima, Washington, USA

Dedicated to Shahnaz Samandari

*fearless teacher of the Bahá'í Faith,
and to her parents,
Mr. Abulfath and Mrs. Bulgais Samandari,
whose ancestors embraced the Báb,
and who suffered much in service
to the Cause of God.*

The Báb: Gate to Bahá'u'lláh

TABLE OF CONTENTS

Introduction 1
Overview 2
To the Organizers 4
    Teachers 4
    Special Role of Youth 4
    Schedule 5
    Handouts 5
    Sample Retreat Flyer with Registration Form 6
    Sample Retreat Schedules 7
To the Teacher 10
Opening Activities and Orientation Program 13

LESSONS
    1. His Birth, Early Life and Station 17
    2. Declaration of the Báb 31
    3. Martyrdom of the Báb 53
    4. The Primal Point 69

Additional Activities 89
Children's Performance 119
Handouts 147
    Song Sheet 149
    Quotations 151
    Stories from the Life of the Báb 153
    Coloring Pages 169
Music 179
Closing Activities and Follow-up 193
References for Teachers 197
Bibliography 217
Works by the Same Author 221
List of Activities by Chapter 225
Index of Activities by Category 227

The Báb: Gate to Bahá'u'lláh

INTRODUCTION

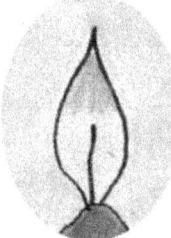

Bahá'u'lláh has prescribed unto all people, "that which will lead to the exaltation of the Word of God amongst His servants, and likewise, to the advancement of the world of being." "To this end," He states, "the greatest means is education of the child."[1]

"My highest wish and desire," proclaims 'Abdu'l-Bahá, "is that ye who are my children may be educated according to the teachings of Bahá'u'lláh...that ye may each become a lighted candle in the world of humanity."[2] He adds that we should "let them make the greatest progress in the shortest span of time."[3]

The Universal House of Justice has likewise called upon us to involve Bahá'í children in "programmes of activity that will engage their interests [and] mold their capacities for teaching and service."[4]

The International Teaching Centre has affirmed that "these young people should then be seen as a door to entry by troops and as a fruitful source of teachers...not simply as children for whom activity must be arranged...but as a living creation of God necessary at this very moment for the purposes of God..."[5]

The purpose of these classes, then, is to systematically familiarize children with the fundamental truths of the Bahá'í Revelation, and to increase their desire and capacity to teach and serve. Additional goals are to strengthen bonds of friendship, and to provide an enjoyable Bahá'í activity which children will enthusiastically look forward to and invite their friends. In the words of some of the adult and youth volunteers:

"Thank you for this amazing and transforming experience! Your curriculum is brilliant!" (Chris Bily)

"I loved every minute! Makes me wish I was still young enough to attend." (Safa Lohrasbi)

"I am amazed and impressed with the quality and quantity of Bahá'í education you provided in such a short time! – and the children got it!" (Anna Fulton)

"I learned a lot about myself and discovered how to help kids learn and grow, and ways to make their experience happy." (Brynne Haug)

References

1. Bahá'í Education: A Compilation, p. 4
2. Selections from the Writings of 'Abdu'l-Bahá, p. 141
3. Bahá'í Education: A Compilation, p. 71
4. Ridván 2000 Message
5. To the Boards of Counselors, 5 Dec. 1988

The Báb: Gate to Bahá'u'lláh

OVERVIEW

TEACHER'S GUIDES FOR CHILDREN'S CLASSES

It is hoped that this easy-to-use teacher's guide, the third in a series for the Bahá'í education of children, will be a useful resource for Bahá'í summer and winter schools, Holy Day programs and weekend retreats. It might also be included in a parent's toolkit for home schooling, or form part of the religious curriculum for a full-time Baha'i-inspired academic school—such as the one our family established in Puerto Rico where many of these lessons were developed.

Anticipating future needs, with a few minor modifications, some of the theme books might also be appropriate for upper elementary public school classrooms. "The Manifestation of God," for example, would be well-suited for a class on comparative religion, and "The Power of Unity," could offer a valuable contribution to a unit on diversity and the oneness of humankind.

Each book is filled with fun, hands-on, kid-tested learning activities designed for ages 8-12. These activities were developed and tested in the field, in response to the needs of teachers and children, and have been used successfully in multiple settings over many years.

The lessons incorporate a variety of instructional strategies as recommended in the Bahá'í Writings on education, such as learning through play, questioning, memorization, consultation, reflection, stories, speeches, music, arts and crafts, science, independent investigation, lectures, group discussion, plays and recreational activities.

When used as part of an intensive program, such as a summer school or weekend retreat, the teacher will need to select activities to fit within the time allotted. If the lessons are part of an ongoing program such as a daily or weekly academic class, one or more activities can be selected for each session, until the entire course has been completed. Utilized in this way, there is sufficient material in each book for several months of weekly classes.

The lessons are user-friendly and ready-to-go with very little outside preparation needed by the teacher. Essentially everything is included, with the exception of craft supplies and common household items. Each book has a sample retreat schedule, detailed lesson plans, instructions and patterns for making classroom materials, copy-ready student handouts, song sheets, music, and plans for a children's performance. When optional materials are recommended (e.g., photographs or videos), the sources are given.

The Báb: Gate to Bahá'u'lláh

Each teacher's guide focuses on a distinct theme, with all of the lessons, songs, crafts and other learning activities integrated around that theme. The series includes:

(1) GOD AND THE UNIVERSE
- The Kingdoms of Creation
- God, the Creator
- Prayer, Our Connection with God
- What Is a Human Being?

(2) THE MANIFESTATION
- Station of the Manifestation
- Introduction to the Prophets
- Progressive Revelation
- One Common Faith

(3) THE BÁB: GATE TO BAHÁ'U'LLÁH
- His Birth and Early Life
- Declaration of the Báb
- Martyrdom of the Báb
- The Primal Point

(4) BAHÁ'U'LLÁH: THE GLORY OF GOD
- His Birth, Early Life and Station
- Declaration of Bahá'u'lláh
- Exiles and Imprisonment
- Clouds of Glory

(5) THE POWER OF UNITY
- The Power of Unity
- Unity in Diversity
- The Colors We Are
- Overcoming Prejudice

Additional theme books are being prepared on 'Abdu'l-Bahá, Bahá'í Principles, Bahá'í Laws and Institutions, Consultation for Kids, and The Bahá'í Community.

CHILDREN'S RETREAT PLANNING GUIDE

These theme books can be used in conjunction with the *Bahá'í Children's Retreat Planning Guide,* which is available from **www.UnityWorksStore.com**. It covers the following topics:

- ❏ Scheduling
- ❏ Sponsorship
- ❏ Participants
- ❏ Teachers
- ❏ Other volunteers
- ❏ Facility
- ❏ Publicity
- ❏ Finances
- ❏ Pre-registration
- ❏ Materials
- ❏ Site preparation
- ❏ Sample schedule
- ❏ On-site registration
- ❏ Orientation
- ❏ Outdoor activities
- ❏ Children's performance
- ❏ Closing activities
- ❏ Food, forms, signs

The Báb: Gate to Bahá'u'lláh

TO THE ORGANIZERS

Teachers

This teacher's guide includes four lessons on *The Báb: Gate to Bahá'u'lláh*. One individual could teach all four lessons; the classes can be team-taught; or a different person might be asked to lead each class.

Special Role of Youth

Capable youth and junior youth can be invited to assist with the classes and activities. We have found that many former participants are eager to return to the children's retreats as volunteers. Inspired by this experience, a high percentage of them have gone on to complete junior youth animator training, and several have arisen to organize children's classes or junior youth groups in their own neighborhoods.

The participation of youth volunteers at the retreat is also a great help for the adults and a joy for the younger children, while offering the youth an opportunity to apply their institute training and to acquire new skills. The youth are given guided experience and hands-on teaching practice. They return home with new confidence, encouraged and motivated to support local children's classes. In addition, a wonderful community atmosphere is created with all age groups working together to educate the children.

In the words of one youth:

> *"The retreats have been an integral part of my growing up experience, and I'm so grateful for the opportunity to come and help out now as a youth. It's really special to see my brothers and cousins and their friends, and know that they'll grow up with the same wonderful friendships and learning experiences and shared memories that my generation of youth gained.*
>
> *"I learned a lot about myself and discovered how to help kids learn and grow, and ways to make their experience happy. Although I went through all the same lessons myself, it's still great to hear and see the lessons again. Us kids have so much fun every time and I am always looking forward to the next retreat."* (Brynne Haug, age 16)

Youth volunteers: Kierra, Yuri, Alonso, Layli, Alex, Brynne, Carew

Schedule

If planning a weekend retreat, the lessons can be scheduled over a two-day or a three-day period. Sample schedules for both are included below. The two-day schedule offers participants a choice of some of the crafts and activities. The three-day schedule includes more of the crafts and classroom activities, additional time for memorization practice, an evening talent show, and a group consultation on how to share with others the concepts learned at the retreat. For an ongoing class, all of the activities can be included.

Handouts

Some handouts are included with the lessons, while others have been grouped near the end of this book for convenience in photocopying. They can also be downloaded from: **www.UnityWorksStore.com** (click on Children's Classes > The Báb > student handouts). The handouts can be copied one at a time as needed for a particular class, or all at once as part of the handout packet for a summer school or weekend retreat.

The **Schedule, Songs** and **Quotations** should be photocopied for all participants and included in their folders during registration. If each item is copied on paper of a different color, it will be easier for the children to find. The songs and quotations should each be copied on two sides of the page to save paper and for ease of use.

The 16-page packet on *Stories from the Life of the Báb* (from the title sheet through the quiz and references) should be copied back-to-back on white paper, stapled together and included in the folders. This packet will be used in various lessons.

Each instructor should be given **To the Teacher** (pages 10-12), a copy of the appropriate lesson plan, and **References for Teachers** (found at the end of this book), along with the handouts mentioned above. Teachers should also make copies of any additional handouts needed for their specific lessons.

The coordinator of the children's performance will need copies of the entire **Children's Performance** section (pages 119-145), in addition to the schedule, song sheet, page of quotations, and the "Stories from the Life of the Báb" handout packet.

The song leader will need **To the Music Coordinator** and sheet music for each song, found in the section on music (pages 179-184).

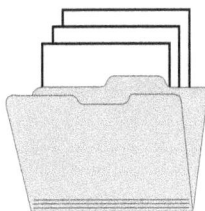

The Báb: Gate to Bahá'u'lláh

— Sample Flyer —

BAHÁ'Í CHILDREN'S RETREAT #3
Sponsored by the Bahá'ís of Our Town

KIDS: AGES 8–12

Join us for a fun weekend of Bahá'í classes, prayers, singing, arts & crafts, archery, games, storytelling, tasty food & more!

THEME: The Báb: Gate to Bahá'u'lláh

October 7-9
Noorani Home, 1919 Unity Lane
Our Town, WA 98765 - (919) 765-4321

COST: $35 per child or $30 if paid before September 7. Additional children from same family, $20 each. Scholarships available. Make checks payable to: Bahá'ís of Our Town. Space is limited, apply now!

Participants should bring: sleeping bag, pillow, towel, toothbrush and paste, comb, any medicines with clear instructions, bathing suit, sturdy shoes, pajamas and change of clothes.
Please do NOT bring: electronic games, radios, CDs, iPods, etc.

Starts Friday at 5:30 p.m. with registration and dinner. Ends at 2:00 p.m. on Sunday

··

BAHÁ'Í CHILDREN'S RETREAT

Mail this form to: Lua Smith, 1863 Ridván Lane, Our Town, WA 98765
Email: lsmith@gmail.com - Tel: (919) 123-4567

Child's name (print): _____ Age: _____ Sex: _____

Address: _____ Phone: _____

Email: _____ Fee enclosed: $ _____ Partial scholarship requested: $_____

Emergency contact: _____ Phone: _____

Medical or dietary information: _____

The child named above has my permission to attend the Bahá'í Children's Retreat on Oct. 7-9, 2011, at the Noorani home in Our Town. I understand that s/he is participating at her/his own risk. If necessary, I hereby give the event organizers permission to administer first aid and obtain emergency medical treatment.

_____ _____ _____
Parent or Guardian (print name)   Signature   Date

— Sample **2-Day** Schedule —

 Bahá'í Children's Retreat

Noorani home, Our Town, October 7-9, 2011

"The Báb: Gate to Bahá'u'lláh"

FRIDAY
5:30 pm	Registration, decorate folders
6:00	Dinner
7:30	Prayers, singing, orientation
8:00	**Orientation program**
9:00	Volunteer briefing
9:30	Group song, prayers and bedtime
10:00	Lights out

SATURDAY
7:30 am	Morning prayers
8:00	Breakfast
8:30	Singing
8:45	**Class #1: The Báb: His Birth, Early Life and Station** (90 min.)
10:15	Break
10:45	**Class #2: Declaration of the Báb** (90 min.)
12:15 pm	Lunch and quiet time
1:30	**Class #3: Martyrdom of the Báb** (90 min.)
3:00	Snack and outdoor activities (including treasure hunt)
4:30	Rehearsal for children's performance
6:00	Dinner
7:00	Prepare refreshments, rehearse songs
8:00	**Children's performance**
9:15	Refreshments and socializing
10:00	Group song, prayers and bedtime
10:30	Lights out

SUNDAY
8:00 am	Morning prayers
8:30	Breakfast
9:00	Singing
9:15	**Class #4: The Primal Point** (90 min.)
10:45	Outdoor activities
12:00 pm	Lunch
12:30	Clean-up
1:00	Closing activities, evaluation, graduation
1:30	Group photo
1:45	Dessert
2:00	Check lost-and-found; farewells

– Sample **3-Day** Schedule –

 Bahá'í Children's Retreat

Noorani home, Our Town, October 7-10, 2011

"The Báb: Gate to Bahá'u'lláh"

FRIDAY

5:30 pm	Registration, decorate folders
6:00	Dinner
7:30	Prayers, singing, orientation
8:00	**Orientation program**
9:00	Volunteer briefing
9:30	Group song, prayers and bedtime
10:00	Lights out

SATURDAY

7:30 am	Morning prayers
8:00	Breakfast
8:30	Singing
8:45	**Class #1: His Birth, Early Life and Station** (90 min.)
10:15	Break
10:45	**Class #2: Declaration of the Báb** (90 min.)
12:15 pm	Lunch and quiet time
1:30	Craft activities
3:00	Snack and outdoor activities (including treasure hunt)
4:30	Memorization practice (alone, pairs or groups)
5:15	Group singing practice or free time
6:00	Dinner
7:30	Singing and share memorized quotes
8:15	Evening snack
8:30	Evening program (Bahá'í video, talent show, etc.)
9:30	Group song, prayers and bedtime
10:00	Lights out

SUNDAY

8:00 am	Morning prayers
8:30	Breakfast
9:00	Singing
9:15	**Class #3: Martyrdom of the Báb** (90 min.)
10:45	Outdoor activities
12:00 pm	Lunch and quiet time
1:30	**Class #4: The Primal Point** (90 min.)
3:00	Snack and outdoor activities
4:15	Rehearsal for children's performance
6:00	Dinner

➡

The Báb: Gate to Bahá'u'lláh

— Sample **3-Day** Schedule, continued —

SUNDAY
- 7:00 pm — Prepare refreshments, rehearse songs
- **8:00** — **Children's performance**
- 9:15 — Refreshments and socializing
- 10:00 — Group song, prayers and bedtime
- 10:30 — Lights out

MONDAY
- 8:30 am — Morning prayers
- 9:00 — Breakfast
- 9:30 — Singing
- **9:45** — **Group consultation on how to share what we learned**
- 10:30 — Outdoor activities
- 12:00 pm — Lunch
- 12:30 — Clean-up
- 1:00 — Closing activities, evaluation, graduation
- 1:30 — Group photo
- 1:45 — Dessert
- 2:00 — Check lost-and-found; farewells

Youth volunteer, Layli Gannaway, with Gareth, studying about the life of the Báb.

The Báb: Gate to Bahá'u'lláh

TO THE TEACHER

> "Among the greatest of all services that can possibly be rendered by man to Almighty God is the education and training of children."
>
> 'Abdu'l-Bahá, Selections from the Writings of 'Abdu'l-Bahá, p. 133

Teacher's Guide

The teacher's guide on the following pages contains detailed lesson plans with fun, hands-on, kid-tested learning activities. It includes copy-ready student handouts and simple patterns for making instructional materials. The lessons are user-friendly and ready-to-go with little outside preparation needed by the teacher. They are organized in a sequential, step-by-step format, with each activity building on the previous one. Each lesson can also stand alone. The activities can be used for Bahá'í summer and winter schools, Holy Day programs, cluster gatherings and weekend retreats. They can also form part of the religious curriculum for an academic school.

This teacher's guide begins with an overview of the *Children's Classes and Retreats* series, sample schedules, an orientation program and lesson plans. These are followed by additional activities (a treasure hunt, research projects, puzzles and coloring pages), plans for a children's performance, student handouts, a section on music (with song sheets, musical scores and instructions for group singing), and closing activities with suggestions for follow-up. A comprehensive list of the activities in each lesson, and a separate index of activities by category (music, crafts, stories, etc.), can be found at the end of the book. A compilation of selected passages on the theme of each lesson is included as a reference for teachers. A bibliography completes the manual.

Four Lessons

Each teacher's guide includes four lessons on the chosen theme. The lessons are designed to present basic Bahá'í teachings to children ages 8–12. The suggested time for each activity is in parentheses after the heading. However, if students need additional time to practice a skill, or if the class is engaged in a fruitful discussion and wishes to continue, the time can be extended, and another part of the lesson can be omitted or saved for a future class session. Be flexible.

When the lessons are used as part of an intensive program, such as a summer school or weekend retreat, you will need to select activities to fit within the time allotted. If the lessons are part of an ongoing program such as a daily or weekly academic class, one or more activities can be selected each time, until the entire course has been completed. Utilized in this way, there is sufficient material in the book for several months of weekly classes.

An ongoing class can begin with a welcome for new students, followed by singing, prayers, a review of the previous lesson (including student presentations), and the selected activities. At the beginning of each class, consider scheduling "circle time," to give children an opportunity to share news of interest to the group or to consult on pressing concerns. End the class with a review of the lesson, recitation of any memory quotes, more singing, and refreshments.

Preparing to Teach

In order to present these lessons effectively, you will need to read the lesson plan and become familiar with the objectives and the concepts to be taught. For a deeper understanding of each topic, you can also study the *References for Teachers* found at the end of this book. Your presentation should be practiced until it feels smooth and comfortable.

Explanatory notes to the teacher are not meant to be read as a script, but are intended only as a guide. Key phrases and highlights from these notes can be written on the board before or during the lesson.

All instructional materials should be made or obtained well in advance. Handouts should be photocopied for students and volunteers, and either included in their folders when they arrive, or distributed during each class as needed.

Class Discussions

During class discussions, all students should be encouraged to participate, not just the ones who speak first or loudest. A child who is silent can be asked, "Maria, what do you think about this?" Have students raise their hands rather than shouting out the answer. A simple comment like, "I'm happy to see so many of you raising your hands quietly," will reinforce this rule.

If a student's answer is incorrect, rather than saying, "No, that's wrong," it is better to respond with, "Good try. You're on the right track," or "That's an interesting thought!" Then ask another question or give a small hint that will help the child succeed. Be patient and enthusiastic. Encouragement is generally more motivating than criticism. Do not allow the children to laugh at or tease each other.

With a larger group, you may find it useful to ring a bell or develop a hand signal to bring the children back to order after a discussion or other class activity. Raising your hand while standing quietly in front of the class can be very effective. As soon as one person notices the teacher, that person should stop talking and raise his/her hand. As others notice, they should join in. Teach children the signal, and practice it a few times before starting the discussion.

Volunteers

Youth and adult volunteers can be asked to assist you with learning activities and classroom management. Volunteers can be put in charge of discussion groups. They can help with craft projects, lead the singing, teach one of the classes, work one-on-one with students who need extra assistance, and remove a disruptive child if necessary. Discipline is easier to maintain if volunteers are spaced throughout the room during the lesson.

The Báb: Gate to Bahá'u'lláh

Children's Performance*

This guidebook includes instructions for a children's performance that will give students an opportunity to demonstrate and reinforce what they have learned. Friends, families, neighbors and co-workers can be invited to the show. The fact that children will be performing in front of a live audience serves as excellent motivation for them to learn the material presented in class. The presentation may include prayers, singing, stories, recitation of Bahá'í passages, demonstrations to illustrate various concepts, an exhibition of arts and crafts, a readers' theater and a quiz show.

The children's performance also provides an opportunity for home visits to parents before and after the show, to invite them and to talk in more depth about some of the themes presented.

A detailed agenda and plans for the performance are included in this manual. The children will need time to rehearse. If the program is part of a larger summer school or weekend retreat, the planning committee may schedule rehearsal time and appoint someone to coordinate the program. During class sessions, the teacher should make note of those children who seem to grasp the material well, and who could present it in front of an audience.

> *"It is the hope of 'Abdu'l-Bahá that those youthful souls ...will be tended by one who traineth them to love."*
> 'Abdu'l-Bahá, Selections from the Writings of 'Abdu'l-Bahá, p. 134

* Note: While our student presentations have typically been scheduled for the evening, they could be held at any time. In the two-day weekend retreat format, Saturday evening is often the most convenient time for inviting neighbors and friends. This means that activities from the fourth class on Sunday morning will not be included in the presentation. If the performance follows a three-day retreat schedule or a weekly format, these activities can easily be added to the final show.

The Báb: Gate to Bahá'u'lláh

OPENING ACTIVITIES

If these lessons are being used as part of an intensive program, such as a summer school or weekend retreat, it is usually a good idea to provide some self-directed activities for children during the registration period, while they are waiting for others to arrive. After checking in, they can be shown to a table to decorate their folders or to work on other projects (see theme book #1 on *God and the Universe* for ideas). If desired, a separate table with the appropriate materials can be set up for each station. The instructions should be posted and volunteers can be asked to assist the children. These activities can also be incorporated into an ongoing class.

Orientation Program

The orientation program on the first day is designed to make everyone feel welcome and to help them get to know each other. Explain to the group that we will be learning about **The Báb**, Who was a Manifestation of God and Forerunner to Bahá'u'lláh. We will focus on four main topics:

(1) His Birth, Early Life and Station
(2) Declaration of the Báb
(3) Martyrdom of the Báb
(4) His Important Role in the Faith of God

A sample orientation program is outlined below:

1. Welcome
2. Opening music
3. Selected prayers
4. Letter from the sponsoring institution
5. Introductions ^{A}
6. Orientation ^{B}
7. Review of the schedule
8. Ice-breakers and warm-up activities (see below)
9. Group singing (see song sheet in handout section)

A. <u>Introductions</u>: Each person can be asked to introduce him or herself, sharing their name, town, and one interesting personal fact. As a variation, people can be asked to act out a hobby or favorite activity, without using any words, and the group can guess what it is.

B. <u>Orientation</u>: This should cover information about classes, supervision, the role of volunteers, any house rules, food, safety, recreation and relating to others. See the *Bahá'í Children's Retreats Planning Guide* for details.

After the orientation and review of the schedule, you can organize one or two warm-up activities (see next page) which will serve as ice-breakers and help to introduce the theme. The orientation program can be followed by a snack and a short video (e.g., segments from a recent Bahá'í Newsreel), which can be played for the children during the briefing for volunteers.

The Báb: Gate to Bahá'u'lláh

Warm-up Activities

1. Unity Bingo (20-30 min.)

This is a fun mixer which has become a favorite activity at all our children's retreats. A sample Bingo sheet is included in the *Bahá'í Children's Retreats Planning Guide,* along with a blank form that can be downloaded and customized with your own set of questions (available from: **www. UnityWorksStore.com** > click on Children's Classes).

2. The Light Dance (10-15 min.)

This activity foreshadows the search for the Báb in Lesson #2. The Báb was "hidden" in plain sight, and only those with spiritual eyes were able to recognize Him. His first disciples were instructed not to tell others. People had to find the Báb on their own. In the same way, this game requires each player to discover the "truth" for him or herself. The answer to the riddle becomes obvious once you recognize the secret clue.

Before the game begins, privately share the secret (see box below) with about one third of the participants. Then have everyone (children, youth and adults) sit or stand in a circle. The "first followers" who know the secret should be dispersed throughout the group. Starting with someone who is in on the secret, have participants pass a flashlight from hand-to-hand around the circle.

Tell the group:

There is a trick to doing this correctly. When you discover the secret, don't share it with others. Let them use their powers of observation to discover it on their own. When everyone has learned the secret, the game ends.

<u>Tell the first followers</u>: When you receive the flashlight, pass it back and forth, from your right hand to your left, while chanting the following refrain: *"I can do the light dance, light dance, light dance. I can do the light dance! Can you?"* With the words, *"Can you?"* the flashlight is passed to the next player.

<u>Here is the secret</u>: When it is your turn to speak, **first clear your throat**. The words and the movements only serve to distract the others. After a while, if no one catches on, you should modify the routine, for example, by changing your movements, or speaking more slowly, using a higher voice, or eliminating some or all of the words.

The Báb: Gate to Bahá'u'lláh

"The education and training of children is among the most meritorious acts of humankind."
- 'Abdu'l-Bahá, Selections from the Writings of 'Abdu'l-Bahá, p. 129

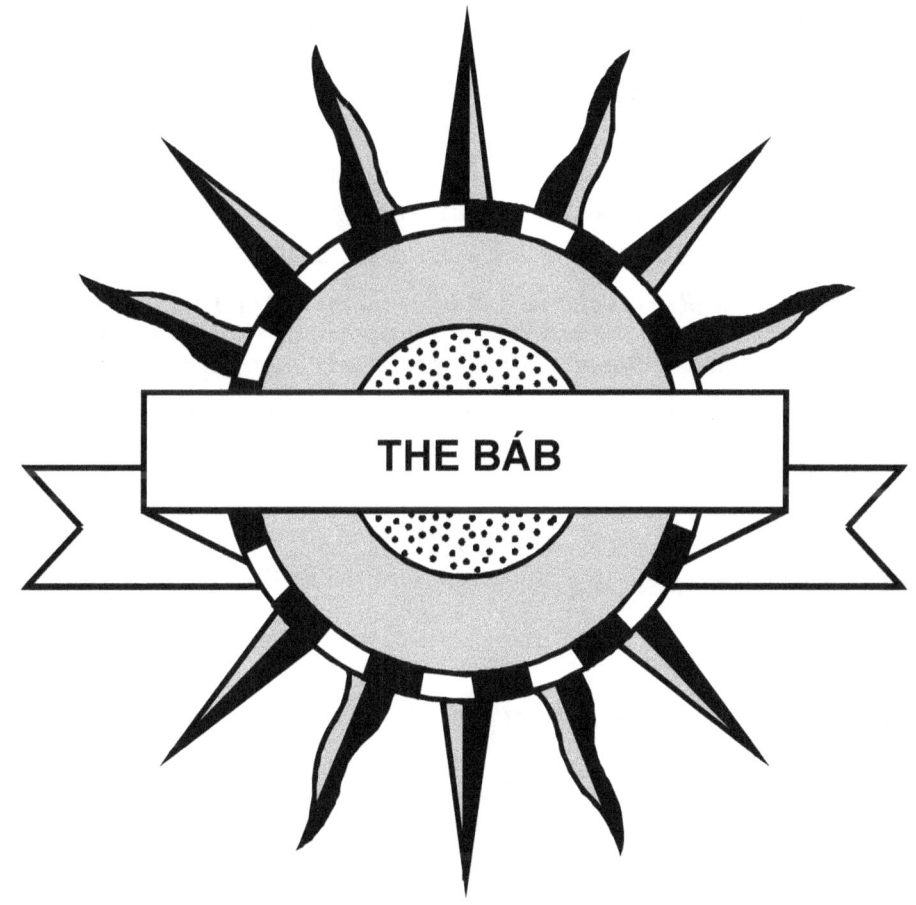

LESSON #1

His Birth, Early Life and Station

The Báb – Lesson #1

His Birth, Early Life and Station

Objectives: Students will be able to:
- Explain that God speaks to humankind through His Manifestations.
- Explain that the Báb was a Manifestation of God and the Forerunner to Bahá'u'lláh.
- Compare the role of a Forerunner to that of a farmer preparing the soil.
- Locate Persia on a map and describe conditions there around the time of the Báb's birth.
- Recount significant stories from the Báb's early life.

Before class, prepare all instructional materials on the list at the end of this lesson. Write memory quote neatly on the board with one phrase on each line. Set up felt board, post wall map and any pictures. Orient volunteer assistants. Distribute folders and pens to all.

---

1. SONG: "O God, My God" (5 min.)

Have students take out their song sheets and sing along. Ask the music coordinator for assistance if needed.

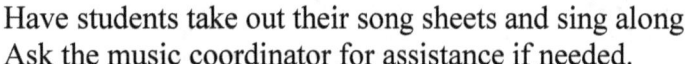

Ask students:

- Who gave us this beautiful prayer? *(The Báb)*
- Does anyone know Who the Báb is?
  (A Manifestation of God and the Forerunner to Bahá'u'lláh)
- Today we're going to learn a little about the life of the Báb.
  It's an amazing story! First let's do a quick review of the kingdoms of creation.

2. REVIEW: "Kingdoms of Creation" (5-10 min.)
(Use felt lesson from previous theme book, *The Manifestation*)

- Ask: Who remembers the four kingdoms of creation?
  (Mineral, plant, animal, human)

- Good. Can you say them in order, starting with the lowest?

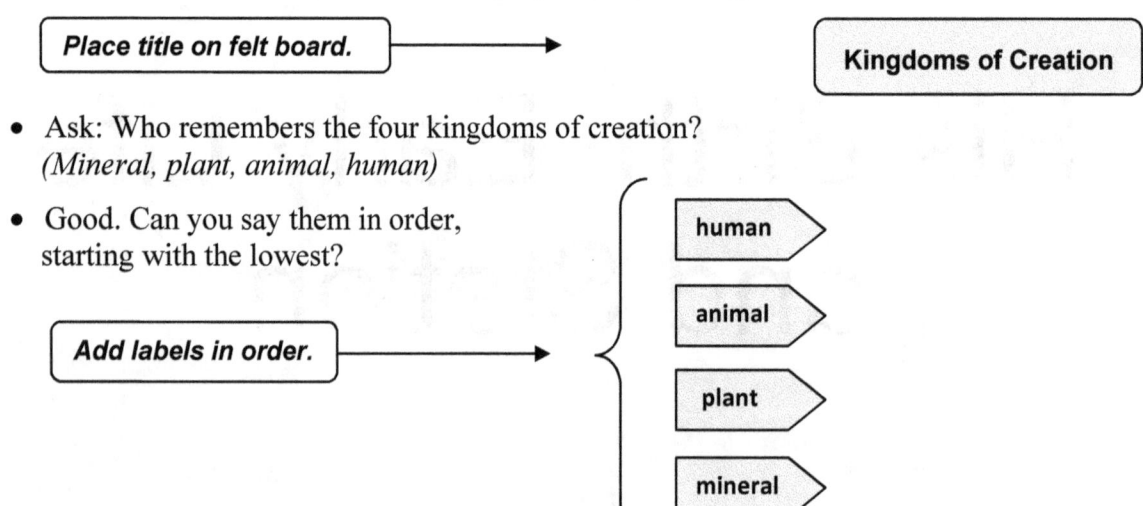

Bahá'í Children's Classes and Retreats: Theme 3, p. 18

The Báb – Lesson #1

- Do you remember the powers of each kingdom?

  > Have a volunteer add each circle as it is mentioned.

  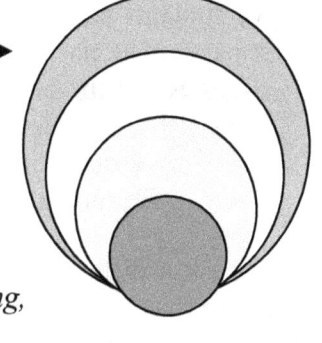

  That's right.
  Minerals have cohesion.
  Plants have cohesion and growth.
  Animals add feelings, senses and movement from place to place.
  Humans add conscious thought, free will to choose right or wrong, and the ability to know and love God.

- Who created all these things? *(God)*

- What do we know about God? *(He is a mystery, unknowable, called by many names.)*

- Why did God create people? *(He loves us and wants us to love Him too.)*

- How can we speak to Him? *(Through our prayers.)*

- How does God speak to us? *(Through His Prophets or Manifestations of God)*

  > Add Prophet circle and label to felt board.

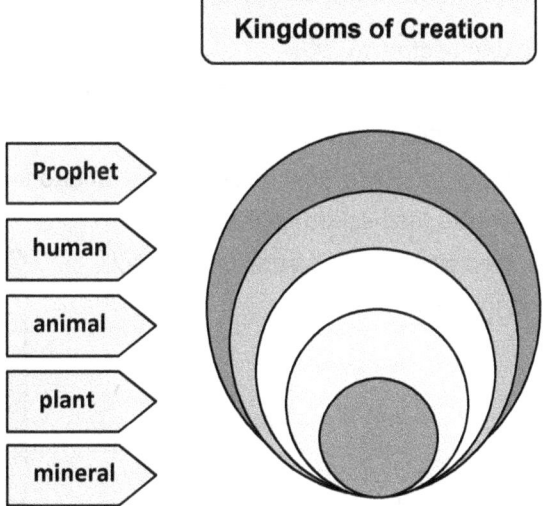

- What powers do the Prophets have?
  (All the powers of the lower kingdoms plus the Holy Spirit; superhuman knowledge; they speak with the Voice of God; they are specially chosen by God to bring us His Word.)

Bahá'í Children's Classes and Retreats: Theme 3, p. 19

The Báb – Lesson #1

3. READING: "Preparing the Soil of the Heart" (10-15 min.)

Have students take out the stapled packet on *Stories from the Life of the Báb,* and turn to the first page. (The packet is in the handouts section of this book, and the first reading is included at the end of this lesson.) Explain that we are going to learn about the life of the Báb, starting with why He was sent by God. Read the first paragraph and make up a question based on what you read, for example, "What do farmers do to prepare the soil so plants can grow?" Call on students to answer.

Then ask a different student, youth or adult volunteer to read each remaining paragraph out loud, to make up a question or two about it, and to call on other children to answer. Choose those with expressive voices who read well, or give brief lines to those who read less fluently. If necessary, encourage them to call on someone who hasn't yet had a chance to respond.

4. DEMONSTRATION: "Preparing the Soil" (10-15 min.)

Display objects for the soil demonstration on a table in front of the class. (See list of materials at the end of this lesson.)

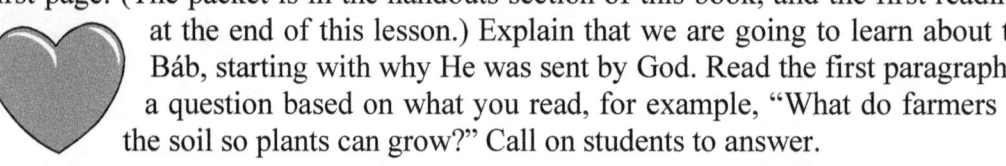

Ask the class:

- Who has planted a garden?

- What are some of the steps?
  (Have children raise their hands to answer, and allow for a variety of responses.)

SOIL DEMONSTRATION

A. Call on two students for the demonstration.
B. Give each one some large seeds and a planter pot or tray filled with hard-packed dirt.
C. Give one of the students some "fertilizer" and a metal fork or sturdy tool to loosen the dirt.
D. Ask that student to "plow" the soil (carefully so it doesn't spill), and to fertilize the ground.
E. Then ask both students to sprinkle their seeds on the dirt.
F. The student with the fork should also mix the seeds into the soil.
G. Then pass both pots around the room.

Ask the class:

- What happens to the seeds if the hard soil is not prepared?
  (They stay on top and won't grow.)

- What do you think will happen when the wind blows?
  (The seeds that stayed on the surface will blow away.)

- What can this teach us about the role of a Forerunner or Herald who prepares us for the next Messenger of God? *(Ask students to think first, then discuss their thoughts with a partner before responding. Encourage a variety of responses.)*

The Báb – Lesson #1

5. READING: "Stories from the Life of the Báb" (45-60 min.)

Explain to the students that they will be working in small groups to learn about the life of the Báb. There are six numbered stories in their packets, starting with #1: "The Promise." Each group will read a different story, then share what they have learned with the entire class. (Point out any pictures on the walls to help illustrate the stories.)

Organizing the Activity

A. First determine how many groups, and thus how many stories, you will need. Groups should have at least two and preferably three people. If there are 18 children, for example, you might form six groups with three children per group. The groups do not need to be exactly even. Some may have five children and some only two, but 3-4 is ideal, as it gives everyone a chance to speak and allows for a variety of opinions. A class with 14 children, for example, might be divided as follows:

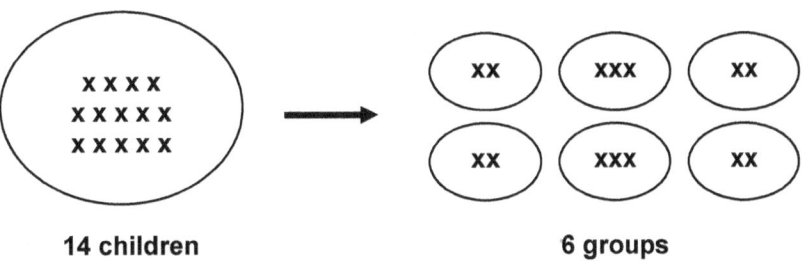

14 children → 6 groups

With fewer children, you will have fewer groups. As a variation, if this lesson is part of an ongoing class, you might select two or three stories each time, or have the entire class read the same story together, choosing a different one each week.

B. Next determine which stories to use and assign each story to a youth or adult volunteer. Give each volunteer a copy of the instruction sheet (included at the end of this lesson).

1. The Promise
2. 19th Century Persia
3. Birth and Early Life
4. School Days
5. An Honest Merchant
6. Wife and Child

C. Then have the volunteers stand in three different corners of the room depending on the reading level of their assigned story.

- Easier (story #2 and #5)
- Medium (story #3 and #4)
- Harder (story #1 and #6)

"Younger children go with Sue or Leon. Those who like to read difficult books, go with Yuri or Farzam. Spanish speakers should go with Carmen."

D. Ask students to choose a story based on their age or reading level. Have them stand with the volunteer in charge of that story. If children need help deciding, use their grade level as a guide. If some students are more comfortable in a different language (e.g., Spanish), you can group them by language if a suitable volunteer is available.

E. Groups can move to another room or outside if desired. Allow them about 15 minutes to work, and walk around to observe their progress.

F. Call the groups back together and ask each one to report, starting with story #1. Students should stand up and speak in a strong, clear voice. This is good practice for the children's performance. Help them stick to the time limit so there will be time for the remaining activities.

Note: When sharing story #3 (Birth and Early Life of the Báb), the children may wish to hear a recording of nightingale songs. For some online samples, visit:

- **www.soundboard.com**/sb/Nightingale_Bird_Sounds.aspx
- **www.youtube.com** – Enter "nightingale sound of nature" in the search box. Click on the first image for 5:27 min. of peaceful music with nature photos.
- **www.youtube.com** – Enter "nightingale paxton" in the search box. Click on the first image for a 1:33 min. close-up video of a nightingale singing.

6. PEER QUESTIONS (15-20 min.)

Who	Where
What	Why
When	How

Say the following words and write them in large print on the board:

Ask students to take out the notebook paper from their folders and write 2-3 questions about the story they just read. The questions should begin with one of the words on the board. For example: "**What** name was the Báb given by his parents?" and "**Why** did the Báb wear a green turban?" Give them a few minutes to work.

When they are finished, proceed around the room, calling on each student to ask one of their questions. Then call on another student to answer it. Have the children raise their hands. Continue with a second round of questions if there is time, and praise students for their efforts.

The Báb – Lesson #1

7. MAP ACTIVITY (10 min.)

A. Have students locate the map near the end of their story packets.

B. On a large wall map, ask different students to point out the country you are in, then the state or province, then the city. (For example: the United States, Washington State, Yakima.)

C. Then on the large map, ask them to point out the country of Iran and the city of Shiraz, where the Báb was born.

D. On their own maps, have them write in "Persia" in the parentheses below "Iran," and print "Shiraz" on line next to the star. Using crayons or colored pencils, they can also color in Iran and the other countries on the map.

8. QUIZ ON THE LIFE OF THE BÁB (20-30 min.)

Have children locate the quiz at the end of their story packets. (A teacher's version with answers is included at the end of this lesson.) Divide the class into the same story groups with the same leaders, and have each group answer the quiz questions together. Allow about 15 minutes to work. Students should know most of the answers from reading the stories. The quiz serves as a review and as preparation for the quiz show during the children's performance.

Call the class back together and ask each quiz question again. Ask the questions quickly and have students raise their hands to answer. Repeat the correct answer to help reinforce learning.

9. MEMORY QUOTE: "Good news!" (10-15 min.)

Ask students to take out their page of quotations and locate quote #16: "GOOD NEWS! GOOD NEWS!" (This quote, which prepares students for the following lesson, should already be written on the board.)

You may wish to have students memorize only a part of this quotation, depending on their ability levels. For example, you might start with the third line, or stop with the word *awake* or *joy*.

See the following pages for ways to help children understand and memorize the quote.

"GOOD NEWS! GOOD NEWS!
The Trumpet is sounding!
...O Ye that sleep, Awake!
...Be Happy! Be full of Joy!

...This is the day of the Proclamation of the Báb!"

'Abdu'l-Bahá

The Báb – Lesson #1

A. **Understanding:** Read the quote aloud slowly, then ask students:

- Who said these words? *('Abdu'l-Bahá, the son of Bahá'u'lláh)*

- What does "proclamation" mean? *(An announcement; an open or public statement. It refers to the time when the Báb told people He was a Manifestation of God.)*

- Why is this good news? Why should we be happy and full of joy?
  (It signals the coming of God's Messenger with a new Revelation.)

- What is the meaning of the passage, "O Ye that sleep, Awake?"
  (Wake up spiritually and recognize the new Manifestation.)

- What does a trumpet blast sound like—the kind that would wake you up?

(If a trumpet and trumpet player are available, demonstrate the sound. If you have access to the Internet, children may wish to hear the sound of a trumpet playing "reveille"—a military bugle call used to wake the troops at sunrise. Go to the following website and click on the 21-second audio file at the top right of the page: **http://en.wikipedia.org/wiki/Reveille**)

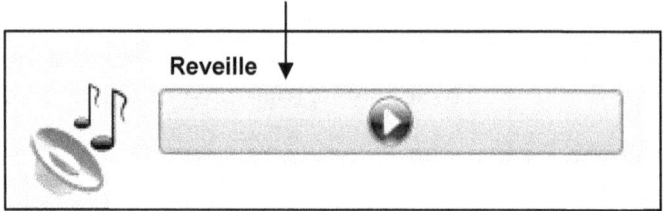

- Why do you think the proclamation of the Báb is compared to the sound of a trumpet?
  (Accept a variety of responses. See box below for ideas.)

Note to the teacher: A trumpet carries much farther than the human voice. It can sound a warning, serve as a call to arms, and loudly proclaim a special event or celebration—such as the return of a king to his kingdom.

Biblically, a trumpet blast is a symbol of warning, resurrection of the dead, the judgment of the latter day when all people are called to account, and the return of Christ. (Refer to Ezekiel 33:2-6, 1 Corinthians 15:52, 1 Thessalonians 4:15-17, Revelation 8:2, 8:13, and Matthew 24:30-31 for some examples.)

There are similar passages in the Qur'án (e.g., Sura 6:73, 36:51, 39:68-69, 69:13, 74:8), and in the Bahá'í writings (Epistle to the Son of the Wolf, p. 132-333; Gleanings from the Writings of Bahá'u'lláh, p. 31; and Selections from the Writings of 'Abdu'l-Bahá, p. 13).

Just as reveille pierces the silence to wake the troops at sunrise, the Báb's revelation signals the dawn of a new Day.

The Báb – Lesson #1

B. **Repetition:** Read the quote again slowly and have students repeat after each phrase. Read it again, faster. Then read two phrases at a time as students repeat. (You can use gestures as a memory aid. (Visit www.signingsavvy.com to see signs for "trumpet," "sleep," "wake up" and other words, or make up your own.)

C. **Backwards Buildup:** Read the last phrase and have students repeat until it is memorized. Then add the previous phrase and read through to the end. Continue in this manner until you have reached the beginning. By that time, most children will have the entire passage memorized. If you are only using part of the quote, you might have the children repeat:

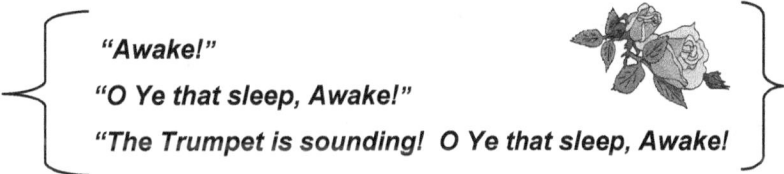

"Awake!"
"O Ye that sleep, Awake!"
"The Trumpet is sounding! O Ye that sleep, Awake!"

D. **Disappearing Act:** Then, using an eraser, swipe a narrow diagonal path through the entire passage on the board. This will leave a blank space on each line. Ask for student volunteers to read the passage again. Let everyone take a turn. Then make another eraser swipe and ask for another round of volunteers. Continue until the passage has completely disappeared.

E. **Recitation:** Ask for student volunteers to recite the whole quote from memory. Call on the most capable ones first so they can serve as models.

> *Tell students they can work with a friend and use these techniques to memorize other quotes for the children's performance. Encourage them to memorize additional passages after returning home.*

10. SONG: "The Báb Blew His Trumpet" (5 min.)

Have students take out their song sheets and sing along. Ask the music coordinator for assistance if needed.

(Note: Some of the words have been changed and some verses added to this popular Bahá'í song.)

Collect all folders and pencils.

The Báb – Lesson #1

Teacher's version of reading for activity #3

Preparing the Soil of the Heart

In early spring, when it is still cold outside, farmers work to prepare the soil so plants will be able to grow. They pull out weeds and remove stones. They spread fertilizer, and they plow[1] the earth so it is ready to receive the seeds. **[Point to a stone, trowel, seeds or other items to illustrate.]**

Then, when the sun warms the earth and the spring rains come once again, it is time to plant and the seeds are put into the ground. They grow strong because the farmers have prepared the soil.

The same thing happens when a new Age[2] begins. First, God sends a herald[3] or forerunner[4] to tell people that a Messenger of God is about to appear. The herald prepares people's hearts so they can recognize God's Manifestation when He comes.

Before Jesus came, God sent John the Baptist to tell people that soon someone much greater would appear. This also happened when God sent Bahá'u'lláh to the world. First, the Báb appeared in the land of Persia. **[Point to Persia, now Iran, on the map.]**

The Báb announced that He was a Messenger from God whose main mission was to prepare the way for Bahá'u'lláh. God sent Him to warn the people that the Promised One of all religions was coming soon.

The Báb's religion was called the Bábí Faith and His Holy Book is the Bayán. In the Bayán, the Báb told His followers to have good conduct, not to smoke or drink, to show respect for women, and to always take care of the poor.

His laws and teachings were very strict in order to show that the new Faith was a sharp break from the old ways. The Báb's Message was like a plow, digging up the soil of human hearts, or a trumpet blast waking them from a long sleep. It was time to get ready for the new Age.

Thousands and thousands of people heard about the Báb and believed His message. He had prepared them for the coming of Bahá'u'lláh.

1. **plow:** To break up the soil in preparation for planting
2. **Age:** A very long, long time; the start of a new period in history. In religious terms, a new cycle marked by the coming of a new Manifestation of God with new ideas and new laws
3. **herald:** Forerunner, messenger, bringer of important news, one who announces that something is going to happen
4. **forerunner:** One who comes before another to prepare the way

Bahá'í Children's Classes and Retreats: Theme 3, p. 26

The Báb – Lesson #1

Instructions for group leaders for activity #5

Stories from the Life of the Báb

You will have about 15 minutes to work. Take your group to a quiet place and help the children with the following tasks:

1. **Have children write their names** on the front of their story packets.

2. **Read the story out loud** with the children taking turns.

3. **Define any difficult words**, checking the dictionary if necessary.

4. **Ask the questions** at the end of the story and encourage children to share their thoughts. Give hints and encouragement if needed, but don't answer for them. Do not allow the children to laugh at or tease each other.

5. **Take notes below** and prepare children to share the story with the class using their own words. Your group will have 3 minutes to report back, so have the children practice being brief and to the point.

6. **Make sure each child has a part.** Older or more capable students might have a larger role. For example, one student might recount the main points of the story, calling on other students to fill in certain details. Some groups have added music or sound effects to their presentation—much to the enjoyment of the rest of the class.

Bahá'í Children's Classes and Retreats: Theme 3, p. 27

The Báb – Lesson #1

Teacher's version of map for activity #7

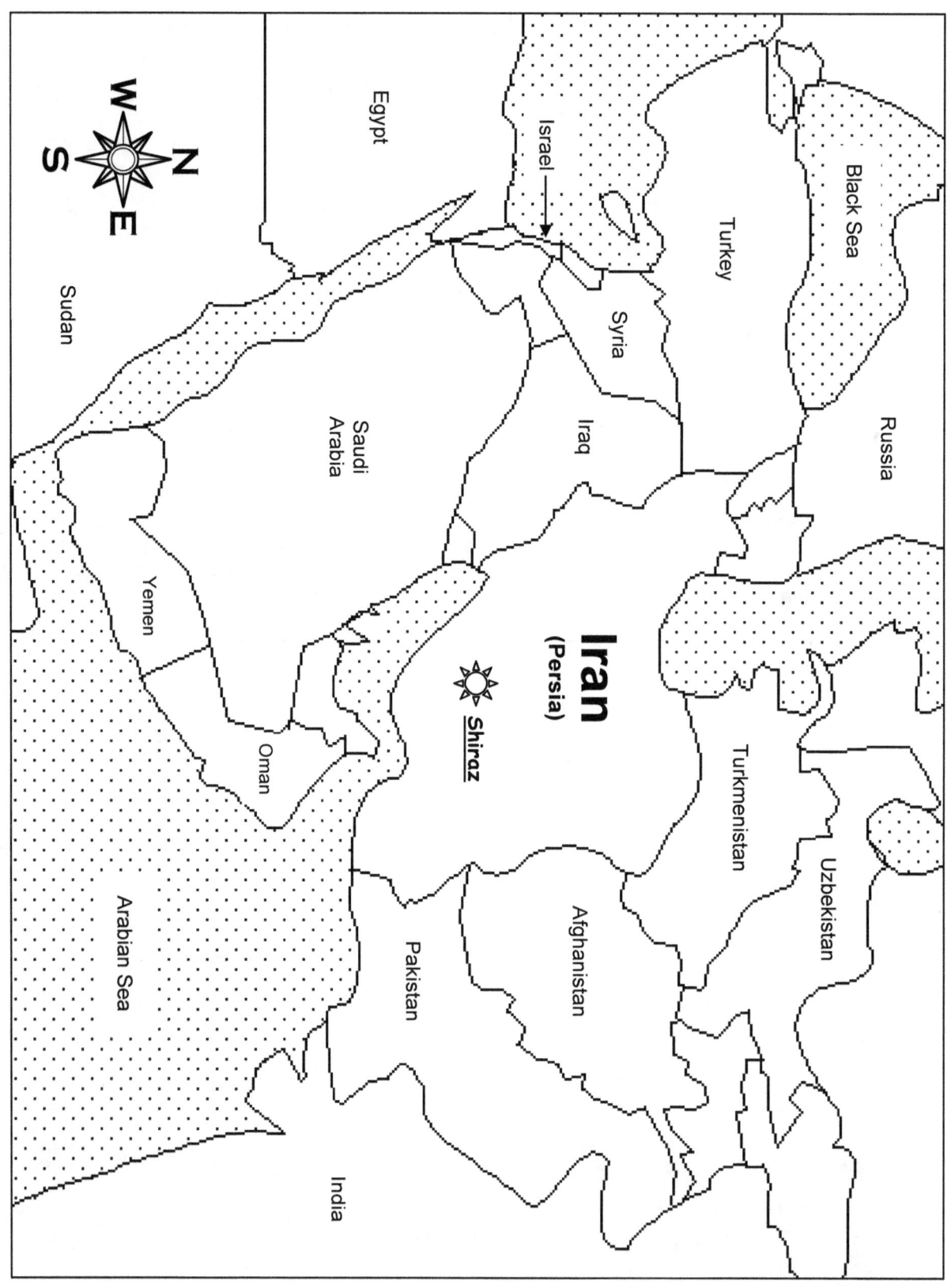

Bahá'í Children's Classes and Retreats: Theme 3, p. 28

The Báb – Lesson #1

Teacher's version of quiz for activity #8

Quiz on the Life of the Báb

1. Who was Siyyid 'Alí-Muhammad? *(The Báb)*

2. What does "the Báb" mean? *(Gate or door)*

3. Why was He called a Siyyid? *(Descendent of the Prophet Muhammad)*

4. When and where was He born? *(The city of Shiraz in Persia, October 20, 1819)*

5. Describe the city of Shiraz. *(Roses, poets, gardens, trees, flowers, nightingales)*

6. Why was the Báb raised by his uncle? *(Father died)*

7. When His uncle sent the Báb to school, why did the teacher send Him home? *(Knew more than the teacher; had innate knowledge)*

8. Where did the Báb's knowledge come from? *(From God)*

9. What work did the Báb do after leaving school? *(Cloth merchant with uncle)*

10. Did the Báb ever have His own family? *(Wife; baby son died at birth)*

11. What did the Báb look like? *(Handsome, slender, dark hair, dark eyes, light skin)*

12. Why did He wear a green turban on his head? *(As a symbol, to show He was descended from the Prophet Muhammad)*

13. What kind of person was He? *(Courteous, gentle, honest, trustworthy, prayerful)*

14. What is Persia called today, and what was it like at the time of the Báb? *(Iran; a lot of ignorance, prejudice, fighting, dishonesty, violence)*

15. Was the Báb a Manifestation of God? *(Yes)*

16. Were most people expecting Him when He came? *(Expecting their Promised One)*

17. What is the name of the Báb's religion and Holy Book? *(Bábí Faith, the Bayán)*

18. Why is the Báb also called a Herald? *(Announced the coming of another Manifestation)*

19. What was His main message? *(Prepare your hearts for the coming of Bahá'u'lláh)*

The Báb – Lesson #1

MATERIALS NEEDED

- ❑ White board, easel, markers, eraser
- ❑ Folder, notebook paper, pen or pencil for each student
- ❑ Dictionary
- ❑ Song sheets and page of quotations for each student [A]
- ❑ Felt lesson on "The Kingdoms of Creation" with additional circle and label for the Prophet (from theme books #1 and #2)
- ❑ Felt board and easel
- ❑ Packet of readings for each student on "Stories from the Life of the Báb" [A]
- ❑ Teacher's version of the first reading on "Preparing the Soil" (included here)
- ❑ Pictures to illustrate "Stories from the Life of the Báb" [A]
- ❑ Instructions for group leaders
- ❑ Materials for soil demonstration [B]
- ❑ Large world map posted on the wall
- ❑ Student outline maps of the Middle East (found in their story packets)
- ❑ Teacher's version of the map (included here)
- ❑ Crayons or colored pencils to color in the student maps
- ❑ Quiz on the Life of the Báb for each student (in story packets)
- ❑ Teacher's version of the quiz (included here)
- ❑ References for teachers (included at the end of this manual)

A. The song and readings are included in the Handouts section of this manual. The student handouts, along with full-page color illustrations to accompany the lessons, are available in the download packet for this teacher's guide: www.UnityWorksStore.com > Children's Classes > The Báb > student handouts. The illustrations can be posted on the walls during class as an aid for visual learners and to help bring the lessons and readings to life.

B. Prepare the following items for the soil demonstration (activity #3 and #4)
- ❑ Small table to display all the materials
- ❑ Two small planter pots or other open containers filled with hard-packed dirt
- ❑ A tray to hold the pots of dirt (for easier clean-up)
- ❑ A metal fork or other sturdy tool to break up the soil
- ❑ A small container of sand or flour to represent fertilizer
- ❑ A spoon to scoop out the fertilizer
- ❑ Sunflower seeds, dried beans or other seeds
- ❑ A few items to illustrate the reading (e.g., a trowel or shovel, picture of a plow, a stone, watering can)

Tip: Add water and pack the dirt down firmly so the top of the soil is about an inch (2.5 cm) below the rim to avoid spills. Let dry.

* * * * *

LESSON #2

Declaration of the Báb

The Báb – Lesson #2

Declaration of the Báb

Objectives: Students will be able to:
- Identify Mulla Husayn as the first to recognize the Báb in 1844.
- List some of the clues by which Mulla Husayn was able to recognize Him.
- Recount the circumstances of the Báb's declaration to Mulla Husayn.
- Explain why the Báb did not want Mulla Husayn to tell anyone else yet.
- Use the analogy of a gate to explain the role of the Báb in relation to Bahá'u'lláh.

---

*Before class, prepare all instructional materials on the list at the end of this lesson.
Post photos and illustrations. Set up craft activity. Orient volunteer assistants.
Write the memory quote on a second white board, with one phrase on each line.
Distribute folders and pencils to each student.*

---

1. SONG: "Hoy Es el Día" (5 min.)

Have students take out their song sheets and sing along. Ask the music coordinator for assistance if needed.

2. INTRODUCTION (5 min.)
- This class is about the Declaration of the Báb.
- Does anyone know what "declaration" means?
  (an announcement, a proclamation, an open or public statement)
- That's right. The Báb announced that He was a Messenger of God.
- Before He declared, some people were already expecting a Messenger of God.
- They didn't know Who it would be or where to look, but they had some clues from their Holy Book, the Qur'án, and they began to search for Him.

3. READING: "Spiritual Treasure Hunt" (20-30 min.)

Have students take out their packet of readings and turn to the page titled "Spiritual Treasure Hunt." (A copy is included at the end of this lesson for convenience.) Read the title and the first paragraph, and make up a question based on what you read, for example, "Who was the Qá'im?" Call on students to answer and remind them to raise their hands.

Then call on capable children, youth or adults to read each remaining paragraph out loud. Choose people with expressive voices who read well. Have each reader make up one or two questions about that paragraph and call on other students to answer—just as you did. Encourage them to call on someone who hasn't yet had a chance to respond.

The Báb – Lesson #2

4. PICTURES (5 min.)

Show students pictures of Iran at the time of the Báb, and the photograph of the room where He declared to Mulla Husayn.

5. MAGNET DEMONSTRATION (5 min.)

Ask the class:

- Remember that Mulla Husayn said he felt drawn **like a magnet** to the city of Shiraz? What do you think he meant by this?

  (He felt an invisible spiritual attraction to the Báb. It was not a wandering type of search, looking here and there for the Promised Qá'im. Rather, Mulla Husayn felt pulled directly to the city where the Báb lived.)

- Who knows what a magnet is?

  (An object that attracts iron or steel and produces a magnetic field. We can't see a magnetic field. It's invisible, but we can see its effects.)

"FEEL THE FORCE"

A. Ask for a volunteer to hold up a string with a large metal paper clip or nail tied to one end.

B. Have another student hold up a magnet, and slowly approach the nail until they click together.

C. You can also put some paper clips on top of a piece of thin cardboard or a manila folder, and slowly move the magnet around underneath. The clips will follow your movements.

D. Another option is to place a handful of paper clips in a clear plastic box, and move the magnet around to attract the clips. You can also use iron filings, black sand, staples, BBs or other magnetic objects inside the box.

Pass the items around so all the children can feel this invisible force.

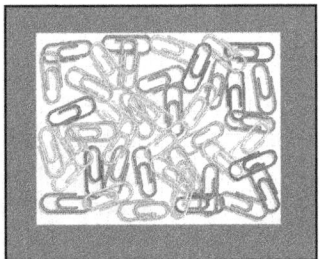
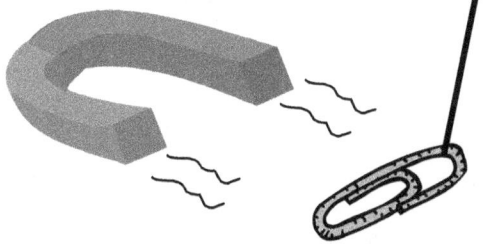

The Báb – Lesson #2

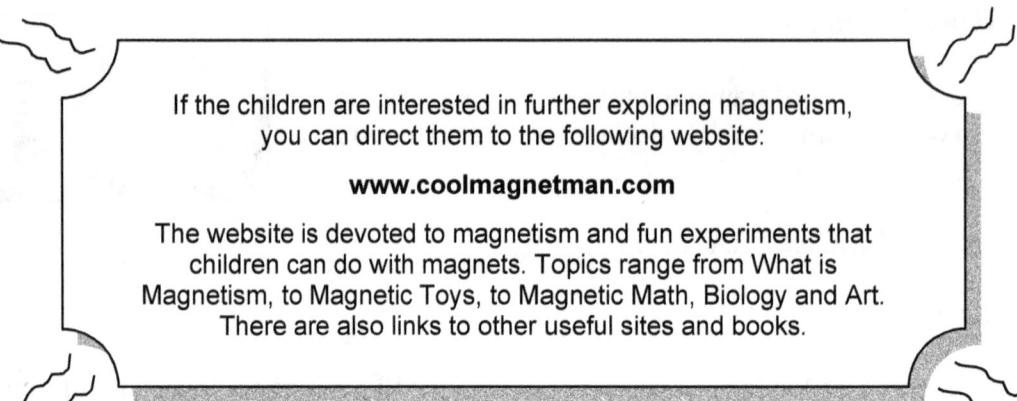

If the children are interested in further exploring magnetism, you can direct them to the following website:

www.coolmagnetman.com

The website is devoted to magnetism and fun experiments that children can do with magnets. Topics range from What is Magnetism, to Magnetic Toys, to Magnetic Math, Biology and Art. There are also links to other useful sites and books.

6. GROUP DISCUSSION: "Clues to the Báb" (10 min.)

Hold up the poster with the list of clues that Mulla Husayn used to find the Báb. Read the clues out loud and ask students what each one means, in order to ensure understanding. Then write the following question on the board:

Clues to the Báb
1. Noble lineage
2. His name
3. His age
4. Innate knowledge
5. Medium height
6. Non-smoker
7. Year 1260

"If the Báb knew He was a Manifestation of God, why didn't He just tell people?"

Have students think about the question on their own for a minute. Then ask them to share their thoughts with a partner. Give them a few minutes to consult. Then call on different individuals to share their understanding with the class.

7. MEMORY QUOTE: "Awake, awake..." (10-15 min.)

Have students take out their page of quotations and locate quote #7: "Awake, awake, for, lo! the Gate of God is open..." (The quote should already be written on the board.)

A. <u>Understanding</u>: Read the quote aloud slowly, then ask students:

- Who said these words and to whom? *(The Báb to Mulla Husayn)*
- Who or what is the Gate of God? *(The Báb)*
- What does "awake" mean, and why do you think the Báb says it twice?
- What does "radiance" mean? *(brightness, light, glow)*
- The word "lo" means "look."
- What do you think the Báb is saying?
  (He was sent by God to spiritually awaken people to the dawn of a new Day. Also, the coming of Bahá'u'lláh would be like the bright sun at mid-day. The Báb was like the rising sun at dawn, telling us it is time to wake up.)

"Awake, awake, for, lo! the Gate of God is open, and the morning Light is shedding its radiance upon all mankind!"

The Báb

The Báb – Lesson #2

B. **Repetition:** Read the quote again slowly and have students repeat after each phrase. Read it again, faster. Then read two phrases at a time as students repeat. You can use gestures as a memory aid. (For ideas, see: *www.signingsavvy.com*. Non-members are allowed to view five free signs per day.)

C. **Backwards Buildup:** Read the last phrase and have students repeat until it is memorized. Then add the previous phrase and read through to the end. Continue in this manner until you have reached the beginning. By that time, most children will have the entire passage memorized.

{
"... upon all mankind!"
"...is shedding its radiance upon all mankind!"
"... and the morning Light is shedding its radiance upon all mankind!"
}

D. **Disappearing Act:** Then, using an eraser, swipe a narrow diagonal path through the entire passage on the board. This will leave a blank space on each line. Ask for student volunteers to read the passage again. Let everyone take a turn. Then make another eraser swipe and ask for another round of volunteers. Continue until the passage has completely disappeared.

E. **Recitation:** Ask for student volunteers to recite the whole quote from memory. Call on the most capable ones first so they can serve as models.

> *Tell students they can work with a friend and use these same techniques to memorize other quotes for the children's performance. Encourage them to memorize additional passages after returning home.*

If time allows, ask for volunteers to recite the quote learned in the previous lesson:

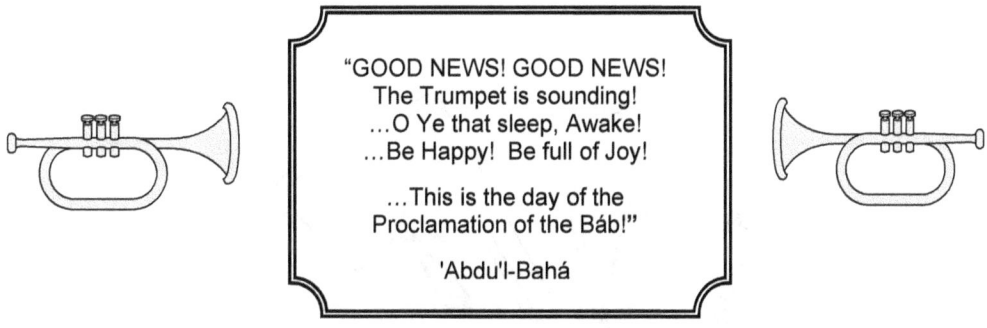

"GOOD NEWS! GOOD NEWS!
The Trumpet is sounding!
...O Ye that sleep, Awake!
...Be Happy! Be full of Joy!

...This is the day of the
Proclamation of the Báb!"

'Abdu'l-Bahá

Collect all folders and pencils.

8. CRAFT: The Gate of God (45-90 min*)

Craft projects are designed to reinforce the material presented during class. The children will be making a gate to symbolize the role of the Báb as the Gate to Bahá'u'lláh. The completed project can be used as a teaching tool.

If your class consists of older children and there are capable volunteers willing to take on a challenging project, you can make the wooden model of the gate. If time is limited or you are working with younger children, you can make the simpler cut-and-paste version. Instructions for both crafts can be found at the end of this lesson. Volunteers should be oriented beforehand.

The time for the wooden model can be reduced to about 60 minutes if doors are pre-cut and teachers are familiar with the project. The paper version should take about 45 minutes or less.

Begin by showing students a sample of the craft, then ask:

- How would you enter a building if it had no door? *(Not easily!)*
- What is the purpose of a door or gate? *(It lets people in or keeps them out.)*
- How does this relate to the Báb? *(He was the gate through which people could enter to find the Promised One. He helped prepare their hearts to recognize Bahá'u'lláh.)*

* * * * *

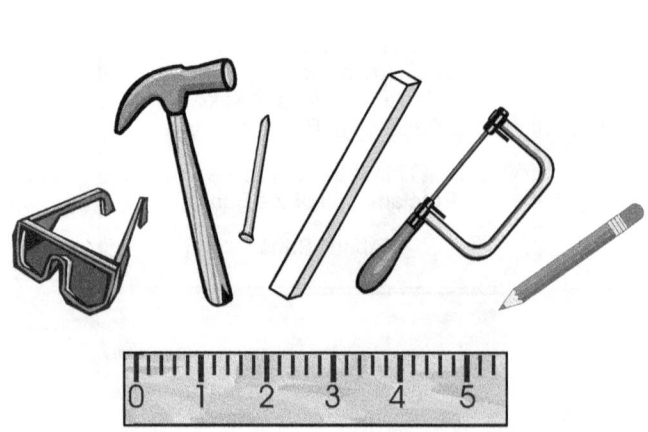

Spiritual Treasure Hunt
Mulla Husayn and the Search for the Báb

It was springtime in Persia in 1844, just before the coming of the Báb. Many people had heard about the Qá'im[1], a Divine Teacher like Jesus or Muhammad, who had been promised by God in the Muslim holy book, the Qur'án.

Many people thought that the Promised Qá'im would not come for a very long time. Others felt certain He was coming soon, while a few believed that He was already living in the world.

Whenever God sends a new Messenger, only a few people recognize Him at first. Some might see Him on the street or hear Him talk, but do not realize that He is a Manifestation because their hearts have not been prepared.

Others may be too busy thinking about their own problems, and still others just don't want to listen. But there are always some whose hearts are ready, and they are expecting Him.

One very brave and pure-hearted man, Mulla Husayn, was expecting the Qá'im and wanted to go search for Him. He decided to leave his home and family and travel throughout the land of Persia.[2]

Mulla Husayn could only find two people to go with him—his brother and his nephew. In order to prepare their hearts for this "holy adventure," the three young men went to a quiet place for 40 days to pray.

When they started out on their journey to find the Promised One, they didn't know who to look for or where to search, but Mulla Husayn felt drawn **"like a magnet"** to the city of Shiraz.

The three men traveled on foot across the desert for many days. Finally they reached Shiraz with its fragrant flower gardens and beautiful green trees. They were tired and thirsty after their long walk under the hot sun.

Mulla Husayn told his companions to go to the mosque[3] and he would meet them there later for evening prayers.

As Mulla Husayn walked alone near the gate of the city, praying with all his heart that God would lead him to the Promised One, a Young Man approached. He wore a green turban and on His face was a smile of loving welcome.

Mulla Husayn did not know that this was the One he had been searching for. The stranger put His arms around Mulla Husayn as if they were old friends, and invited him to His home to rest after such a long journey. But Mulla Husayn explained that his traveling companions were waiting for him.

"Commit them to the care of God," said the Young Man. "He will surely protect and watch over them."[4]

He was so kind and confident that Mulla Husayn felt unable to refuse the invitation, and he followed the Báb into the city. He thought perhaps this kind stranger could help him find the promised Qá'im.

---

1. **Qá'im:** "He Who arises" – the Promised One of Islam (Shoghi Effendi, God Passes By, p. 57)
2. **Ref:** For the story of Mulla Husayn's search, see The Dawnbreakers, p. 50-65
3. **mosque:** A Muslim house of worship
4. **Ref:** The Dawnbreakers, p. 52

The Báb – Lesson #2

When they arrived at the Báb's house, the Báb poured water over Mulla Husayn's hands to wash away the dust of travel, and served him tea. They prayed together and Mulla Husayn again begged God to help him find the Promised One. He still did not know who the Báb was. →

Finally, the Báb asked about Mulla Husayn's quest,[5] and how he would recognize the Promised Qá'im. Mulla Husayn replied that his teacher had given him specific clues to look for.

The Promised One would be…

- Descended from the Prophet Muhammad.
- Between 20 and 30 years old.
- Of medium height.
- A non-smoker.
- In His name, "Ali" will come before the name of the Prophet.
- He will have innate knowledge that comes from God.
- He will reveal His Mission in the year 1260 (1844 on our calendar).

"The Báb paused for a while and then with a vibrant[6] voice declared: 'Behold, all these signs are manifest in Me!'"[7]

Mulla Husayn was so shocked that at first he could not believe it. But as the Báb continued speaking, Mulla Husayn realized that this was the One he had been searching for.

The Báb explained that He was a Messenger of God and also the Herald of a second Manifestation with a mission even greater than His own.

The Báb's declaration took place on the eve of May 23, 1844. He was only 25 years old.

This was the first time that the Báb had told anyone who He was. Mulla Husayn was the first* to believe in Him, but the Báb asked him not to tell anyone yet.

He said that 17 more pure-hearted souls would have to find Him on their own, searching by themselves, just as Mulla Husayn had done. He said that God would guide their steps.

Then, when all 18 had discovered the Báb, He would send them out across the land to tell people that the Promised Qá'im had come, and to prepare them for the coming of Bahá'u'lláh. It was the dawn of a new Day.

5. **quest:** Special mission, or search for something of great importance
6. **vibrant:** Lively, dynamic, energetic, full of life
7. **Ref:** The Dawnbreakers, p. 57

* Earlier, the wife of the Báb had recognized that He was a Holy Person but she did not know He was the Promised Qá'im. (Hour of Dawn, p. 27; Adib Taherzadeh, The Revelation of Baha'u'llah v 2, p. 382, 385)

The Báb – Lesson #2

Poster for activity #6

7 Clues to the Báb

1. Descended from Muhammad

2. Between 20 and 30 years old

3. In His name, "Ali" will come before the name of the Prophet

4. Innate knowledge

5. Medium height

6. Non-smoker

7. Will appear in the year 1260

The Báb – Lesson #2

THE GATE OF GOD

— Wood Model —

> Craft activities are designed to reinforce the material presented during class. The gate symbolizes the role of the Báb as the Gate to Bahá'u'lláh. When children have completed their project and cleaned up their work area, they may assist others who need help. Remind them to label all projects with their names. Quiet music can be played in the background if desired.

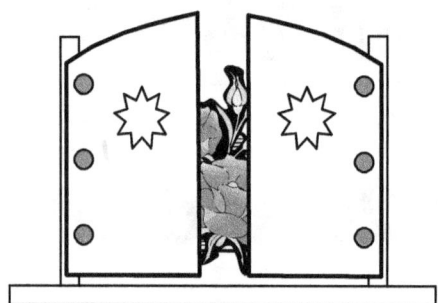

MATERIALS

Wood

(1) Plywood for base, approx. ¼-inch thick, cut into 8 x 10-inch pieces (6.5 mm thick, 20 x 25 cm.), one base per child. Note: A half-panel (4 feet x 4 feet) will yield 24 pieces.

(2) Masonite or plywood for gates, ⅛-inch thick, cut into 8 x 12-inch pieces (3 mm thick, 20 x 30 cm.), one per child. Note: The lumber yard may cut the pieces for a small fee.

(3) Square dowels for gate posts, ⅜-inch thick (or 9.5 mm). Children will cut these into 9-inch (23 cm) lengths to yield two posts per child.

Tools

- ❑ Miter box or vise
- ❑ Hacksaw (for dowels)
- ❑ Jigsaw (for doors)
- ❑ Extension cords if needed
- ❑ Clamps
- ❑ Sandpaper
- ❑ Sanding blocks (optional)
- ❑ Electric drill with drill bits
- ❑ Hammers
- ❑ A few large flat-head nails
- ❑ Scissors
- ❑ Wire cutters (for flowers)
- ❑ Screwdrivers

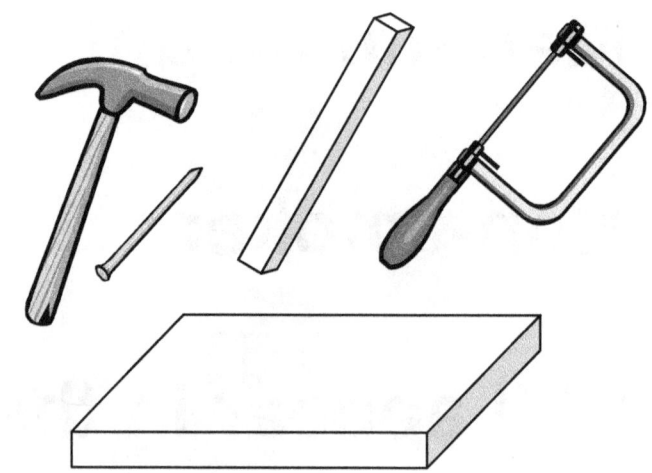

The Báb – Lesson #2

Additional Tools and Supplies

- [ ] Tarps to protect tables
- [ ] Utility cloth to wipe off sawdust
- [ ] Several gate patterns
- [ ] Pencils
- [ ] Rulers or T-squares
- [ ] Safety goggles
- [ ] Thick board to protect work table from drilling
- [ ] Black electrical tape (approx. 4.5 feet or 1.5 meters per child)
- [ ] Gold-colored upholstery tacks (6 per child + extras)
- [ ] Flat-head wood screws (#6 x ¾-inch, 2 per child + extras)
- [ ] Fake grass or green indoor-outdoor carpet. (Avoid grass with rubber backing since glue won't stick. Children will each cut one piece: 4 x 10 in., or 10 x 25 cm.)
- [ ] Artificial flowers
- [ ] Modeling clay (to hold the flowers upright)
- [ ] Stick-on gold notary seals or other decorations (for doors)
- [ ] Laminated quotes (1 per child)
- [ ] Glue stick or white craft glue

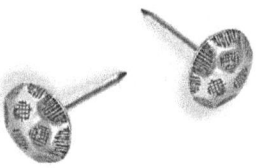

The Báb – Lesson #2

SET UP WORK STATIONS

Set up the following tables, each with an adult supervisor, tools and instructions. Label each work station with a sign.

(A) SAND (steps #1, 7, 11)
Sand base, gates, dowels.
Materials: Sandpaper, dust cloth

(B) MARK (steps #2, 3, 5, 9)
Write name on base; mark holes; measure and mark dowels for gate posts; trace gate patterns on wood.
Materials: Pencils, rulers or T-squares, gate patterns

(C) DRILL (step #4)
Drill holes in base.
Materials: Drill, safety goggles, backing board to protect work table

(D) CUT POSTS (step #6)
Cut two gate posts.
Materials: Dowels, miter box or vise, hacksaw

(E) NAIL (steps #8, 13)
Nail hole in each post; tack gates to posts.
Materials: Hammers, nails, upholstery tacks

(F) CUT GATES (step #10)
Cut two gates.
Materials: Jigsaw, clamps, safety goggles, optional sawhorse

(G) FINISH (steps #12, 14)
Add edging and attach posts to base.
Materials: Electrical tape, scissors, screws, screwdrivers

(H) DECORATE (steps #15, 16, 17)
Add decorations.
Materials: Grass, scissors, quotes, glue, upholstery tacks, clay, artificial flowers, wire cutters, stickers, contact paper (optional)

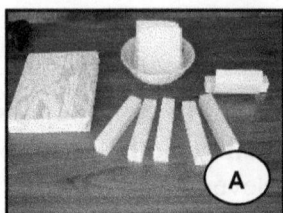
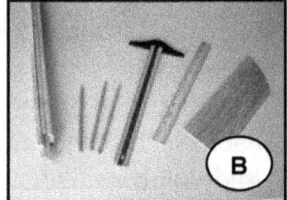
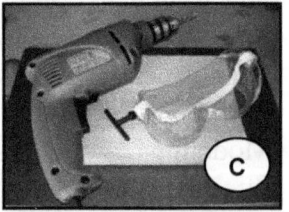

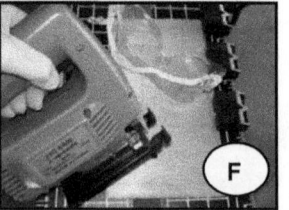

Bahá'í Children's Classes and Retreats: Theme 3, p. 42

The Báb – Lesson #2

Table cards for The Gate of God craft.
Copy onto heavy paper, cut on lines, and display one card at each station.

(A) SAND

Step #1, 7, 11

(Sand base, gates and dowels.)

(B) MARK

Step #2, 3, 5, 9

(Write name; mark holes and dowels; trace gates.)

(C) DRILL

Step #4

(Drill two holes.)

(D) CUT POSTS

Step #6

(Cut two gate posts using hacksaw.)

(E) NAIL

Step #8, 13

(Nail hole in each post; tack gates to posts.)

(F) CUT GATES

Step #10

(Cut two gates using jigsaw.)

(G) FINISH

Step #12, 14

(Tape edges; attach posts to base.)

(H) DECORATE

Step #15, 16, 17

(Add flowers and other decorations.)

The Báb – Lesson #2

Instructions

Safety: Have children work under careful adult supervision. They should use safety goggles, with sleeves rolled up and hair tied back. Unplug all power tools and put them away when not in use.

To minimize waiting in line, children can go through these steps in any reasonable order, starting with stations A or B.

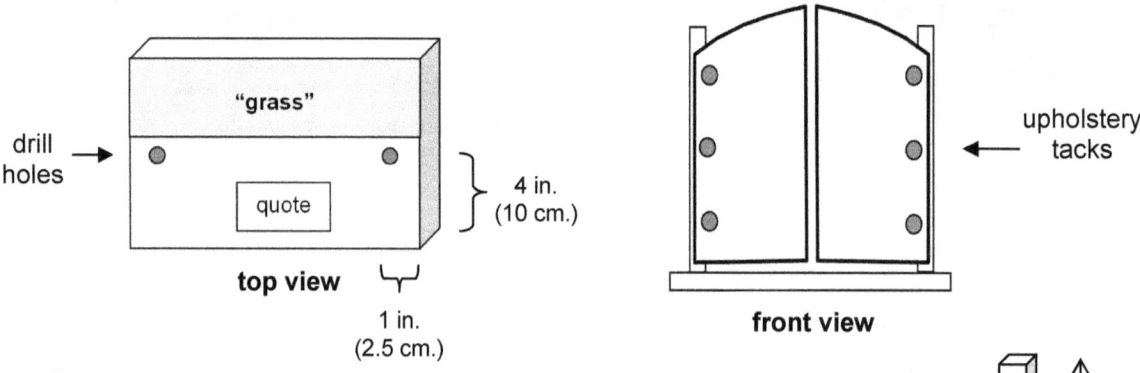

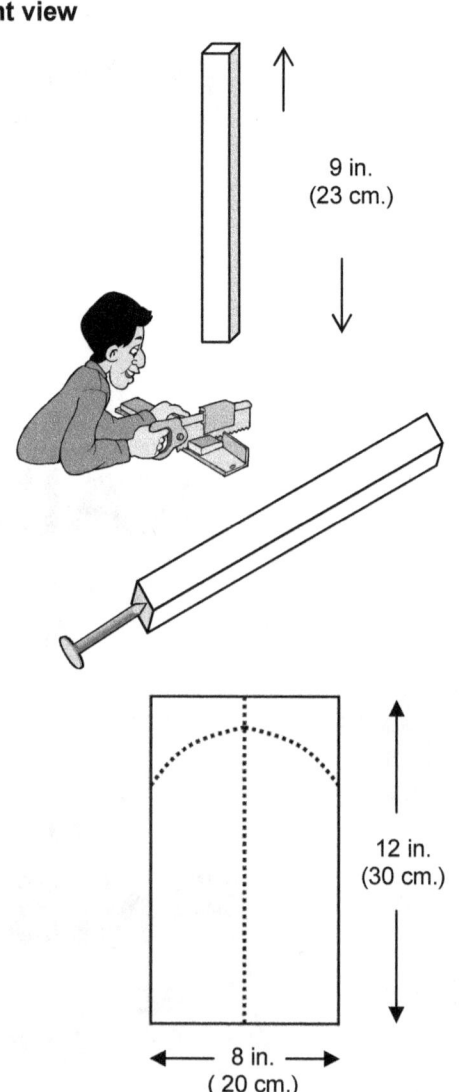

	Task	Station
1	Sand rough edges of wood base.	A
2	Write name on bottom of base.	B
3	Mark two holes on bottom of base, making each hole 4 in. (10 cm.) from the front edge, and 1 in. (2.5 cm.) in from the side. (See "top view" above.)	B
4	Drill holes in base, placing base on top of a thick board to avoid drilling into work table.	C
5	Measure and mark dowels into two 9-inch (23 cm.) lengths for gate posts.	B
6	Using the miter box or vise and hacksaw, cut two gate posts from marked dowels. Cut straight or gates will be tilted.	D
7	Sand rough edges on dowels.	A
8	Using hammer and nail, tap holes in bottom of posts for screws. Hammer on floor or sturdy work table. Tap lightly and don't make holes too large or screws will wobble.	E
9	Trace gate pattern onto 1/8-inch (3 mm.) wood. Flip pattern for 2nd gate. Extend center line to edge of wood for easier cutting later.	B
10	Using the jigsaw, cut gates through center line. Then fold gates together backwards (with pattern facing out). Clamp and cut along curve, cutting through both pieces at once.	F

Bahá'í Children's Classes and Retreats: Theme 3, p. 44

	Task	Station
11	Sand rough edges on gates.	A
12	For a finished look, cover top and side edges of each gate with black electrical tape. Do one side at a time. Don't tape bottom.	G
13	Attach gates to posts with upholstery tacks. (See "front view" above.) Nail through gate first. Let post extend slightly below bottom of gate so gate will swing freely when attached.	E
14	Attach posts to base using wood screws through holes in bottom of base. Do not over-tighten or gate will not swivel easily.	G
15	Cut fake grass and glue it to base, covering only the side behind the gate. (See "top view" above.)	H
16	Glue quote to base in front of gate. If quote is not already laminated, cover with contact paper after glue dries.	H
17	Add decorations. Gold upholstery tacks can be stuck into the post tops as a decorative cap. Small silk roses on wire stems can be pressed into a ball of clay which has been pressed into the grass. Gold notary seals or stickers can be attached to the front of each door, etc.	H

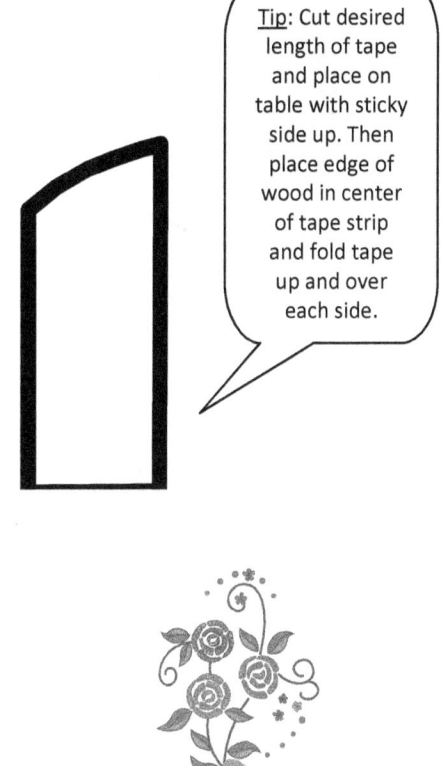

Tip: Cut desired length of tape and place on table with sticky side up. Then place edge of wood in center of tape strip and fold tape up and over each side.

Before Class Begins

Before class begins, orient the volunteers. They should be able to assist children with the tasks at their own station, and know which station to send children to next. It helps to have a sample product at each table. When new students arrive, the assistant should show sthem the model and demonstrate the skill. Offer as much help as is needed. Safety is a primary concern.

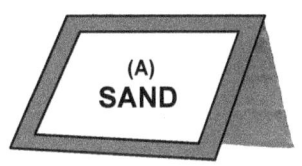

Notes

1. The gates can be made from plywood, but masonite (also called hardboard) is easier to cut.
2. Masonite is relatively inexpensive and one panel (24 x 48 inches) can be cut into 24 pieces that are 8 x 12 inches each.
3. Upholstery tacks are also known as furniture nails.
4. To save time, pre-draw the cut lines on the underside of the grass. →
5. The following websites offer free online videos on how to use a jigsaw:
   - www.ehow.com/video_4420242_basic-tips-cutting-wood-using.html
   - www.ehow.com/video_4420245_how-cut-arc-using-jig.html

The Báb – Lesson #2

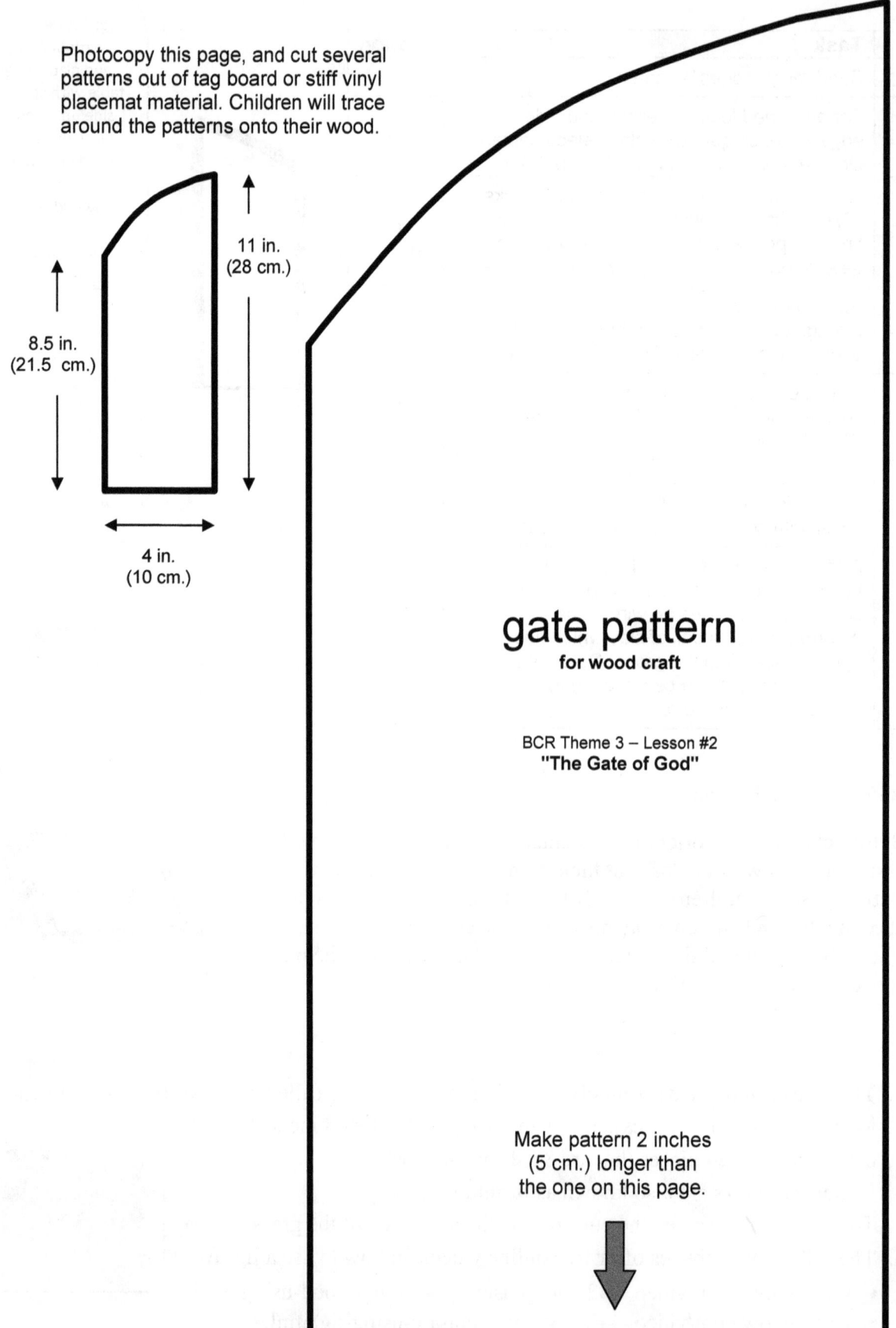

Photocopy this page, and cut several patterns out of tag board or stiff vinyl placemat material. Children will trace around the patterns onto their wood.

11 in. (28 cm.)
8.5 in. (21.5 cm.)
4 in. (10 cm.)

gate pattern
for wood craft

BCR Theme 3 – Lesson #2
"The Gate of God"

Make pattern 2 inches (5 cm.) longer than the one on this page.

Bahá'í Children's Classes and Retreats: Theme 3, p. 46

The Báb – Lesson #2

Quotation for The Gate of God craft.
Photocopy onto heavy paper, laminate (for wood craft), and cut one per child.

"Awake, awake, for, lo! the Gate of God is open and the morning Light is shedding its radiance upon all mankind."
The Báb

"Awake, awake, for, lo! the Gate of God is open and the morning Light is shedding its radiance upon all mankind."
The Báb

"Awake, awake, for, lo! the Gate of God is open and the morning Light is shedding its radiance upon all mankind."
The Báb

"Awake, awake, for, lo! the Gate of God is open and the morning Light is shedding its radiance upon all mankind."
The Báb

The Báb – Lesson #2

Working on the "Gate of God" wood craft

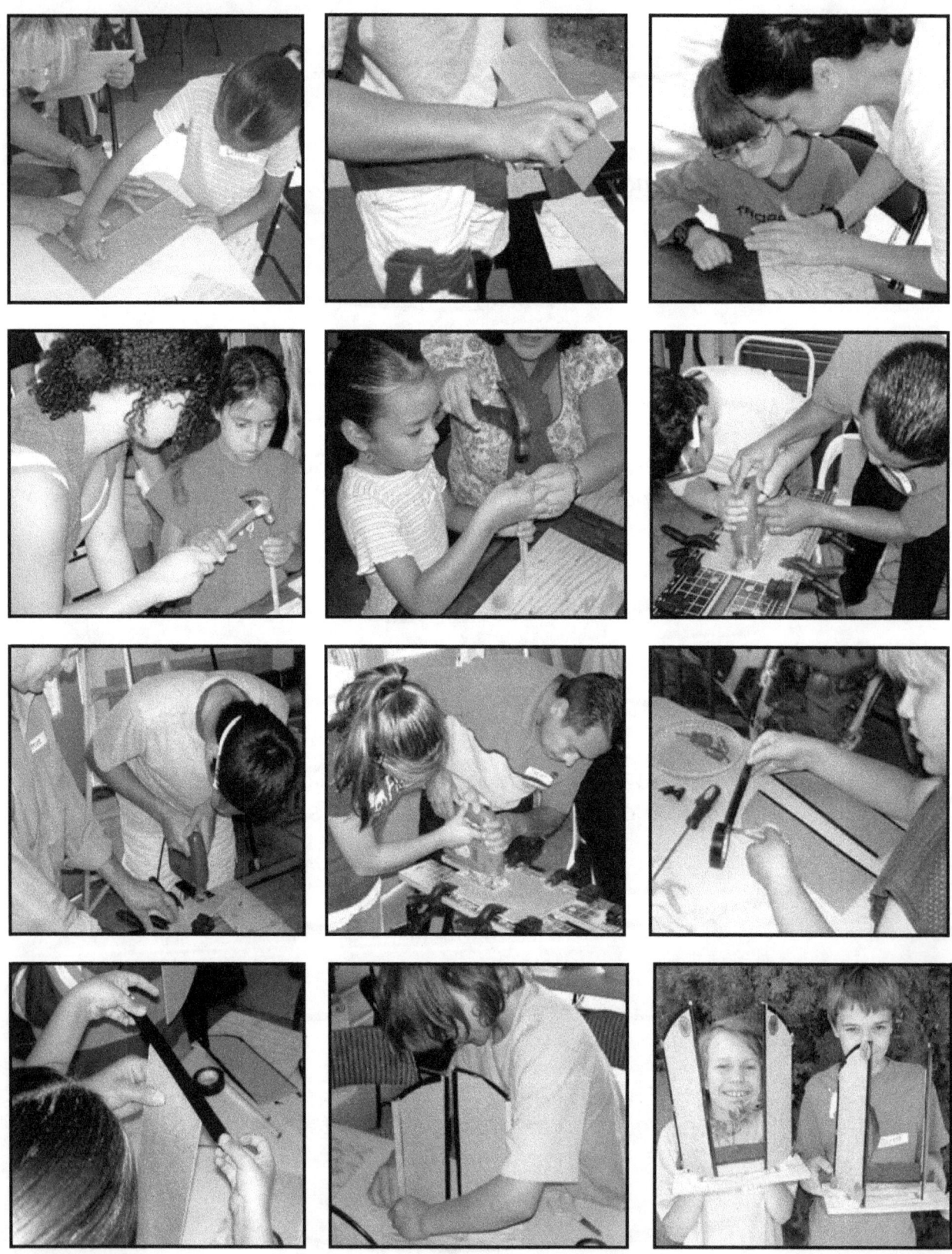

The Báb – Lesson #2

THE GATE OF GOD

— Paper Model —

Craft activities are designed to reinforce the material presented during class. The gate symbolizes the role of the Báb as the Gate to Bahá'u'lláh. When children have completed their project and cleaned up their work area, they may assist others who need help. Remind them to label all projects with their names. Quiet music can be played in the background if desired.

Materials

- ❑ Sheets of cardstock or heavy paper
- ❑ Poster board in a variety of colors
- ❑ Gate patterns
- ❑ Pencils
- ❑ Rulers
- ❑ Scissors
- ❑ Glue sticks
- ❑ Floral wrapping paper
- ❑ Quotes (use quotes from wood craft, above)
- ❑ Crayons or colored markers (optional)
- ❑ Gold notary seals or other appropriate stickers

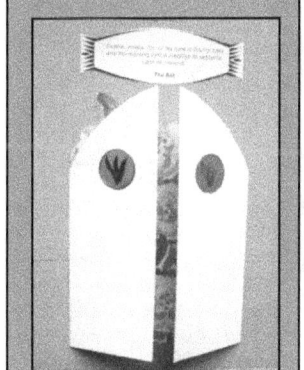

Instructions

1. Trace the gate pattern onto the cardstock, placing the longest edge of the pattern along one edge of the paper, with the corners aligned (see illustration on next page).

2. Flip the pattern, placing the long edge along the other side of the paper, and trace a second gate.

3. Using the dotted line as a guide, measure and draw a straight line from the top to the bottom of each gate hinge.

4. Using the scissors, carefully cut out both gates with the hinges attached.

5. Fold each hinge along the line.

6. If desired, color the front of the gates with crayons or markers.

7. Find one of the quotations ("Awake, awake…") and trim close to the outline.

8. Position the quotation and both gates on a piece of poster board, making sure the center edges of the gates are touching. Then glue each item into place, only putting glue on the back of the gate hinges so the gates can swing open and closed.

9. Glue the poster board to another larger poster board, using a different color to make a frame.

10. Decorate the project with gold seals or stickers on the gates, and with floral wrapping paper or other designs on the inside. Remember to write your name on the back.

The Báb – Lesson #2

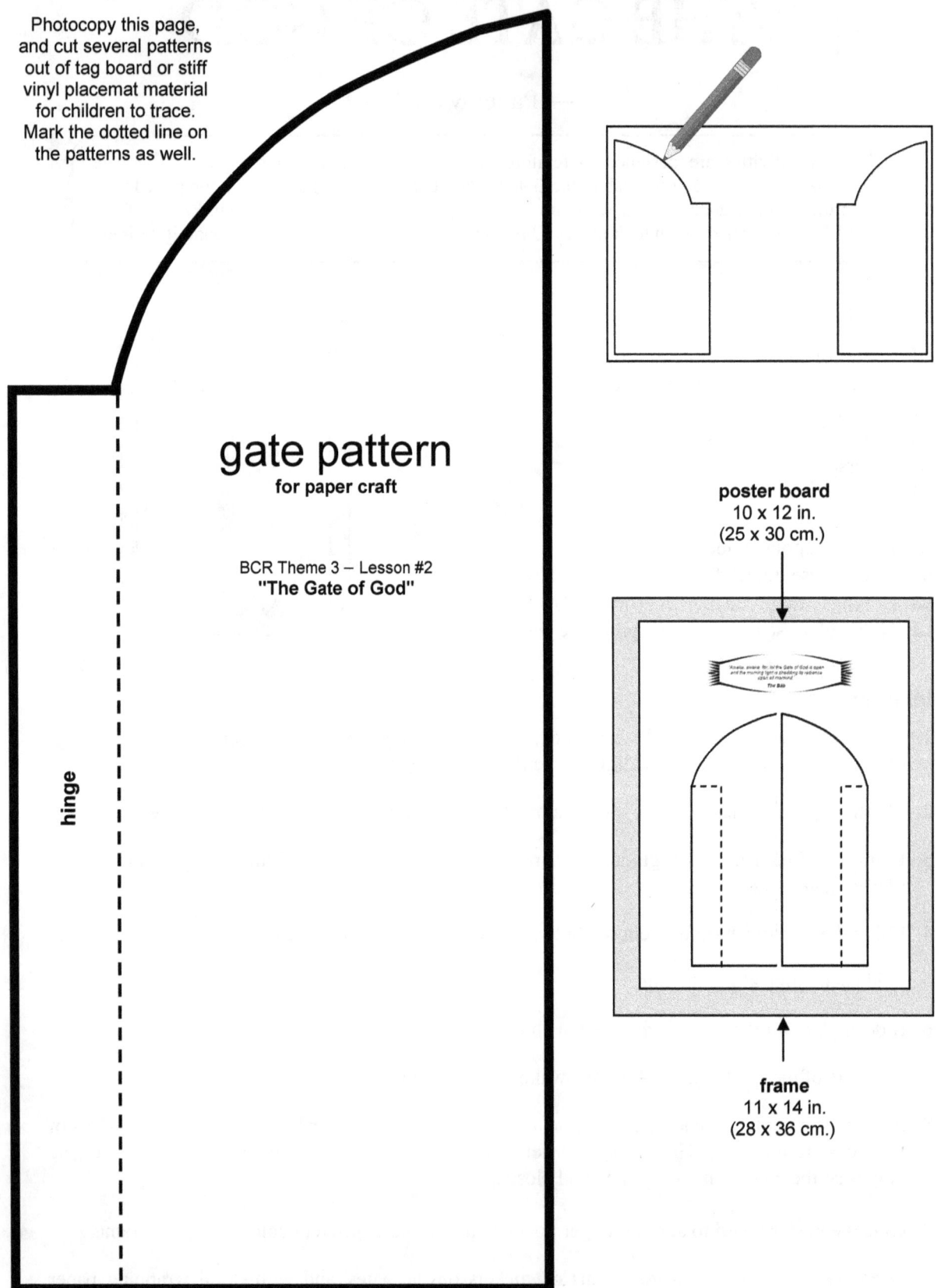

Photocopy this page, and cut several patterns out of tag board or stiff vinyl placemat material for children to trace. Mark the dotted line on the patterns as well.

gate pattern
for paper craft

BCR Theme 3 – Lesson #2
"The Gate of God"

hinge

poster board
10 x 12 in.
(25 x 30 cm.)

frame
11 x 14 in.
(28 x 36 cm.)

The Báb – Lesson #2

MATERIALS NEEDED

- ☐ White board, easel, markers, eraser
- ☐ Folders with song sheets and page of quotations for each student [A]
- ☐ Packet of readings on "Stories from the Life of the Báb" [A]
- ☐ "Spiritual Treasure Hunt" handout (included with this lesson)
- ☐ Pictures of Iran at the time of the Báb, including the photograph of the room where He declared to Mulla Husayn [B]
- ☐ Items for magnet demonstration (activity #5)
  - String or thread with large metal paper clip or nail tied to one end
  - Small magnetic objects (e.g., paper clips, iron filings, black sand, staples, BBs)
  - Clear plastic box and/or thin cardboard or manila folder
  - One or more magnets
- ☐ Poster with clues to recognizing the Báb (included with this lesson)
- ☐ Materials for craft activities (see separate lists), sample of each project, and page of instructions for the assistant at each station
- ☐ References for teachers (included at the end of this manual)

A. Included in the Handouts section of this teacher's guide. The student handouts, along with full-page color illustrations designed to accompany the lessons, are available for download from: **www.UnityWorksStore.com**. Click on Children's Classes > The Báb > student handouts. Illustrations can be printed on cardstock and posted on the wall during class as an aid for visual learners and to help bring the lessons and readings to life.

B. Photographs of Iran can be found online at:
  - < www.google.com > click on "Images" on the top left menu and enter "Iran photos 19th century" in the search box. You can also type "Shiraz photos 19th century."
  - < www.wikipedia.org > enter "Shiraz" in the search box.
  - A photograph of the Báb's declaration chamber is included in the download packet for this teacher's guide (see note above).

* * * * *

Bahá'í Children's Classes and Retreats: Theme 3, p. 51

LESSON #3

Martyrdom of the Báb

The Báb – Lesson #3

Martyrdom of the Báb

Objectives: Students will be able to:
- Recount the story of the martyrdom of the Báb.
- Based on the story, give an example of God's power.
- Explain why the Báb was sent away, imprisoned and finally killed by the authorities.
- Give the date and place of the Báb's martyrdom, and tell how old he was.
- Recognize the Shrine of the Báb and tell where it is located.
- Explain the meaning of martyrdom for one's faith.

---

*Before class, prepare all instructional materials on the list at the end of this lesson.
Post the story illustrations. Set up craft activities. Orient volunteer assistants.
Write the memory quote on a second white board, with one phrase on each line.
Distribute folders and pencils to each student.*

---

1. SONG: "Remover of Difficulties" (5 min.)

Have students take out their song sheets and sing along. Ask the music coordinator for assistance if needed.

2. MEMORY QUOTES (5 min.)

Ask for a few volunteers to recite from memory the quotes learned during previous lessons:

- "GOOD NEWS! GOOD NEWS! The Trumpet is sounding! ...O Ye that sleep, Awake! ...Be Happy! Be full of Joy! ...This is the day of the Proclamation of the Báb!" ('Abdu'l-Bahá)

- "Awake, awake, for, lo! the Gate of God is open and the morning light is shedding its radiance upon all mankind." (The Báb)

3. READING: "Imprisonment and Martyrdom of the Báb" (30-45 min.)

Have students take out their packet of readings and turn to the page titled "Imprisonment and Martyrdom of the Báb." (A copy is included at the end of this lesson for convenience.)

Read the title and ask:

- What does "imprisonment" mean? *(To put someone in prison or jail.)*

- What does "martyrdom" mean? *(To give up your own life for a higher cause. For example, many people around the world have sacrificed their lives for human rights like freedom or justice. Others have been killed for refusing to give up their religious beliefs.)*

Bahá'í Children's Classes and Retreats: Theme 3, p. 54

The Báb – Lesson #3

Introduce the story with a demonstration:

- Have students bring the story with them, and stand around the room in a large circle.

- Pass out the "thousand chain" and have each child hold onto the chain with both hands.

- Tell the children to imagine that each bead represents one bullet (or musket ball).

- Point to the 750th "bullet." *(There should be a red ribbon tied at the spot.)*

- If available, pass a metal object around the circle that is approximately the size and shape of a musket ball (for example, a large ball bearing or a black marble).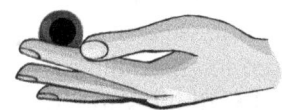

- Then ask students to remain in the circle and sit down quietly.

- Explain that every time they hear the words **"750"** in the story, they should silently hold up the chain. *(This will help them to get a sense of how many bullets were aimed at the Báb, all at close range, and just how miraculous it was that, with the noise and smoke, not one hit its target the first time around.)*

> As an alternative to the chain, provide a bucket or clear plastic tub filled with 750 beads or marbles. This can be set on a small table in the center of the circle. Supervise children carefully if they will be handling the beads.

Begin reading the story as students follow on their handouts.

Read the title again and the first paragraph. Then make up a question based on what you read, for example, "Including Mulla Husayn, how many pure souls first recognized the Báb?" *(18)* Call on students to answer and remind them to raise their hands.

Then call on capable children, youth or adults to read each remaining paragraph out loud.* Choose people with expressive voices who read well. Have each reader make up one or two questions about that paragraph and call on students to answer—just as you did. Encourage them to call on someone who hasn't yet had a chance to respond.

*Note: Since this is quite a long story, if the children are young or have limited attention spans, rather than selecting different people to read each paragraph, you may wish to read the entire story yourself.

Bahá'í Children's Classes and Retreats: Theme 3, p. 55

The Báb – Lesson #3

4. DISCUSSION: "Martyrdom of the Báb" (30-40 min.)

Explain to the students that they will be working in small groups to share their thoughts about the martyrdom of the Báb. Divide children into groups of 3-4 and assign a youth or adult volunteer to each group.

Give each volunteer a copy of the "Martyrdom of the Báb" instruction sheet (included at the end of this lesson). As group facilitators, they should ask the questions and encourage the children to share their thoughts. Groups can move to another room or outside if desired. Allow about 15 minutes to work, and walk around to observe their progress. Call the groups back to share a summary of their discussions.

5. MEMORY QUOTE: "Remover of Difficulties" (10-15 min.)

Have students take out their page of quotations and locate quote #9: *"Is there any Remover…"* It should already be written on the board.

> "Is there any Remover of difficulties save God? Say: Praised be God! He is God! All are His servants, and all abide by His bidding!"
>
> The Báb

Read the quote aloud slowly, then ask:

- Who gave us this prayer? *(The Báb)*

- What is a servant? *(Someone who performs duties for another, especially a person of lower rank who works in the home of their master or an employer of higher status.)*

- What does "abide" mean? *(To act in accordance with, to submit to, follow or obey—as in "abide by the rules," to exist or live.)*

- What does "bidding" mean? *(A command or request to do something; an order; authoritative instructions.)*

- What do you think this prayer means? *(Accept all responses, for example: We give praise to God. He is the One who can resolve our greatest problems. All are alive by His command and are subject to His Will.)*

- How does this apply to the story we just read? *(Ask students to think for a moment on their own, then to share their thoughts with a partner before responding. Encourage a variety of responses.)*

   If necessary, point out that the Báb told Sam Khan to follow his instructions, and if he were sincere, God would remove his difficulties—which is exactly what happened. The Báb also correctly told the guards that no earthly power could stop Him until He was ready. They too, had to abide by God's bidding. Even the soldiers who finally killed the Báb, were playing their part in the divine Plan. The Báb had completed His mission and His soul returned to God.

The Báb – Lesson #3

After discussing the meaning of the quote, ask for student volunteers to recite it from memory. Call on the most capable ones first so they can serve as models. They should already be familiar with the words from singing the song, but if additional practice is needed, use some of the memorization techniques outlined in Lesson #1.

6. SONG: "Queen of Carmel" (5-10 min.)

Have students take out their song sheets and sing along. Ask the music coordinator for assistance if needed. Before singing, show the class a color picture of the Shrine of the Báb. Point out that "Queen of Carmel" refers to the Shrine, which is "robed in white" (the superstructure itself) and "crowned in gold" (the golden dome).

> "Queen of Carmel enthroned on God's Mountain, crowned in glowing gold, robed in shimmering white, girdled in emerald green, enchanting every eye from air, sea, plain and hill."
>
> Words of the Guardian joyously announcing the completion of the Shrine of the Báb.
> (Shoghi Effendi, Messages to the Baha'i World: 1950-1957, p. 169)

Collect all folders and pencils.

7. CRAFT: "A Candle for the Báb" (40 min.)

Craft projects are designed to reinforce the material presented during class. For a weekend retreat, there may only be time for one or two craft activities. For an ongoing class, you might try a different craft each time. Volunteers should be oriented beforehand.

Begin by showing the class a sample of each craft. When students have completed a project, they should clean up their work area, then assist others who might need help. Remind them to label all projects with their names. Quiet music can be played in the background if desired.

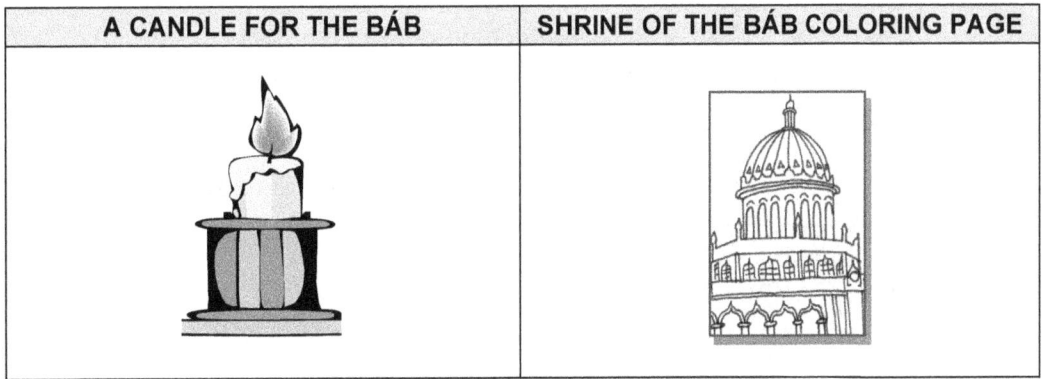

The Báb – Lesson #3

The children will be making a sculpted play dough candle holder (see instructions at the end of this lesson). The candle is a symbolic offering to the Báb, since in prison, He had no light. And yet, like a candle, the Báb sacrificed His own life in order to bring light to the world. The candle also serves as a symbol of the Báb's Revelation itself, which He likened to the "morning light...shedding its radiance upon all mankind."

As an additional or an alternative project, the children may wish to color a picture of the Shrine of the Báb. They will need a coloring page (included with this lesson) and crayons or markers. For a slightly more challenging project, students can cut out the Shrine and glue it to a sheet of blue construction paper (for the sky). Provide construction paper, scissors and glue sticks.

Full-color photos of the Shrine are available in the download packet for this teacher's guide: www.UnityWorksStore.com

Note to the teacher: The Shrine of the Báb, designed by Canadian architect William Sutherland Maxwell, is full of symbolism. For example, the eighteen stained-glass windows ringing the upper level of the Shrine, symbolize the eighteen Letters of the Living—the Báb's first disciples. The golden dome which crowns the structure is an expression of the majesty of the "Queen of Carmel," enthroned on God's Holy mountain. Light is another integral feature of the design, and the Shrine is brightly lit each evening to recall the time when the Báb was kept in a dark prison and denied access to even a candle. A lantern tops the entire structure of the Shrine.

References:
Shoghi Effendi, God Passes By, p. 411
Shoghi Effendi, Messages to the Bahá'í World – 1950-1957, p. 22
Shoghi Effendi, Unfolding Destiny of the British Baha'i Community, p. 321
Ugo Giachery, Shoghi Effendi – Recollections, p. 100
http://news.bahai.org/documentlibrary/643/ShrineOfTheBab.pdf

Imprisonment and Martyrdom of the Báb

After the Báb declared to His first follower, Mulla Husayn, He waited for other disciples[1] to discover Him as well. Soon 18 pure souls, including Mulla Husayn, had recognized Him. The Báb sent these first believers throughout Persia to teach the new Faith and to prepare people for the coming of Bahá'u'lláh.

The Báb's Message spread quickly. Before long, He had thousands of enthusiastic followers. This made the religious and government leaders jealous. They were afraid of losing their own power, just like the authorities during the time of Jesus.

The Prime Minister[2] thought he could destroy the Báb's influence by sending Him far away. Although the Báb hadn't done anything wrong, He was arrested and sent to the prison of Mah-Ku, a stone castle in the remote[3] mountains of northern Persia. The Prime Minister thought that now everyone would forget about the Báb.

It was so cold in the prison, that when the Báb washed His face, the water would freeze to ice on His skin. There was no light in the prison either, not even a lamp, so the Báb spent every night in complete darkness. Can you imagine how cold and dark it was, all alone in that faraway place?

But the people of Mah-Ku found out about their innocent prisoner and soon came to love the Báb. Those who lived nearby would go to the prison every morning on the way to work, and ask for the Báb's blessing. Even the prison guards became His friends. They let the Báb's followers visit Him in prison, too.

Before long, all the people were talking about the great Light that was shining out of that dark prison. Do you know what they meant? Yes, they were talking about the Báb.

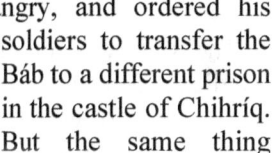

When the Prime Minister heard about this, he became very angry, and ordered his soldiers to transfer the Báb to a different prison in the castle of Chihríq. But the same thing happened again. The guards learned to love their gentle prisoner, and many people came to visit Him.

This time, when the news reached the Prime Minister, he demanded that the Báb be brought to the city of Tabriz immediately. He wanted to find a way to get rid of the Báb once and for all. The king's soldiers put chains on the Báb's hands and feet and around His neck, and brought Him to Tabriz.

As soon as He reached the city, the Báb was arrested and put on trial, but He was not afraid. He boldly told the religious leaders that He was a Messenger of God and that they should follow Him.

This made them even angrier. They took Him outside to be whipped and beaten with a stick across His bare feet. Then they took Him back to prison and sentenced Him to be killed the next day.

That night, in His prison cell, the Báb's face seemed to glow with a special radiance[4] and joy. He knew that He would soon be in Heaven with God.

1. **disciple:** Follower, believer, supporter
2. **Prime Minister:** Head of the government, chief officer appointed by the king
3. **remote:** Far away, distant, isolated, hard to find, difficult to get to
4. **radiance:** Brightness, glow, sparkle, happiness, joy, warmth

The Báb – Lesson #3

Early the next morning, a guard came and took the Báb out to be shot by a firing squad.[5] The Báb was giving final instructions to His secretary and asked the guard to wait, but the guard refused. The Báb told him that nothing on earth could stop Him from finishing His conversation, but the guard still said no.

The Báb was brought before a group of soldiers. Ten thousand people had climbed onto the rooftops to watch the execution. Many were laughing. Some were shouting insults and throwing garbage at the Báb.

Sam Khan, the captain of the soldiers, had been ordered to shoot the Báb. But Sam Khan didn't want to kill an innocent man. He was afraid that God would be angry with him, and he told the Báb how troubled he was. The Báb told Sam Khan not to worry, and to follow his instructions. If he were sincere, God would help him.

The soldiers tied a rope around the Báb's arms and over a nail in the wall, suspending[6] Him above the ground. **Seven hundred and fifty** soldiers lined up in three rows and pointed their rifles at the Báb.

Then Sam Khan shouted, **"Fire! Fire! Fire!"** one row at a time. Can you imagine the loud noise and all of the smoke from **750** rifles? With all those bullets, can you imagine what happened to the Báb?

But when the smoke cleared, everyone gasped in astonishment. The bullets had cut the ropes, and the Báb had disappeared!

The soldiers rushed all around looking for Him. They found Him back in His cell talking with His secretary again. "I have finished My conversation....," He said calmly. "Now you may proceed to fulfill your intention."[7] But Sam Khan and his soldiers knew that a miracle had occurred. God had saved them from killing the Báb, and they refused to shoot at Him again.

Another **750** soldiers were brought in and the Báb was suspended once more. When the soldiers raised their guns to fire, the Báb spoke His last words to the crowd: "The day will come when you will have recognized Me; that day I shall no longer be with you."[8] The people became very quiet.

This time, the soldiers succeeded in killing the Báb. It was noon on July 9th, 1850. The Báb was only 30 years old.

The moment the shots were fired, a great storm suddenly broke over the city. A strange wind blew through the streets. Thick dust blocked out the sunlight and blinded the eyes of those who were watching. The entire city was in darkness. The crowd became frightened and stood in complete silence.

The Báb's friends took His body, and hid it from His enemies for many years. Finally, they carried Him to the Holy Land,[9] where He is buried on Mount Carmel in a beautiful shrine with a golden dome. Today, the Shrine of the Báb is a holy place visited by people from all over the world.

---

5. **firing squad:** A group of soldiers who carry out an execution by gunfire
6. **suspend:** To hang something from above
7. **meaning:** Now you may carry out your plan (Ref: Shoghi Effendi, God Passes By, p. 53)
8. **Ref:** Shoghi Effendi, The Dawn-Breakers, p. 514
9. **Holy Land:** Refers to present-day Israel

The Báb – Lesson #3

Instructions for group leaders for activity #4

Martyrdom of the Báb

> Gather your small group and find a quiet place. You will have about 15 minutes to work. Your job is to ask the questions below and encourage all of the children to share their thoughts. Give hints and encouragement if needed, but don't answer for them. A child who is silent can be asked, "What do you think about this?" Do not allow the children to laugh at or tease each other. Take notes below. If there is time to report back, prepare the group to share a brief summary of their thoughts.

1. Why was the Báb sent away, imprisoned and finally killed by the authorities?

2. Why do you think they used 750 rifles, when just one would have been enough?

3. Do you think the Báb knew He would be killed at a young age?

4. Why do you think He openly proclaimed His Faith instead of hiding for His own safety?

5. What miracle is associated with the martyrdom of the Báb?

6. What does "martyrdom" mean?

> Note: Your students may raise the issue of terrorism. Suicide bombers and other terrorists are sometimes referred to as martyrs because they give their lives for a cause, but they also use violence to hurt innocent people. Their goal is to create fear among the general public and to gain publicity for their political aims. If appropriate, you might ask: What is the difference between a martyr and a terrorist; between willingly giving up one's own life for a higher purpose, and the murder of others supposedly carried out in the name of God?

Bahá'í Children's Classes and Retreats: Theme 3, p. 61

The Báb – Lesson #3

A CANDLE FOR THE BÁB

"I am the Lamp which the Finger of God hath lit…I am the Flame of that supernal Light…"
(Selections from the Writings of the Báb, p. 74)

Materials

- ❑ Votive candles in a variety of colors (one for each child)
- ❑ Play dough ingredients (makes enough for 2-3 children)
    - 1 cup flour
    - 1 cup salt
    - 1 cup water
    - 1 tablespoon cooking oil
    - 1 teaspoon cream of tartar [A]
    - food coloring [B]

For other play dough recipes:
www.playdoughrecipe.com

- ❑ Measuring cups and spoons
- ❑ Sturdy cooking pot
- ❑ Large mixing spoon
- ❑ Sculpting tools (plastic knife, fork, rolling pin, cookie cutters, egg slicer, toothpicks)
- ❑ Cutting board or clean counter top (cover with wax paper or placemat for easy clean up)
- ❑ Sponge or paint brush for smoothing rough edges of the dough
- ❑ Airtight container (plastic bag or tub)
- ❑ Cookie sheet

Instructions for Making Dough

1. Mix all ingredients together in a cooking pot.
2. Stir over medium-low heat until mixture clumps together in a ball.
   (It will look like mashed potatoes. If it's sticky, cook a little longer.)
3. Cool by spreading mixture on a cutting board or a clean counter top.
4. When cool, knead until smooth and form a ball.
5. Store in an airtight container until ready to use.
   (If the dough dries out, it can be softened by adding a little water to the mix.)

> A. Cream of tartar is available in the spice section of most supermarkets.
>   (Salt preserves the dough. Oil makes it smooth. Cream of tartar makes it more elastic.)
>
> B. Tempera paint, powdered jello or any unsweetened powdered drink mix can be used instead of food coloring. You can make the entire batch one color, or make the dough without color, then divide into parts and add a different color to each part. If the children are working in small groups, each group could make a batch of a different color which others can then use.

The Báb – Lesson #3

Instructions for Making Candle Holder

1. Mold dough into desired shape.
   (A variety of kitchen utensils can be used as sculpting tools.)
2. Gently press candle into the dough to make an indentation, then remove.
3. Smooth rough edges with a wet sponge or a paint brush dipped in water.
4. To dry candle holder, place on cookie sheet and bake on low heat (about 200 degrees Fahrenheit or 100 degrees Celsius) for two hours—or longer if dough is very thick.
   (Candle holder can also be air dried, which may take 1-2 days depending on humidity.)
5. When done baking, turn oven off and leave dough inside oven overnight.
   (This will allow it to cool down slowly and prevent cracking.)
6. When completely dry, spray with shellac to preserve (optional).

> Tip: For a large group of children, it may be easier to schedule 2-3 small groups at a time, with a separate set of utensils for each group.

For play-dough making photos:
www.instructables.com/id/How-to-Make-Playdough-Play-doh

The Báb – Lesson #3

Samples of "A Candle for the Báb" craft

 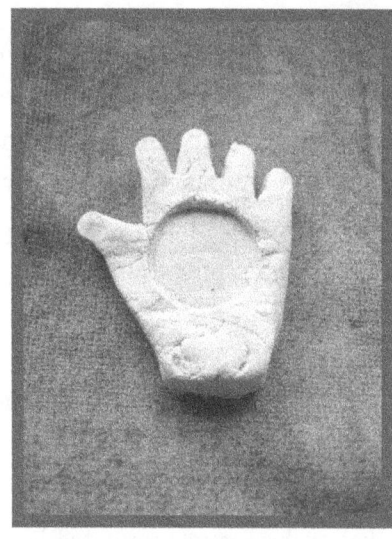 
 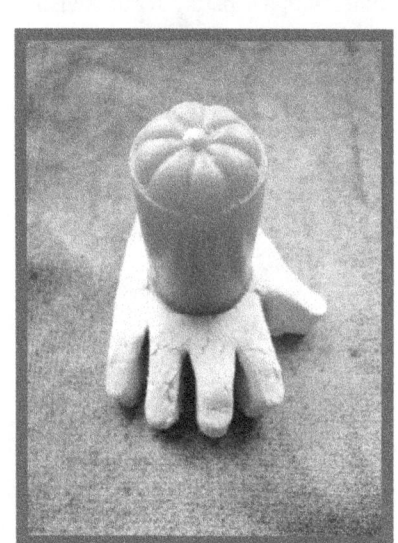 

"So grievous was His plight while in that fortress that, in the Persian Bayan, He Himself has stated that at night-time He did not even have a lighted lamp…" (Shoghi Effendi, God Passes By, p. 18)

"I remember how often [Shoghi Effendi] would tell the visiting pilgrims that because a simple candle was denied the beloved Báb during His imprisonment in Mah-Ku, His resting-place was to be eternally a temple of light." (Ugo Giachery, Shoghi Effendi - Recollections)

The Báb – Lesson #3

**The Báb is buried on Mount Carmel
in a beautiful shrine with a golden dome.**

Bahá'í Children's Classes and Retreats: Theme 3, p. 65

The Báb – Lesson #3

MATERIALS NEEDED

- ❑ White board, easel, markers, eraser
- ❑ Second white board or some chart paper
- ❑ Folders with song sheets and page of quotations for each student[A]
- ❑ Handout on "Imprisonment and Martyrdom of the Báb" (from story packet)[A]
- ❑ Color photograph of the Shrine of the Báb and other illustrations for the story[A]
- ❑ A large black marble or ball bearing to represent a single bullet or musket ball[B]
- ❑ Something to represent 750 bullets, for example:
  - A "thousand chain" with a red ribbon tied at the 750th bead[C]
  - A length of "standard ball chain"[D]
  - A bucket or clear plastic tub filled with 750 beads or marbles[B]
- ❑ Instruction sheet on "Martyrdom of the Báb" for each group leader (activity #4)
- ❑ Materials for craft activities (see separate list), sample of each project, and page of instructions for the assistants at each station
- ❑ References for teachers (included at the end of this manual)

A. Included in the Handouts section of this teacher's guide. The student handouts, along with full-page color illustrations designed to accompany the lessons, are available for download from: **www.UnityWorksStore.com**. Click on Children's Classes > The Báb > student handouts. Illustrations can be printed on cardstock and posted on the wall during class as an aid for visual learners and to help bring the lessons and readings to life.

B. A musket ball is made of solid lead and is approximately 1/2-inch (1.25 cm) in diameter. A 14 mm opaque round black marble (available from aquarium supply, craft and dollar stores) would be about the right size. You can also order online. Search for "black marbles" or visit www.mcgillswarehouse.com and enter "frosted black marbles" in the search box on the top right.

C. A "thousand chain" (used in the Montessori system of education for teaching math) is available from a variety of online discount stores. Visit some of the outlets below and enter "bead chain" in the search box.

- www.montessoriconcepts.com
- www.aplusmontessori.com
- www.kidadvance.com
- www.adenamontessori.us
- www.montessorioutlet.com

Used Montessori materials may also be available online, for example, you can search for "Montessori thousand chain for sale Craigslist."

D. Ball chain can be found at the hardware store or online, for example: http://bead-chain.com/Standard-Ball-Chain.htm.

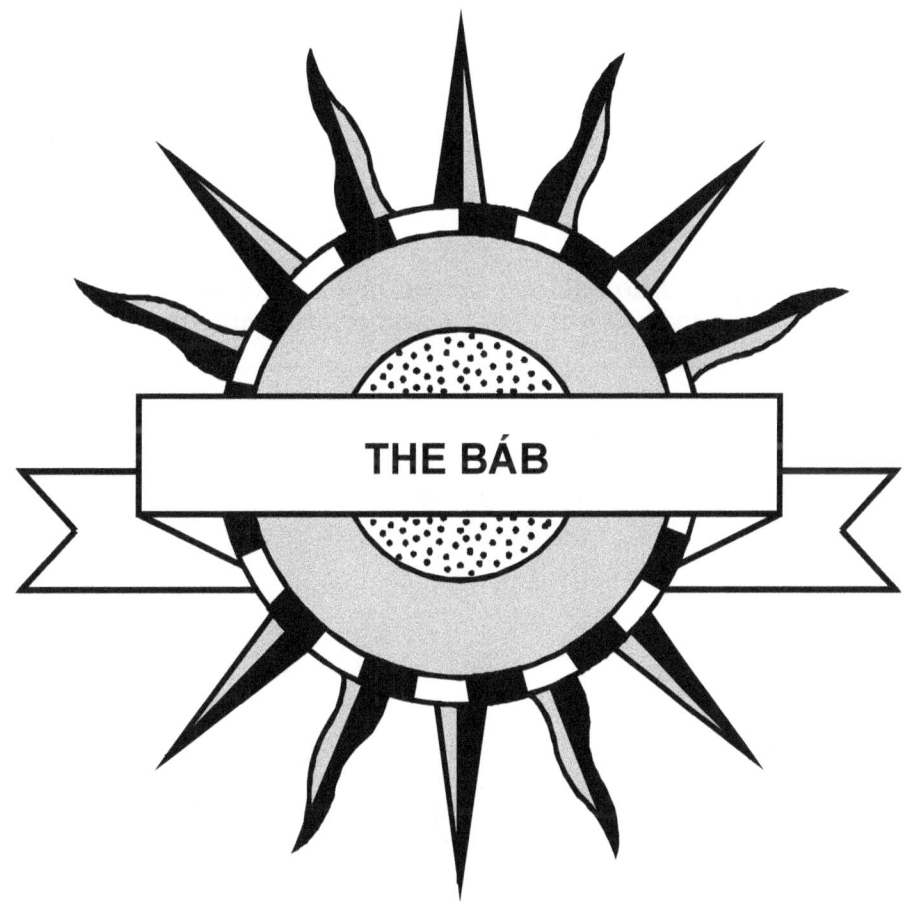

LESSON #4

The Primal Point

The Báb – Lesson #4

The Primal Point

Objectives: Students will be able to:
- Tell someone who the Báb is.
- Relate key facts about the Báb and His life.
- Describe His station as the Primal Point between the Adamic Cycle and the Bahá'í Cycle, between humankind's childhood and its maturity, at once fulfilling the promises of the former Prophets while ushering in the dawn of a new Day.

Before class, prepare all instructional materials on the list at the end of this lesson. Set up felt board and craft activity. Orient volunteer assistants. Distribute folders and pens to all.

---

1. SONG: "The Prophets…" (5 min.)

Have students take out their song sheets and sing along. Students should remember the song from a previous lesson. Ask the music coordinator for assistance if needed.

2. MEMORY QUOTES (5 min.)

Ask for a few volunteers to recite from memory the quotes learned during previous lessons:

- *"GOOD NEWS! GOOD NEWS! The Trumpet is sounding! …O Ye that sleep, Awake! Be Happy! Be full of Joy! …This is the day of the Proclamation of the Báb!"* ('Abdu'l-Bahá)

- *"Awake, awake, for, lo! the Gate of God is open and the morning light is shedding its radiance upon all mankind."* (The Báb)

- *"Is there any Remover of difficulties save God? Say: Praised be God! He is God! All are His servants, and all abide by His bidding!"* (The Báb)

3. REVIEW (15-30 min.)

Choose one or more of the following activities to review the life of the Bab.

A. <u>Three Key Dates</u>: Write the following dates on the board and ask the class what happened on each one. Then explain that Bahá'ís take these special Holy Days off from work or school to commemorate the life of the Báb.

- **Oct. 20, 1819** *(Birth of the Báb)*
- **May 23, 1844** *(Declaration of the Báb)*
- **July 9, 1850** *(Martyrdom of the Báb)*

Bahá'í Children's Classes and Retreats: Theme 3, p. 70

The Báb – Lesson #4

B. <u>Nine Important Facts</u>: Divide the class into small groups and ask each group to develop a list of nine or more important facts about the Báb and His life. Allow about five minutes to work. Reconvene the class and have each group share one fact. Write each fact briefly on the board. Continue until all ideas have been shared. Then praise the students for what they have learned.

C. <u>Who Is the Báb</u>? Have the same small groups consider this question and prepare an answer. Give them about five minutes to work, then share the responses.

D. <u>Peer Questions</u>: Say the following words and write them in large print on the board:

? | Who   Where
  | What   Why
  | When   How
?

Give each student a sheet of notebook paper and ask them to write 2-3 questions about the Báb. The questions should begin with one of the words listed on the board. For example: "**Who** raised the Báb?" and "**Why** did His teacher send Him home from school?"

Proceed around the room, calling on each student to ask one of their questions. Then call on another student to answer it. Have the children raise their hands. Continue with a second round of questions if there is time, and praise students for their efforts.

4. FELT LESSON: "The Primal Point" (15-20 min.)

Present the felt lesson on "The Primal Point" (see patterns and instructions at the end of this lesson). If there is time, ask several children if they would like to try it in front of the class without your help. They may also wish to volunteer for the children's performance.

5. WORKSHEET: "The Primal Point" (5-10 min.)

With the completed felt lesson still on display, give students the worksheet on "The Primal Point" and have them fill in the blanks (see sample at the end of this lesson). If desired, they can also color in the shapes with crayons or colored pencils.

6. SONG: "1844" (10 min.)

Have students take out their song sheets and sing along.
Ask the music coordinator for assistance if needed.

Collect all folders and pencils.

Bahá'í Children's Classes and Retreats: Theme 3, p. 71

The Báb – Lesson #4

7. CRAFT: "The Primal Point" (45 min.)

Craft projects are designed to reinforce the material presented during class. The children will be making a craft-foam diagram to illustrate the pivotal relationship of the Báb's Dispensation to the Adamic Cycle and the Bahá'í Cycle.

Begin by showing the class a sample of the craft. When students have completed the project, they should clean up their work area, then assist others who might need help. Remind them to label all projects with their names. Quiet music can be played in the background if desired. The completed project can be used as a teaching tool.

Dismiss the children for outdoor activities when done.

* * * * *

America displays her illustration of the Primal Point

The Báb – Lesson #4

"The Primal Point"

Teacher's Guide, Script, and Patterns for Felt Lesson

TO THE TEACHER: This packet contains instructions, a script, and patterns for making a felt lesson on "The Primal Point." In order to present the lesson, you will need either a felt board or carpet board (see instructions on following pages). A carpet board is more durable and has a more finished look. After preparing the board and cutting out the pattern pieces, read through the script and repeat the actions until you can present the lesson smoothly. The objectives of the lesson are listed below. The children will be able to:

(1) Recognize the Primal Point as one of the titles of the Báb.

(2) Explain that He is the link between the Adamic and the Bahá'í Cycle.

(3) Tell how His coming is a turning point for humanity.

Bahá'í Children's Classes and Retreats: Theme 3, p. 73

The Báb – Lesson #4

Script for Felt Lesson

"The Primal Point"

	NARRATION	ACTION
1	Throughout the ages, God has sent many divine Teachers to the world. It all started with Adam who taught us there was only one God, and who showed us the difference between right and wrong.	Place felt pointer for Adam at an angle on left side of board.
2	Each Prophet brought the teachings of God to His own people. (Do you remember some of their names? That's right.) And each Prophet told us of a great Teacher who would come in the future, to unite all the religions and bring peace to the world.	Add pointers for the remaining Prophets, except Bahá'u'lláh. (See layout on next page.)
3	The One promised by all of these Manifestations is Bahá'u'lláh. Bahá'u'lláh said that we are all part of one human family and that all of the great religions come from the same God.	Place pointer for Bahá'u'lláh on top right, leaving a space in the middle.
4	The Báb is <u>also</u> a Messenger of God. He came before Bahá'u'lláh to prepare the people for the Promised One. The Báb is the Gate to Bahá'u'lláh, who showed people the way.	Add circle for the Báb.
5	The Báb is called the **Primal Point**. He pointed people towards the Promised One. He is the link between the old and the new. The Báb is the connecting point between the Adamic Cycle (which began with Adam), and the Bahá'í Cycle, which we live in today.	Add signs for Adamic and Bahá'í cycles. Adamic Bahá'í
6	The Adamic Cycle lasted for 6,000 years. The Adamic Cycle is called the Age of Prophecy because during that time, God's Messengers told us about things that would happen in the future.	Point to the left side of the chart.
7	The Bahá'í Cycle is called the Age of Fulfillment because now it is time for God's promises from the past to come true.	Point to the right side of the chart.
8	During the Bahá'í Cycle, many more Prophets will come under the shadow of Bahá'u'lláh. The Bahá'í Cycle will last 500 thousand years. **That's a long time!**	Add remaining pointers on right.
9	The left side also represents mankind's childhood. The right side represents its maturity—when the human race will grow up, and all people will learn to live in unity and peace.	Add child to left of pointers. Add adult to right of pointers.

Bahá'í Children's Classes and Retreats: Theme 3, p. 74

The Báb – Lesson #4

Layout for Felt Lesson on "The Primal Point"

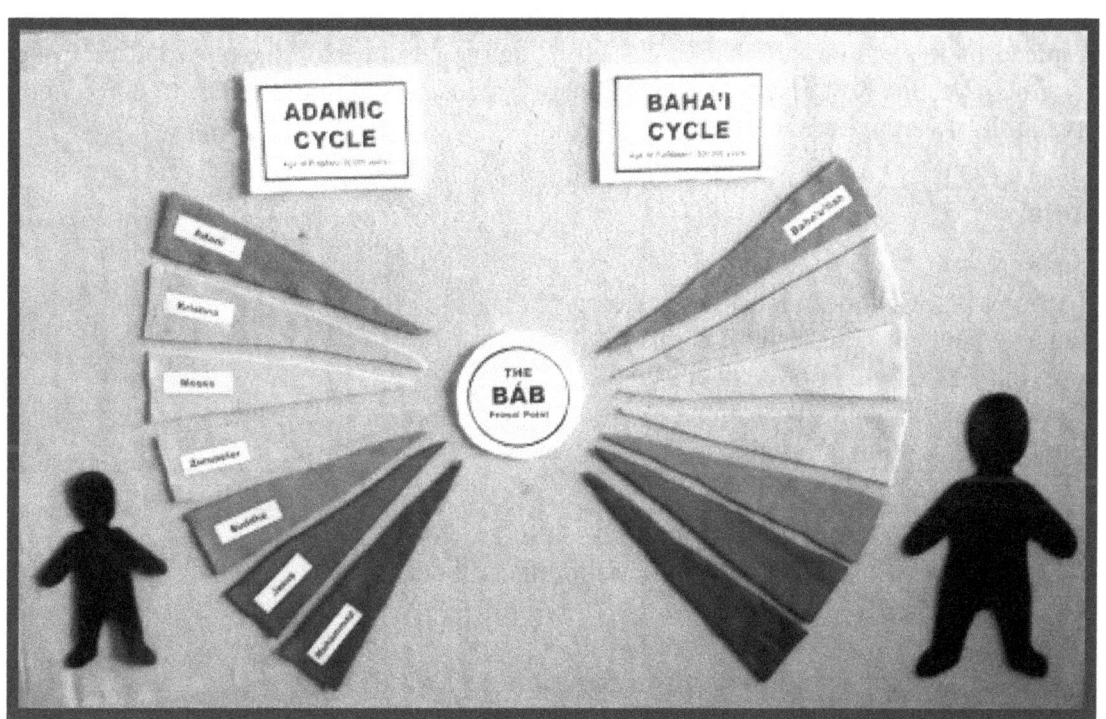

Triangle	Label	Color	Triangle	Label	Color
1	Adam	dark blue	8	Bahá'u'lláh	dark blue
2	Krishna	light blue	9	(no label)	light blue
3	Moses	light green	10	(no label)	light green
4	Zoroaster	yellow	11	(no label)	yellow
5	Buddha	orange	12	(no label)	orange
6	Jesus	red	13	(no label)	red
7	Muhammad	purple	14	(no label)	purple

Suggested Colors for Felt Pieces

The Báb – Lesson #4

Instructions for Making Felt or Carpet Board

A felt board can be purchased at a teacher supply store, or one can be constructed by gluing a large piece of felt onto a stiff backing such as heavy cardboard, thin plywood or masonite. Spray glue gives the best results. A carpet board is constructed in the same way. Felt and glue are available at yardage and craft supply stores.

Materials

- Sharp scissors
- Large piece of felt or indoor-outdoor carpet*
  (choose beige or other neutral color,
  approx. 24 x 36 in. or 60 x 90 cm.)
- Backing board (same size as felt or carpet)
- Spray glue or white craft glue

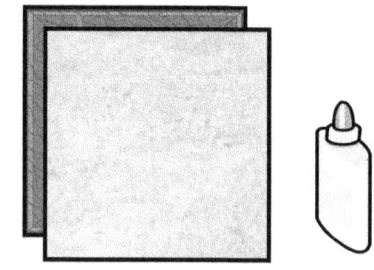

  * If using carpet, test a piece of felt to be sure it sticks.
  Some types of carpeting may work better than others.

Instructions for Making Felt Pieces

1. Photocopy the pattern pages.
2. Laminate the copies, then carefully cut out the patterns and labels.
3. Place each pattern on the correct color of felt and trace.
4. Cut out each felt piece.
5. Glue laminated labels to felt pieces as indicated on previous page.
6. Store the script and felt pieces in a zip-lock plastic bag for ease of use.

Tip: Thicker felt is easier to cut and is more durable.

Materials

- Pattern pieces (on following pages)
- Felt pieces in ten different colors
- Pen for tracing patterns
- Sharp scissors
- White craft glue

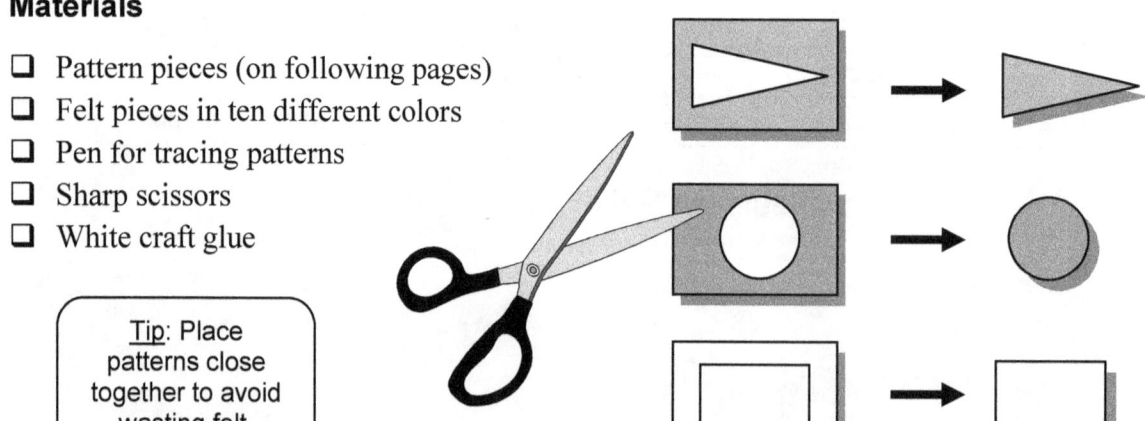

Tip: Place patterns close together to avoid wasting felt.

Bahá'í Children's Classes and Retreats: Theme 3, p. 76

The Báb – Lesson #4

Patterns for Felt Lesson on "The Primal Point"

Photocopy this page and laminate the copy. Carefully cut out patterns and trace onto felt.

The Báb – Lesson #2

Pattern for felt lesson on "The Primal Point"

Cut 2 rectangles from white felt.

Cut 14 felt triangles (2 of each color). ⇨

The Báb – Lesson #2

Pattern for felt lesson on "The Primal Point"

Bahá'í Children's Classes and Retreats: Theme 3, p. 77

The Báb – Lesson #4

Photocopy this page and laminate the copy. Carefully cut out circle pattern and trace onto felt. Cut out laminated labels and glue to felt pointers as indicated. Use a generous amount of glue so it soaks into the felt for a stronger bond.

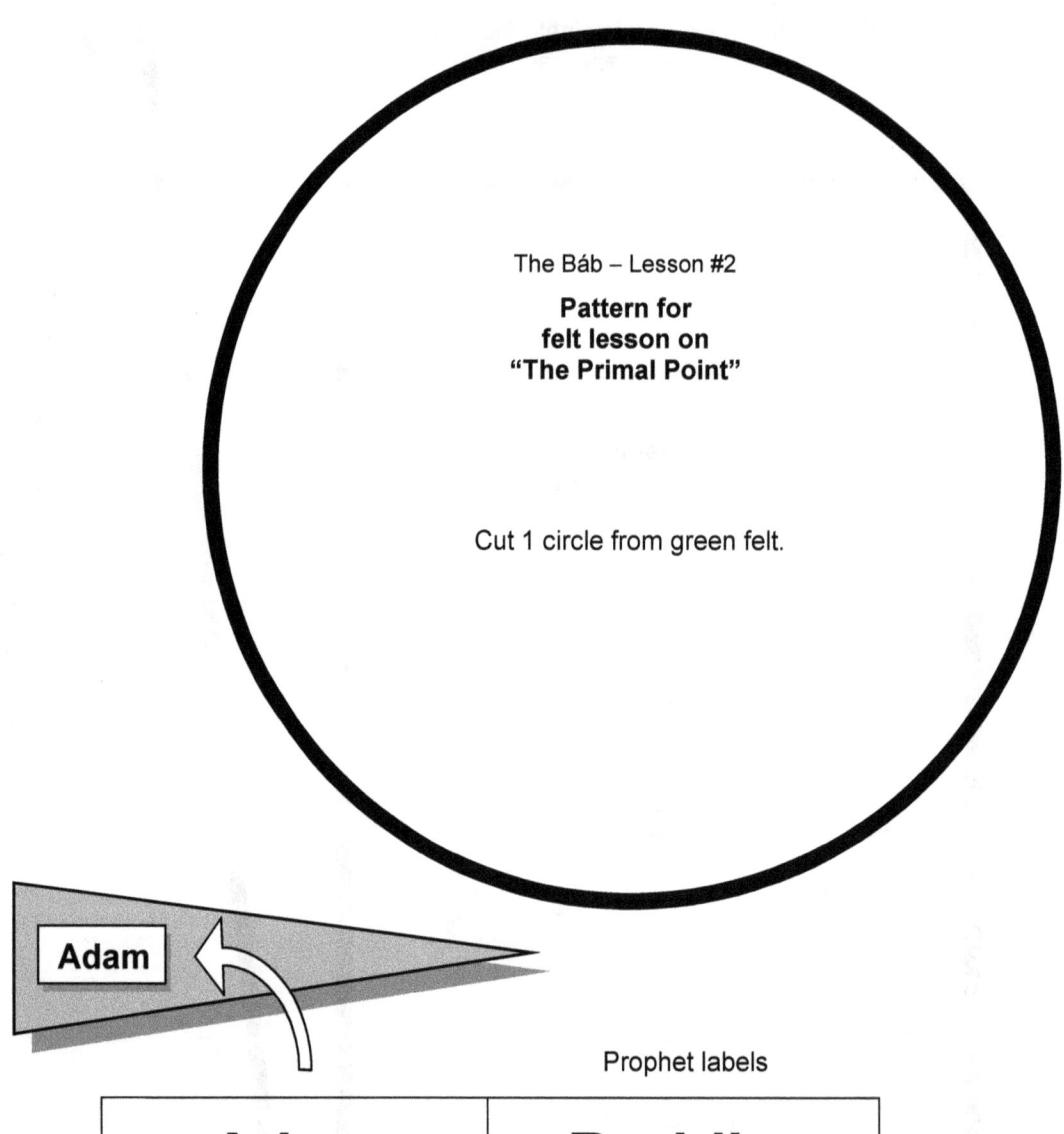

The Báb – Lesson #2
Pattern for felt lesson on "The Primal Point"

Cut 1 circle from green felt.

Prophet labels

Adam	**Buddha**
Krishna	**Jesus**
Moses	**Muhammad**
Zoroaster	**Bahá'u'lláh**

Bahá'í Children's Classes and Retreats: Theme 3, p. 78

The Báb – Lesson #4

Labels for felt lesson on "The Primal Point"

Photocopy this page and laminate the copy. Carefully cut out laminated labels and glue to felt as indicated previously. Use a generous amount of glue so it soaks into the felt for a stronger bond.

THE BÁB — Primal Point

ADAMIC CYCLE — Age of Prophecy (6,000 years)

BAHÁ'Í CYCLE — Age of Fulfillment (500,000 years)

The Báb – Lesson #4

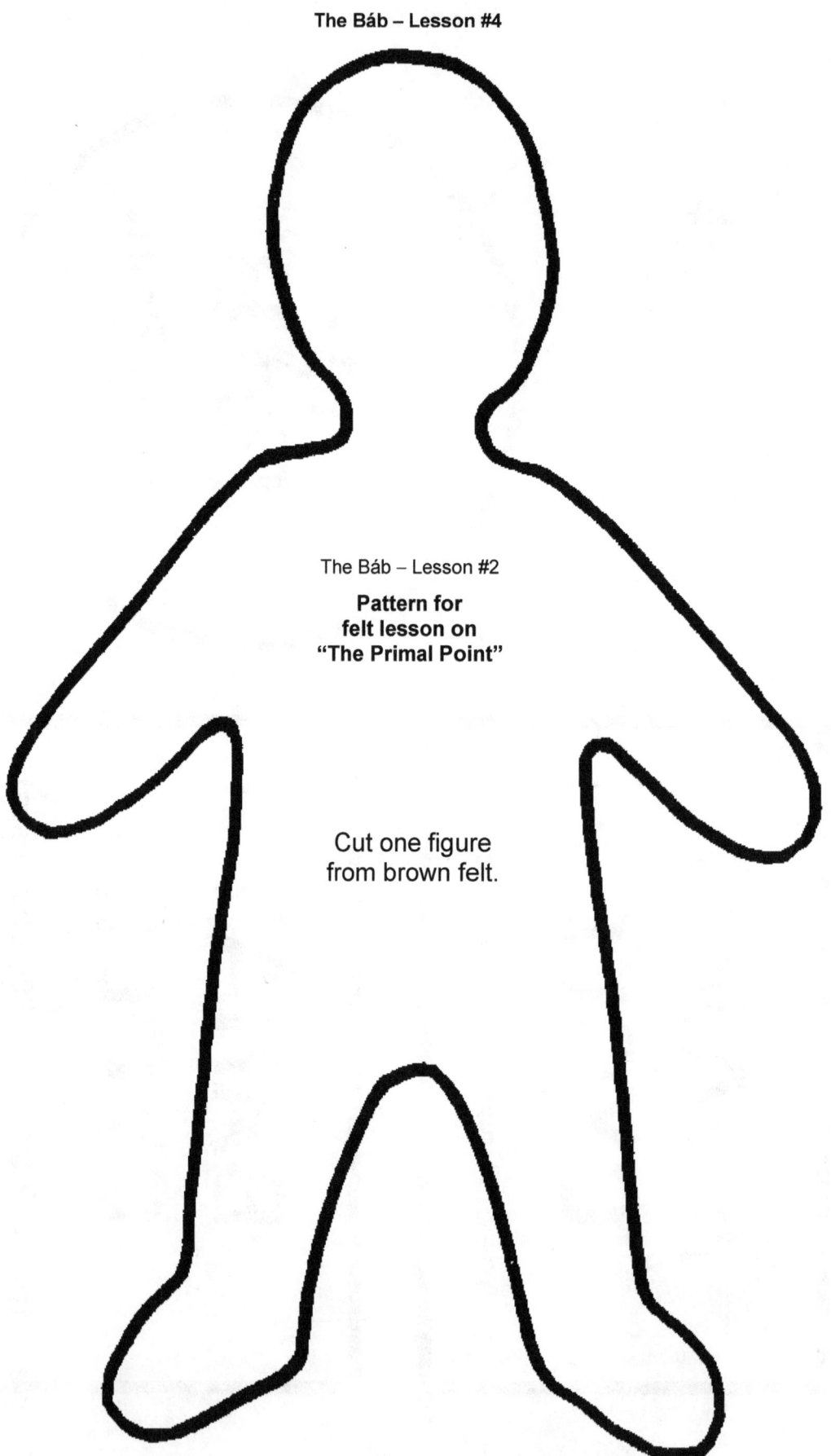

The Báb – Lesson #2

Pattern for felt lesson on "The Primal Point"

Cut one figure from brown felt.

Bahá'í Children's Classes and Retreats: Theme 3, p. 80

The Báb – Lesson #4

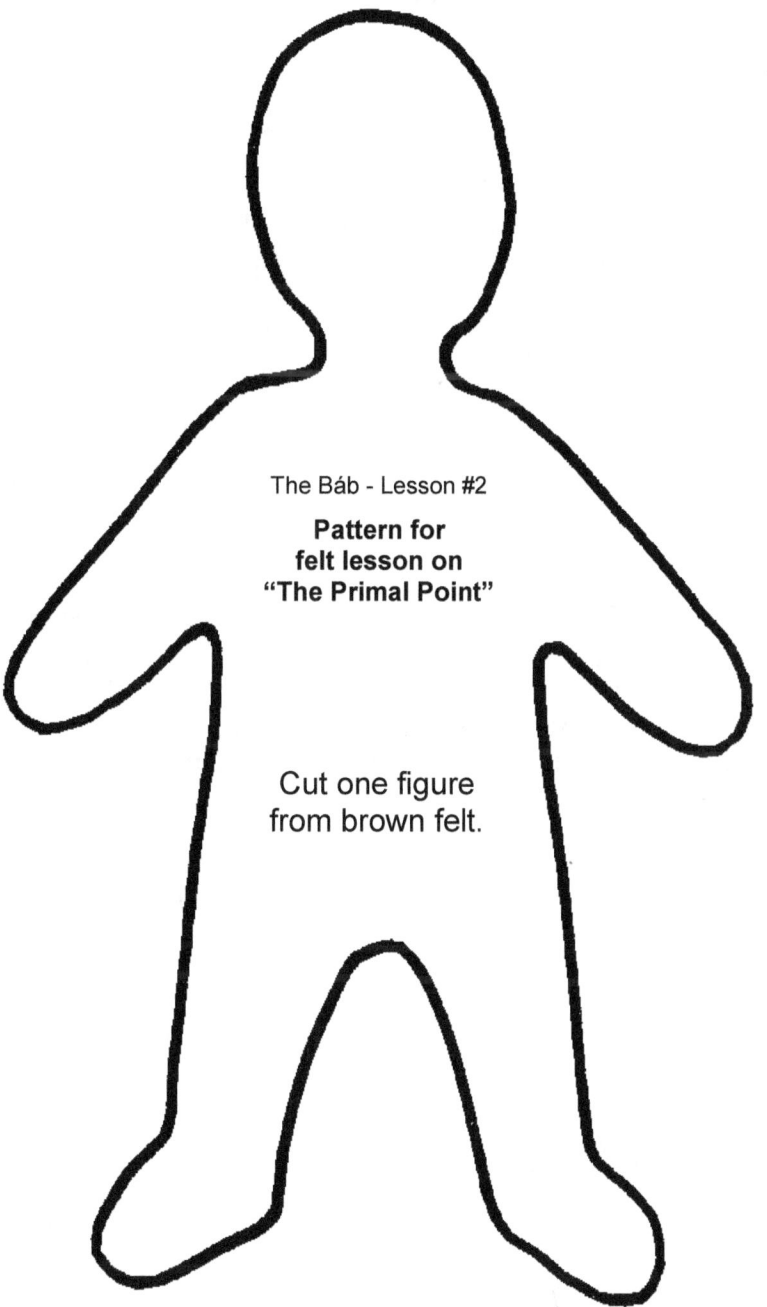

The Báb - Lesson #2

Pattern for felt lesson on "The Primal Point"

Cut one figure from brown felt.

Bahá'í Children's Classes and Retreats: Theme 3, p. 81

The Báb – Lesson #4

Note to the Teacher

> "I am the Primal Point from which have been generated all created things."
> – Selections from the Writings of the Báb, p. 12

Primal means *original* or *first*—like a seed from which life grows. It refers to God, the Creator of all life. Here, the Báb is speaking with the Voice of God.

"In the time of the First Manifestation the Primal Will appeared in Adam; in the day of Noah It became known in Noah; in the day of Abraham in Him; and so in the day of Moses; the day of Jesus; the day of Muhammad, the Apostle of God; the day of the 'Point of the Bayán;' the day of Him Whom God shall make manifest; and the day of the One Who will appear after Him Whom God shall make manifest. Hence the inner meaning of the words uttered by the Apostle of God, 'I am all the Prophets,' inasmuch as what shineth resplendent in each one of Them hath been and will ever remain the one and the same sun." (Selections from the Writings of the Báb, p. 126)

"They resemble the sun which no matter how often it riseth and setteth is still the one and same sun." (Bahá'u'lláh, Prayers and Meditations, p. 50)

Point is the center of a circle. It refers to a central location or hub. The Báb's revelation served as a point of union connecting the dispensations of the past with those of the future. His advent represents a pivot point, fulfilling the promises of the former Prophets, while at the same time ushering in the dawn of a new Day. The Báb also brought a new calendar, creating a new point in time and dating the beginning of a new era from the time of his own declaration.

"Recall the peerless tributes paid to His memory by the Founder of the Faith, acclaiming Him Monarch of God's Messengers, the Primal Point round Whom the realities of all the Prophets circle in adoration." (Shoghi Effendi, Citadel of Faith, p. 81)

"…Blessed Báb, Prophet and Herald of the Faith of Bahá'u'lláh, Founder of the Dispensation marking the culmination of the six thousand year old Adamic Cycle, Inaugurator of the five thousand century Baha'i Cycle." (Shoghi Effendi, Citadel of Faith, p. 80)

The left side of the diagram also represents the childhood of humankind; the center is its adolescence—a transitional period marked by great turmoil and upheaval; and the right denotes its eventual maturity.

"The creative energies released at the hour of the birth of His Revelation, endowing mankind with the potentialities of the attainment of maturity are deranging, during the present transitional age, the equilibrium of the entire planet as the inevitable prelude to the consummation in world unity of the coming of age of the human race." (Shoghi Effendi: Citadel of Faith, p. 81)

* * * * *

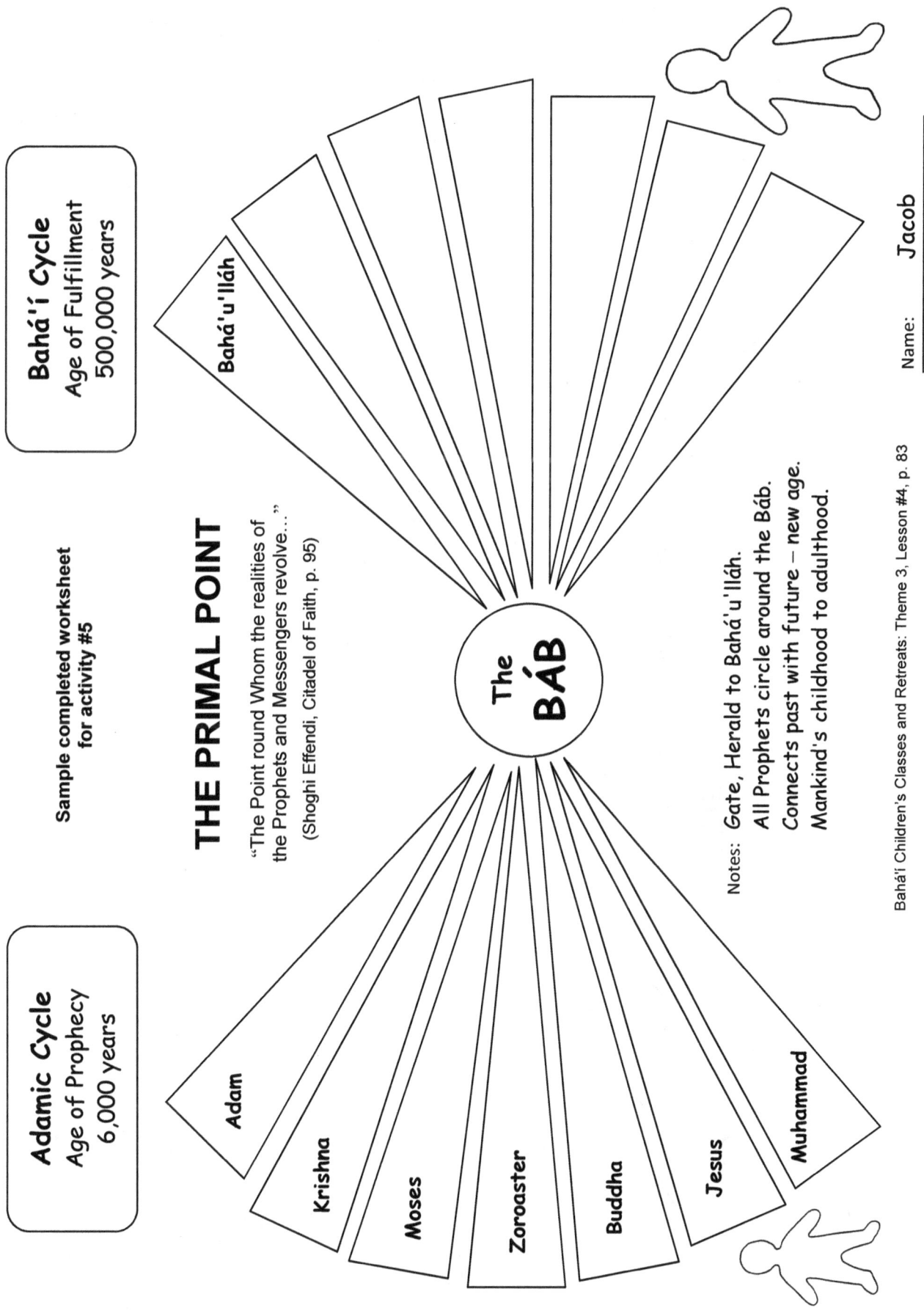

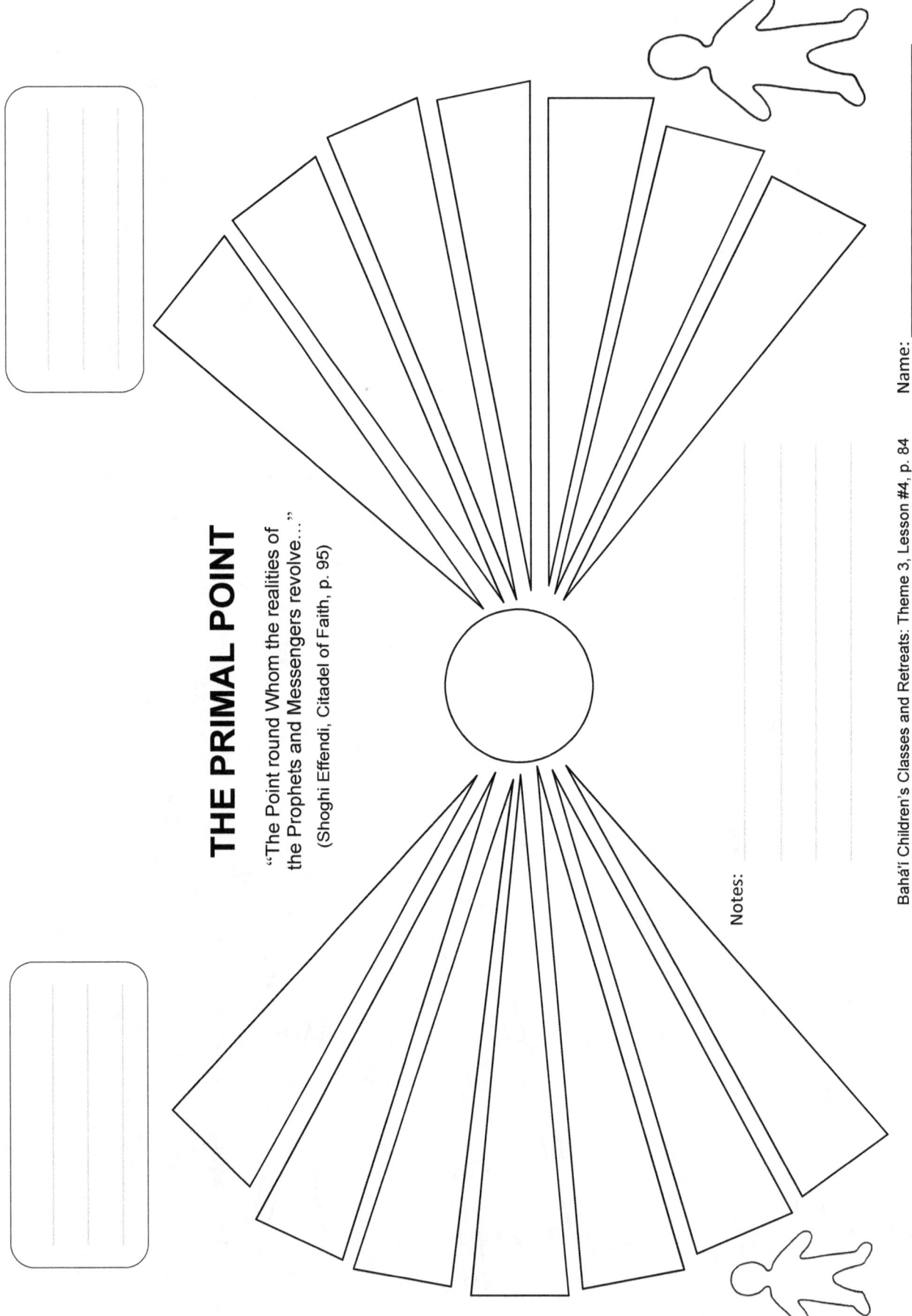

The Báb – Lesson #4

"Primal Point" Craft

> "I am the Primal Point from which have been generated all created things."
> – Selections from the Writings of the Báb, p. 12

Materials
- Poster board, approx. 11 x 14 in. (28 x 36 cm.), one per child
- Craft foam in 8 or 9 different colors (1-2 sheets per child)
- Patterns (Cut from thick vinyl placemat to make one set for every 4-5 children, or laminate next page, then carefully cut out laminated patterns for children to trace.)
- Black markers (don't distribute until needed)
- Black pens (for writing Prophet names)
- Rulers
- Scissors
- Glue sticks (one per child)

Instructions
1. Put name on back of poster board.
2. Using the triangle pattern, cut out 14 foam triangles, two of each color.
3. Turn pieces over so pen marks are facing down. Then label one set of triangles with the Prophet names, as shown on the next page. (Arrows should point to the right.)
4. Label one triangle with "Bahá'u'lláh" using the same color foam used for "Adam" to show that both are the beginning of a new cycle. (Arrow should point to the left.)
5. Using the circle pattern, cut one foam circle. Using the marker, label it "The Báb."
6. Using the rectangle pattern, cut two rectangles from the same color of foam. Using the marker, label one "Adamic Cycle" and the other "Bahá'í Cycle."
7. Using the people patterns, cut one child and one adult from brown or black foam.
8. Using the diagram below as a guide, arrange all the foam pieces on the poster board.
9. Glue each piece in place, starting with the center circle. Glue the middle arrows next.

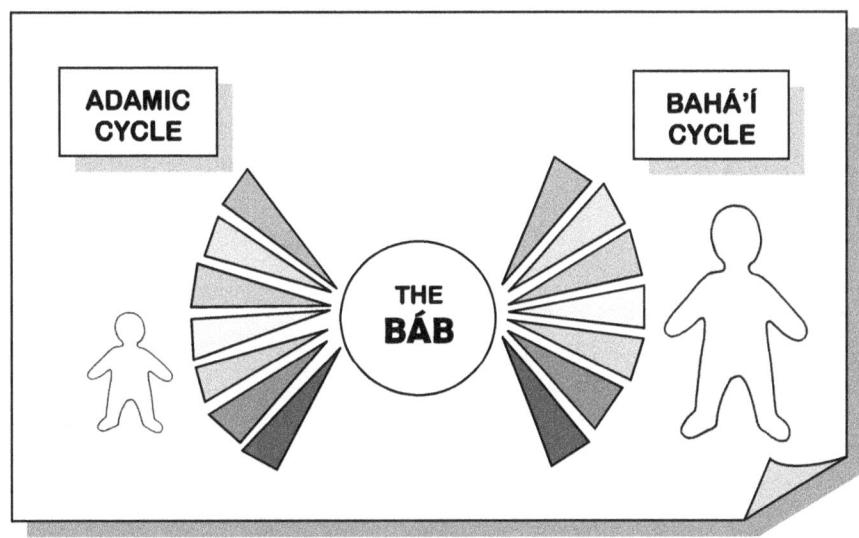

Bahá'í Children's Classes and Retreats: Theme 3, p. 85

The Báb – Lesson #4

Patterns for Primal Point Craft

TIPS

1. Place patterns near edge of foam to minimize waste.

2. Trace around pattern or tape it to foam and cut.

3. Younger children may need help cutting out human figures.

Triangle	Label	Color Suggestion
1	Adam	pink
2	Krishna	light blue
3	Moses	light green
4	Zoroaster	yellow
5	Buddha	orange
6	Jesus	red
7	Muhammad	purple

Cut two from same color of foam.

Cut one.

Cut fourteen, 2 from each color.

Cut one child and one adult from brown or black foam.

Bahá'í Children's Classes and Retreats: Theme 3, p. 86

The Báb – Lesson #4

Children working on the "Primal Point" craft

The Báb – Lesson #4

MATERIALS NEEDED

- White board, easel, markers, eraser
- Folder, notebook paper, pen or pencil for each student
- Song sheets and page of quotations for each student [A]
- Felt lesson on "The Primal Point" (script and patterns included)
- Felt board (with a second easel for convenience if available)
- Worksheet on "The Primal Point" for each student (sample included) [A]
- Materials for craft activity (see separate list), sample project and instructions
- References for teachers (included at the end of this manual)

A. The song sheets, worksheets and quotations are included in the Handouts section of this manual. All handouts, along with full-page color illustrations to accompany the lessons, are available in the download packet for this teacher's guide: **www.UnityWorksStore.com** > Children's Classes > The Báb > student handouts. The illustrations can be posted on the walls during class as an aid for visual learners and to help bring the lessons and readings to life.

* * * * *

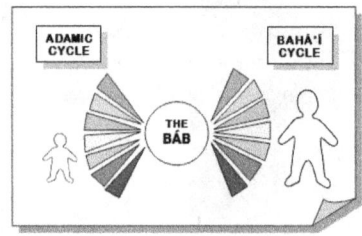

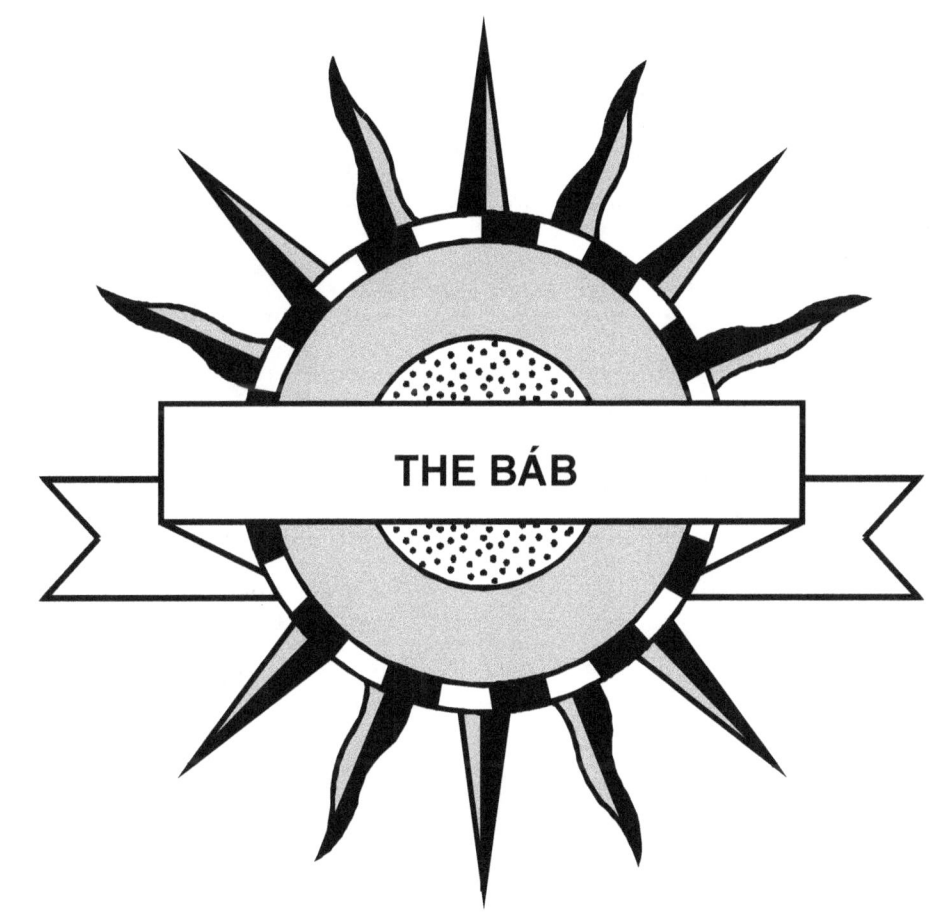

Additional Activities

The Báb: Gate to Bahá'u'lláh

Additional Activities

If time is available, you may wish to plan one or more additional activities related to the theme of *The Báb: Gate to Bahá'u'lláh*.

Treasure Hunt	91-95
Outside Research Project	96-99
Jesus and the Báb	100-106
Puzzles	107-114
Mazes	107-108
Word Search	109
Mystery Dates	110
Number Puzzle	111
Cryptogram	112
Word Scramble	113
Puzzle Solutions	114
Illuminated Prayer	115-116
Online Slide Show	117
Coloring Pages	117, 169-177

The Báb – Additional Activities

TREASURE HUNT

This hour-long activity takes a bit of preparation by the teacher, but it helps to reinforce the concept of a spiritual search and offers an enjoyable challenge that children are not likely to forget. It is also an inexpensive way to get children working together and having fun.

After learning about Mulla Husayn's search for the Báb (Lesson #2), take the children on a treasure hunt. They can be divided into two or more teams. A series of pre-written clues will lead them to the treasure, which should remain a secret until all of the children have discovered it independently and claimed their reward.

Materials

- ☐ Hat or bag containing the names of each child printed on a slip of paper [A]
- ☐ One 3x5 card and a pen or pencil for each team [B]
- ☐ Three sets of clues:
    - Complete list of clues for the teacher and any assistants
    - Second set written on bright paper and cut into separate pieces (for hiding)
    - Third set cut into pieces for distributing a different starting clue to each team [C]
- ☐ Plastic Easter eggs for holding each clue (optional)
- ☐ Hidden treasure (we use a silver teapot with a note leading to the prizes)
- ☐ Small prize for each child (goody bags, snack, candy, dream catchers, polished rocks, plastic gemstones, stuffed animals, mini-puzzles, etc.)

A. Put at least one older child or youth on each team. Form teams by putting the names of the younger children in a hat or bag. Then have each older one pull out several names.

B. Each team will receive a small card for writing down the clues they find along the way. The completed card will be submitted to the teacher in exchange for the final clue which leads to the treasure.

C. If all of the teams will be using the same route, you will need to give each team a different starting point, or have them begin at different times. Otherwise, they will all start together and follow each other to the next clue. This means you will also need more locations than the number of teams, e.g., with five teams, you will need at least six locations.

Bahá'í Children's Classes and Retreats: Theme 3, p. 91

The Báb – Additional Activities

Setting up the Treasure Hunt

1. **Start at the end:** Find a good place to hide the treasure. It can be indoors or out, depending on safety, the weather or other factors, and it should be difficult to find without using clues. Another option is to hide the treasure at the starting point, once children have left the area.

2. **Plan the route:** Do you want children to stay inside the house? Can they go upstairs and downstairs? Are certain areas off limits? Can all or part of the treasure hunt take place outside?

3. **Prepare the clues:** Develop a set of clues appropriate to the reading level and abilities of the children. More challenging clues might consist of riddles, poems with missing words, compass directions, backwards writing, an envelope filled with letters or words to unscramble, puzzle pieces to be assembled, musical notes on a staff that spell out a secret message, or other codes. This is your chance to be creative!

   Easier clues might take the form of simple directions, e.g., "Take 3 giant steps backwards and look under the big rock to find the next clue." (Remember that children may take smaller steps than an adult.) For children with limited reading skills, you can use pictures, e.g., a picture of a bathtub would indicate that the next clue can be found in the bathtub.

   Clues can be written on brightly-colored paper so they are easy to identify, or hidden inside plastic Easter eggs or other small water-resistant containers—especially if the treasure hunt will take place outdoors. Use 5-10 clues (see sample below), depending on the ages of the children and the number of teams.

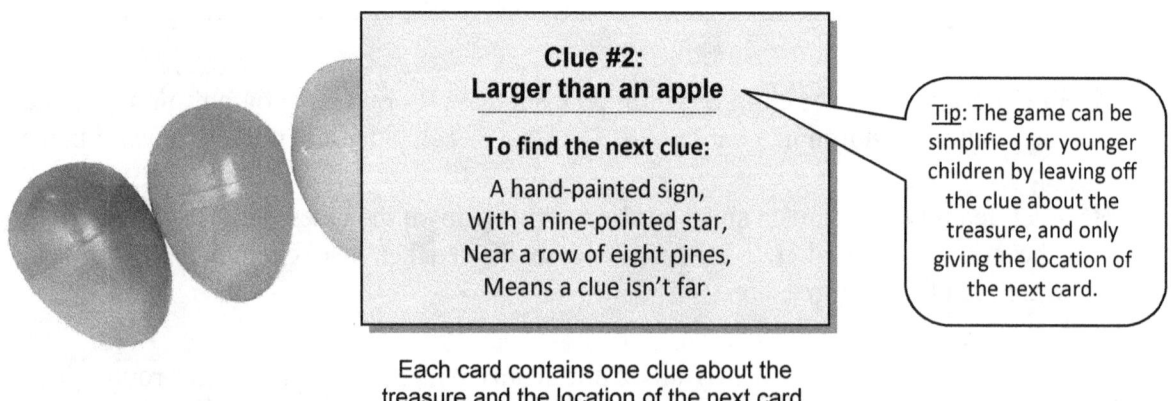

Each card contains one clue about the treasure and the location of the next card.

4. **Hide the clues:** Hide the clues in different locations, as far apart as possible, with each clue leading to the next.

The Báb – Additional Activities

Sample Treasure Routes

Linear Route: Each clue leads to the next one, with the final clue leading to the treasure. This is easier if there is only one team.

Circular Route: In addition to leading to the next location, each card should reveal one characteristic of the treasure (e.g., larger than an apple, smaller than a basketball). The last clue leads back to the first one. Teams must visit every station, collecting all of the clues on a card, which is then submitted to the teacher in exchange for the final clue. A circular route is best if there is more than one team, each with a different starting point.

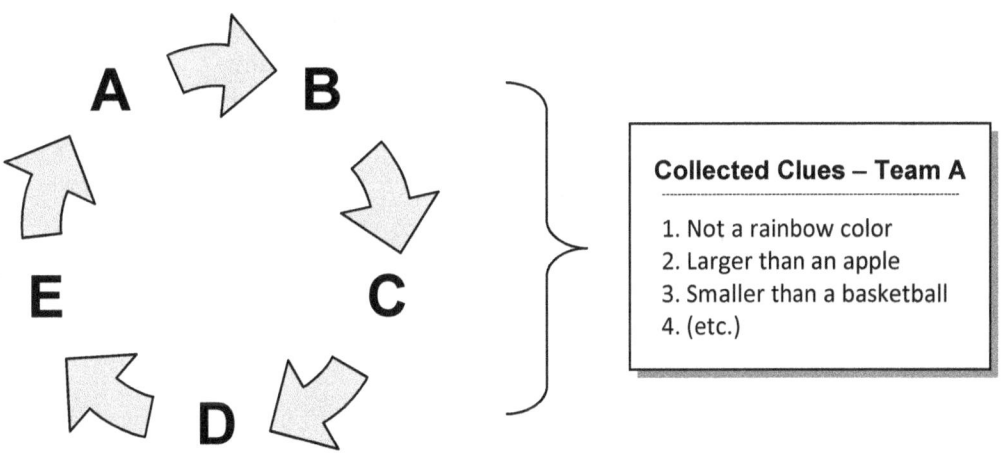

Note: We use a silver teapot to represent the treasure.
Each clue card contains one of the teapot's characteristics:

1. *Not a color found in the rainbow*
2. *Larger than an apple*
3. *Smaller than a basketball*
4. *Has writing in more than one language*
5. *Weighs more than 1 pound*
6. *Too hot to touch when in use*
7. *Hard to break*
8. *Has one moving part*

The final clue is a photo of the teapot, cut into puzzle shapes. When children assemble the puzzle and locate the teapot, they find a small sack of "jewels" inside and a note saying:

Congratulations! You have found the treasure!
One prize per person is on the table in the garage.
Keep the secret!

The Báb – Additional Activities

Sample rhyming clues for the Treasure Hunt

A. Look into your own two eyes.
   Reflect. Behind is your surprise.

B. The next location is not so hot.
   This is the only clue you've got.

C. Roses are red,
   Violets are blue,
   Find the first kind,
   And you've found the next clue.

D. Right by some corn,
   That was planted in March.
   Near a wood fence,
   Under an _____,

E. Tucked inside
   A plastic pouch
   Under a pillow,
   On top of the _____,

F. View this message in a mirror,
   If you want to see it clearer!

Locations
A. Behind the mirror
B. In the refrigerator
C. Next to the rose bush
D. Under the arch in the vegetable garden
E. On the couch

Backwards Text

Tip: To create mirrored text using Microsoft Word 2007 . . .

1. On the **Insert** tab, in the **Text** group, click **WordArt**.
2. Then click the WordArt style that you want.
3. Type your text in the **Text** box and click **OK**.
4. To change the color, shape or style of the letters, click on the text
   to bring up the WordArt Tools menu, then click the **Format** tab.
5. To flip the text, grab the left sizing handle, drag it across to the right and release.

the next clue ⇒ **the next clue** (mirrored)

Look beneath
the apple tree,
and the next clue,
you will see!
(shown mirrored)

The Báb – Additional Activities

Orienting the children for the Treasure Hunt

Remind children that:

When God sends a new Messenger, most people don't recognize Him at first because their hearts have not been prepared, but there are always some whose hearts are ready, and they are expecting Him. One such pure soul, Mulla Husayn, decided to search for the new Messenger and became the first to find the Báb.

Do you remember that the Báb asked him not to tell anyone yet? He said that 17 more pure-hearted souls would have to find Him on their own, searching by themselves, just as Mulla Husayn had done. God would guide their steps.

Then, when all 18 had discovered the Báb, He would send them out across the land to tell people that the Promised Qá'im had come, and to prepare them for the coming of Bahá'u'lláh. These first 18 disciples of the Báb are known as the Letters of the Living.

Sample treasure hunt instructions:

Clues About the Treasure
1. red
2. round
3. (etc.)

Sample 3x5 card

- We're going on a treasure hunt, to remind us of the time when Mulla Husayn went to search for the Báb.
- There's a hidden treasure at the end, and you'll be given clues to find it. (Hint: It's not in the kitchen!)
- We'll search in teams of three (just like Mulla Husayn did with his brother and nephew).
- To form teams, each youth will draw the names of two younger partners from this hat.
- Each team will receive a different starting clue which leads to the location of the next clue.
- There are nine clues in all, with the final clue leading to the treasure.
- As you find each clue, write it down on your 3x5 card.
  (Show children a sample card or draw one on the board and show them how to fill it in.)
- After your team has completed the card, bring it to me to trade for the final clue.
- Please leave each clue where you find it, so it's ready for the next group.
  (This is only necessary if all the teams will be following the same set of clues.)
- Remember to stay with your team rather than hunting for the treasure on your own.
- Also, just like Mulla Husayn kept it a secret when he found the Báb, when you find the treasure, don't tell others where it is. Let each team find the treasure on its own.

Give each team their first clue, a 3x5 card and a pen, and wish them Godspeed!*

* To wish someone *Godspeed* is to ask for God's blessings on his or her endeavor, especially a long or risky journey. It is a more reverent term than "good luck," which calls upon chance rather than divine providence. The word is not in common use today.

The Báb – Additional Activities

OUTSIDE RESEARCH PROJECT

This project encourages students to learn about key individuals associated with the ministry of the Báb, and to gain a greater understanding of the spiritual significance and impact of His Revelation. It is designed for older children, and can take place over a several-week period. Students may work independently, with a partner or in small teams. An older youth or adult mentor can be appointed to work with each team if desired.

A. Ask students to select one of the following historical figures:

> **Anis:** The young follower of the Báb who shared His martyrdom.
> **Mulla Husayn:** The first to declare his belief in the Báb, and the bearer of His message to Bahá'u'lláh.
> **Quddus:** The last Letter of the Living to recognize the Báb, but described by Shoghi Effendi as the first in rank.
> **Tahirih:** An accomplished poet and the only woman among the Letters of the Living. She appeared without her veil to signal the start of a new era.
> **Vahid:** Brilliant religious scholar commanded by the Shah to investigate the truth of the Báb's claim.
> **Zaynab:** Brave young woman who disguised herself as a man to fight in defense of the Bábís of Zanjan.

As a warm-up activity and to help generate enthusiasm for the project, you might first make a "KWL" chart together on the board (see sample below), while students copy on their own charts (next page). This activity also helps the teacher to learn what the students already know, and it gives children from Bahá'í families, who may be more familiar with Bahá'í history, an opportunity to contribute something extra to class.

- **K** = Know (what we already know about that person)
- **W** = Want (what we would like to know)
- **L** = Learned (what we learned—to be filled in after students have shared their research)

Research	Know	Want to Know	Learned
Anis	Died with the Báb	Why he gave his life?	
Mulla Husayn	First to find the Báb	What his friends thought?	
⇩			

The Báb – Additional Activities

Key individuals associated with the ministry of the Báb

Research	Know	Want to Know	Learned
Anis			
Mulla Husayn			
Quddus			
Tahirih			
Vahid			
Zaynab			

Make one copy of this page for each student.

The Báb – Additional Activities

B. Next, ask each team to learn about the life and significance of their selected individual. The teacher or mentor should provide research materials.

Some online resources include:

- *Bahá'í Stories*: http://bahaistories.blogspot.com
- *Core Curriculum Storybooks*: http://www.core-curriculum.org/index.php/the-bab-vol-1
- *Dawnbreakers Study Guide and Outline*: http://bahai-library.com/zamir_dawnbreakers_study_guide
- *Mullá Husayn*, Lowell Johnson: http://bahai-library.com/johnson_mulla_husayn
- *Ocean* (http://bahai-education.org/ocean)
- *Letters of the Living*: search for "huruf hayy" www.bahai-encyclopedia-project.org

Additional resources that may be in your Bahá'í library:

- *Bahá'u'lláh – The King of Glory*, H. M. Balyuzi
- *Children's Stories from the Dawn-breakers*, Zoe Meyer
- *Dawn Over Mount Hira*, Marzieh Gail
- *Eminent Bahá'ís in the Time of Bahá'u'lláh*, H. M. Balyuzi
- *God Passes By*, Shoghi Effendi
- *Hour of the Dawn: The Life of the Báb*, Mary Perkins
- *Martyr-Prophet of a World Faith*, William Sears
- *Memorials of the Faithful*, 'Abdu'l-Bahá
- *Nine Holy Days*, Jacqueline Mehrabi
- *Quddús*, Lowell Johnson
- *Release the Sun*, William Sears
- *Ruhi Book 3A: Teaching Children's Classes* (Lessons 16-20)
- *Ruhi Book 4: Twin Manifestations*
- *Tahirih the Pure*, Martha Root
- *Táhirih*, Lowell Johnson
- *The Báb – The Herald of the Day of Days*, H. M. Balyuzi
- *The Covenant of Bahá'u'lláh*, Adib Taherzadeh
- *The Dawn-breakers*, translated by Shoghi Effendi
- *The Prophets of God*, Mahnaz Afshin
- *The Revelation of Bahá'u'lláh*, vols. 1-4, Adib Taherzadeh

The Báb – Additional Activities

C. When the students have completed their research, have them demonstrate and share what they have learned by developing a presentation for the class. They will each need to choose a format for their presentation, for example:

- Concept map
- Dance or movement
- Diagram
- Dramatic play
- Drawing
- Geographic map
- Music
- Painting
- Poem
- Poster
- PowerPoint slides
- Quiz show
- Sculpture
- Speech
- Timeline
- Written report

By asking students to perform or produce something of their own choosing, the teacher encourages reflection and allows students to draw on their strengths and talents, while also accommodating different learning styles.

Remind the class that we should not portray the Manifestation of God in any form.

D. Encourage students to share their learning at a Feast, Holy Day or other Bahá'í gathering.

> Note: This research project is an example of student-centered, cooperative, inquiry-based learning. It is designed to develop higher-level thinking and problem solving skills. Rather than limiting students to a few responses on a traditional exam, it encourages them to ask useful questions, to search for answers, to organize information and present it to their peers.

The Báb – Additional Activities

JESUS AND THE BÁB

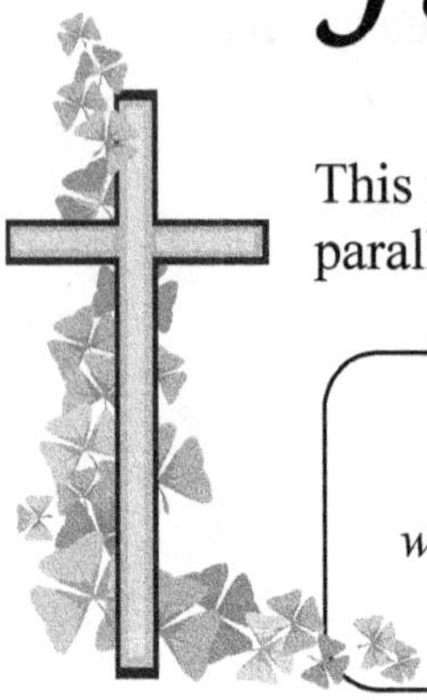

This is a group research project designed to help students recognize some of the parallels between the lives of two of God's Manifestations, Jesus and the Báb.

> *"The passion of Jesus Christ, and indeed His whole public ministry, alone offer a parallel to the Mission and death of the Báb, a parallel which no student of comparative religion can fail to perceive or ignore."*
>
> Shoghi Effendi, *God Passes By*, p. 56

Begin by asking the children what they already know about Jesus, and list their answers on the board. Then study the passages on the following pages together as a class or in small groups. Have the children take notes or highlight key words and phrases as they read.

(Note: These references are available electronically by downloading a free copy of Ocean – http://bahai-education.org/ocean. They are included here for convenience.)

Complete the research project by having the class prepare a comparison chart showing some of the similarities and differences between Jesus and the Báb. The chart below can serve as a model, but students may wish to create their own list of comparisons. Each child should make a personal copy of the completed chart to use as a teaching tool.

Sample comparison chart

COMPARISONS	JESUS	THE BÁB
Given name	Jesus (Yeshua in ancient Hebrew)	Ali Muhammad
Title	The Christ	The Báb
Meaning of title	"Anointed One" in Greek	"Gate" or "Door" in Arabic
Also known as	The Son of God	The Primal Point
Station	Manifestation of God	Manifestation and Herald
Where born and lived		
Immediate family		
Age at declaration		
How did people respond		
Why was He rejected		
Who opposed Him		
Betrayal by someone close		
Number of disciples		
What did He ask them to do		
Arrest and imprisonment		
Circumstances of death		
Age at martyrdom		
Length of ministry		

"The Remarkable Parallel"
From *Thief in the Night* by William Sears, p. 87-88
(Used with permission from George Ronald, Pub.)

I began searching the libraries for all the available documents. You can imagine my feelings of awe and wonder when I uncovered the following facts.

The death of this young man occurred in July 1850. He was slain publicly because of his words and his teaching. Everything I learned about his life reminded me of Christ. In fact, after carefully searching into his background, I could find but one parallel in all recorded history to his brief, turbulent career; only the moving story of the passion of Jesus Christ himself.

As part of my record of 'findings', I here set down the remarkable similarity in the story of their lives:

1. They were both youthful.

2. They were both known for their meekness and loving kindness.

3. They both performed healing miracles.

4. The period of their ministry was very brief in each case, and moved with dramatic swiftness to its climax.

5. Both of them boldly challenged the time-honoured conventions, laws, and rites of the religions into which they had been born.

6. They courageously condemned the unbridled graft and corruption which they saw on every side, both religious and secular.

7. The purity of their own lives shamed the people among whom they taught.

8. Their chief enemies were among the religious leaders of the land. These officials were the instigators of the outrages they were made to suffer.

9. They both had indignities heaped upon them.

10. They were both forcibly brought before the government authorities and were subject to public interrogation.

11. They were both scourged following this interrogation.

The Báb – Additional Activities

12. They both went, first in triumph then in suffering, through the streets of the city where they were to be slain.

13. They were both paraded publicly, and heaped with humiliation, on the way to their place of martyrdom.

14. They both spoke words of hope and promise to the one who was to die with them; in fact, almost the exact same words: "Thou shalt be with me in paradise."

15. They were both martyred publicly before the hostile gaze of the onlookers who crowded the scene.

16. A darkness covered the land following their slaying, in each case beginning at noon.

17. Their bodies were both lacerated by soldiers at the time of their slaying.

18. They both remained in ignominious suspension before the eyes of an unfriendly multitude.

19. Their bodies came finally into the hands of their loving followers.

20. When their bodies, in each case, had vanished from the spot where they had been placed, the religious leaders explained away the fact.

21. Only a handful of their followers were with them at the times of their deaths.

22. In each case, one of their chief disciples denied knowing them. This same disciple, in each case, later became a hero.

23. Each of them had an outstanding woman follower who played a dramatic part in making the disciples turn their faces from the past, and look toward the future.

24. Confusion, bewilderment and despair seized their followers in each case, following their martyrdom.

25. Through their disciples (the Peters and Pauls of each age) their Faiths were carried to all parts of the world.

26. They both replied with the same exact words to the question: Are you the Promised One?

27. Each of them addressed their disciples, charging them to carry their messages to the ends of the earth.

For a similar list see: bahai-library.com/davidmerrick_holydays_martyrdomofbab > scroll to the end

Comparing Jesus and the Báb

Excerpts from *Release the Sun* by William Sears

Just as Jesus had journeyed to Jerusalem, the stronghold of the Jews, to proclaim His Mission, so did the Báb make plans to go to Mecca, the heart of the Moslem world. (p. 23)

An historian of those times, Comte de Gobineau, writes: "From his first public appearances, they sent their most able Mullas [religious leaders] to argue with him and confuse him." …The Báb exposed, unsparingly, their vices and their corruption. Like Jesus, He proved their infidelity to their own belief. He shamed them in their lives. He defeated them with their own Holy Book in His hand. (p. 36)

The priests at Court spoke of the Báb in the same manner the religious authorities had spoken of Jesus, saying: "He is a political revolutionary. He will undermine your state and destroy your influence over your subjects." (p. 57)

Just as Jesus had fallen under the scourge of Pilate following His examination in the judgment hall where He proclaimed Himself as the Redeemer of men, the Báb was also subjected to the same indignity, following the same trial, and the same great proclamation. Seven times the rod of the bastinado was applied to His feet. He was struck across the face with one of the blows. (p. 79)

As Jesus had said: My teaching is not Mine, but His that sent Me; the Báb, too, made it plain that His message was an outpouring from One greater than Himself. His purpose was to proclaim the Word of God as a Messenger of God. The people were free to believe or not, as they chose. (p. 80)

Dr. T. K. Cheyne writes: "It is no doubt a singular coincidence that both [the Báb] and Jesus Christ are reported to have addressed these words to a disciple: 'Today thou shalt be with Me in Paradise.'" (p. 169)

As Jesus had expired on the cross so that men might be called back to God, so did the Báb breathe His last against a barracks wall in the city of Tabriz, Persia. The historian Nicolas in his account of those hours writes, "Christians believe that if Jesus had wished to come down from the cross he could have done so easily; he died of his own free will because it was written that he should and in order that the prophecies might be fulfilled. The same is true of the Báb so [His followers] say…He likewise died voluntarily because his death was to be the salvation of humanity…Christ in His agony in the garden of Gesthsamane cried out, "Father! If Thou be willing, remove this cup from me: nevertheless, not my will, but Thine, be done." The Báb in the frozen winter of Mahku likewise called out to mankind that it was God's will and not His own that impelled Him to "throw Himself headlong into that ocean of superstition and hatred which was fatally to engulf Him." Both Christ and the Báb uttered the same words of warning, "O wayward generation!" (p. 177-178)

These additional passages are beyond the reading level of most children, but can be summarized for them by the teacher.

The Passion of Jesus Christ
From *God Passes By,* Shoghi Effendi, p. 56-57

The passion of Jesus Christ, and indeed His whole public ministry, alone offer a parallel to the Mission and death of the Báb, a parallel which no student of comparative religion can fail to perceive or ignore. In the youthfulness and meekness of the Inaugurator of the Bábí Dispensation; in the extreme brevity and turbulence of His public ministry; in the dramatic swiftness with which that ministry moved towards its climax; in the apostolic order which He instituted, and the primacy which He conferred on one of its members; in the boldness of His challenge to the time-honored conventions, rites and laws which had been woven into the fabric of the religion He Himself had been born into; in the role which an officially recognized and firmly entrenched religious hierarchy played as chief instigator of the outrages which He was made to suffer; in the indignities heaped upon Him; in the suddenness of His arrest; in the interrogation to which He was subjected; in the derision poured, and the scourging inflicted, upon Him; in the public affront He sustained; and, finally, in His ignominious suspension before the gaze of a hostile multitude—in all these we cannot fail to discern a remarkable similarity to the distinguishing features of the career of Jesus Christ.

It should be remembered, however, that apart from the miracle associated with the Báb's execution, He, unlike the Founder of the Christian religion, is not only to be regarded as the independent Author of a divinely revealed Dispensation, but must also be recognized as the Herald of a new Era and the Inaugurator of a great universal prophetic cycle. Nor should the important fact be overlooked that, whereas the chief adversaries of Jesus Christ, in His lifetime, were the Jewish rabbis and their associates, the forces arrayed against the Báb represented the combined civil and ecclesiastical powers of Persia, which, from the moment of His declaration to the hour of His death, persisted, unitedly and by every means at their disposal, in conspiring against the upholders and in vilifying the tenets of His Revelation.

The Báb – Additional Activities

The Cause of Rejection
From *The Dawn-Breakers*, translated by Shoghi Effendi, p. xxxi-ii

The cause of the rejection and persecution of the Báb was in its essence the same as that of the rejection and persecution of the Christ. If Jesus had not brought a New Book, if He had not only reiterated the spiritual principles taught by Moses but had continued Moses' rules and regulations too, He might as a merely moral reformer have escaped the vengeance of the Scribes and Pharisees. But to claim that any part of the Mosaic law, even such material ordinances as those that dealt with divorce and the keeping of the Sabbath, could be altered—and altered by an unordained preacher from the village of Nazareth—this was to threaten the interests of the Scribes and Pharisees themselves, and since they were the representatives of Moses and of God, it was blasphemy against the Most High. As soon as the position of Jesus was understood, His persecution began. As He refused to desist, He was put to death.

For reasons exactly parallel, the Báb was from the beginning opposed by the vested interests of the dominant Church as an uprooter of the Faith. Yet, even in that dark and fanatical country, the mullas (like the Scribes in Palestine eighteen centuries before) did not find it very easy to put forward a plausible pretext for destroying Him whom they thought their enemy.

The Báb – Additional Activities

The Báb's Words to His Disciples
From *The Dawn-Breakers,* translated by Shoghi Effendi, p. 92-94

Ponder the words of Jesus addressed to His disciples, as He sent them forth… "Ye are even as the fire which in the darkness of the night has been kindled upon the mountain top. Let your light shine before the eyes of men. Such must be the purity of your character and the degree of your renunciation, that the people of the earth may through you recognize and be drawn closer to the heavenly Father who is the Source of purity and grace."

…Verily I say, immensely exalted is this Day above the days of the Apostles of old. Nay, immeasurable is the difference! You are the witnesses of the Dawn of the promised Day of God…Scatter throughout the length and breadth of this land, and, with steadfast feet and sanctified hearts, prepare the way for His coming. Heed not your weaknesses and frailty; fix your gaze upon the invincible power of the Lord, your God, the Almighty…Has He not established the ascendancy of Jesus, poor and lowly as He was in the eyes of men…? Arise in His [God's] name, put your trust wholly in Him, and be assured of ultimate victory.

A sample of student work

Jesus and the Báb

- Both were Prophets of God
- Had a very short time to teach
- Willingly sacrificed everything for their Faith
- Died young
- No surviving children
- Came to a country where the old laws and customs had lost their spirit
- Fearlessly challenged the old ways
- Religious and government leaders opposed them
- Suddenly arrested and questioned by the authorities
- Cruelly killed by the same people they had come to teach
- Martyred in front of large hostile crowd

It is also interesting that both sent their disciples out to teach with words such as these: "Ye are even as the fire which in the darkness of the night has been kindled upon the mountain top. Let your light shine before the eyes of men."
(Shoghi Effendi, Dawn-Breakers, p. 92. Also see the Bible, Matthew 5:16)

The Báb – Additional Activities

MAZES

The mazes and word puzzles on the following pages call to mind the search for the Báb. They can be can be photocopied and given to students who would like an extra challenge, especially when waiting for others to finish a task. There are three mazes of different levels of difficulty. Using a pencil, begin at the arrow, enter through the door, and trace a route through the maze until you reach the five-pointed star—a symbol of the Báb.*

* "The five-pointed star is the symbol of our Faith, as used by the Báb…" (On behalf of Shoghi Effendi, Lights of Guidance, p. 110)

The Báb – Additional Activities

Make Your Own Maze

Idea from Kay Dallal

1. Begin by drawing an object in the center of your maze.
2. Draw a wall around the object, leaving an open "door."
3. Draw another wall around the first one, also with an open door.
4. Connect both walls with a short line (not too close to the doors).
5. Continue adding outer walls with open doors, and connect each wall to the previous one.
6. Give your maze to others to solve.

> This line is a dead end that players will bump into as they try to find an open path to the object.

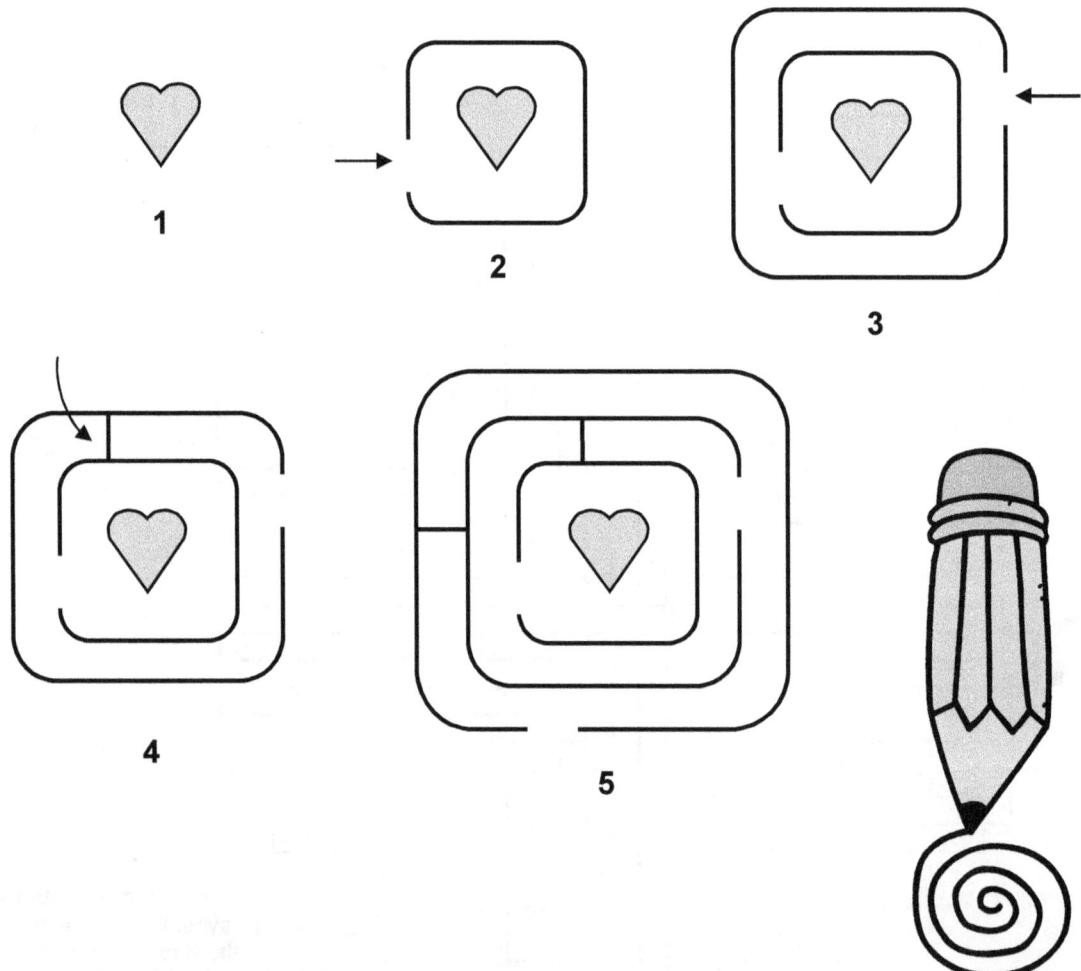

Bahá'í Children's Classes and Retreats: Theme 3, p. 108

The Báb – Additional Activities

Word Search

Word search puzzles can help to reinforce the topics studied during class. Just circle the words that have been hidden in the grid. The first one has been done for you as an example. Words can be written going up, down, forward, backward or diagonally. The terms come from stories of the Báb. The solution is on page 114.

```
k m m r c t k l c o u o g
v a o a e a r u r e p p f
h n d e c n u u t k r v m
s i r z n w n n m o c a s
h f y c p i w u c p g i e
e e t j o a r l r n e r u
r s r g d c a h e e u t l
a t a y l m c t s s r l c
l a m g a t e i a h c o b
d t t t e w s e k z q d f
e i i x p j r a i s r e p
g o n o i t a r a l c e d
n n d i s c i p l e i j e
```

✓ clues	gate	Persia
dawn	herald	proclamation
declaration	magnet	shrine
disciple	manifestation	treasure
forerunner	martyrdom	trumpet

The Báb – Additional Activities

Mystery Dates

Add, subtract or multiply each number in the order indicated, and write the answers in the boxes to the right of the square and below it. The first has been done for you.

1	+	2	−	2	×	1	=	**1**
×		+		×		+		
2	×	1	×	2	×	2	=	
−		×		+		−		
2	×	2	+	1	×	1	=	
+		+		−		×		
1	×	2	×	1	−	2	=	

Copy your answers to the small boxes below.

Bonus Question: What happened on each of these dates?

☐ = _____

☐ = _____

The Báb – Additional Activities

Number Puzzle

The number **19** has special significance in the Faith of the Báb. The Báb referred to His first 18 disciples (the Letters of the Living) along with Himself, as the first "unity" of His religion. He brought a new calendar consisting of 19 months with 19 days each. Bahá'u'lláh declared in 1863, just 19 years after the Báb's declaration in 1844. To solve this puzzle, use the numbers 1– 8 to fill in the missing numbers so that each row and each column add up to 19. You may use each number as often as needed. There is more than one solution.

See answer page for different ways to solve this puzzle.

Bahá'í Children's Classes and Retreats: Theme 3, p. 111

The Báb – Additional Activities

Cryptogram

This puzzle consists of a short piece of encoded text.
Solve the puzzle by writing the correct letter above each Greek symbol.

α	β	χ	δ	ε	φ	γ	η	ι	ϕ	κ	λ	μ
a	b	c	d	e	f	g	h	i	j	k	l	m

ν	ο	π	θ	ρ	σ	τ	υ	ϖ	ω	ξ	ψ	ζ
n	o	p	q	r	s	t	u	v	w	x	y	z

__ __   __ __ __ __ __   __ __ __
ι σ   τ η ε ρ ε   α ν ψ

__ __ __ __ __ __   __ __
ρ ε μ ο ϖ ε ρ   ο φ

__ __ __ __ __ __ __ __ __ __
δ ι φ φ ι χ υ λ τ ι ε σ

__ __ __ __   __ __ __
σ α ϖ ε   γ ο δ

If you need a hint, turn this page upside down.

The words are from a prayer by the Báb.

Baha'i Children's Classes and Retreats: Theme 3, p. 112

The Báb – Additional Activities

Word Scramble

Unscramble each word, then write the correct letters in the box below.

DAMA ☐☐☐☐
         4

CEYCL ☐☐☐☐☐
          6

FLLLUFI ☐☐☐☐☐☐
            3

FRUUTE ☐☐☐☐☐☐
              11

NIKL ☐☐☐☐
       10

PHETPRO ☐☐☐☐☐☐☐
           7 8

TEGA ☐☐☐☐
      5

PROSIME ☐☐☐☐☐☐☐
         1

RELEAV ☐☐☐☐☐☐
        2

TUNIY ☐☐☐☐☐
         9

☐☐☐☐☐☐ ☐☐☐☐☐
1 2 3 4 5 6 7 8 9 10 11

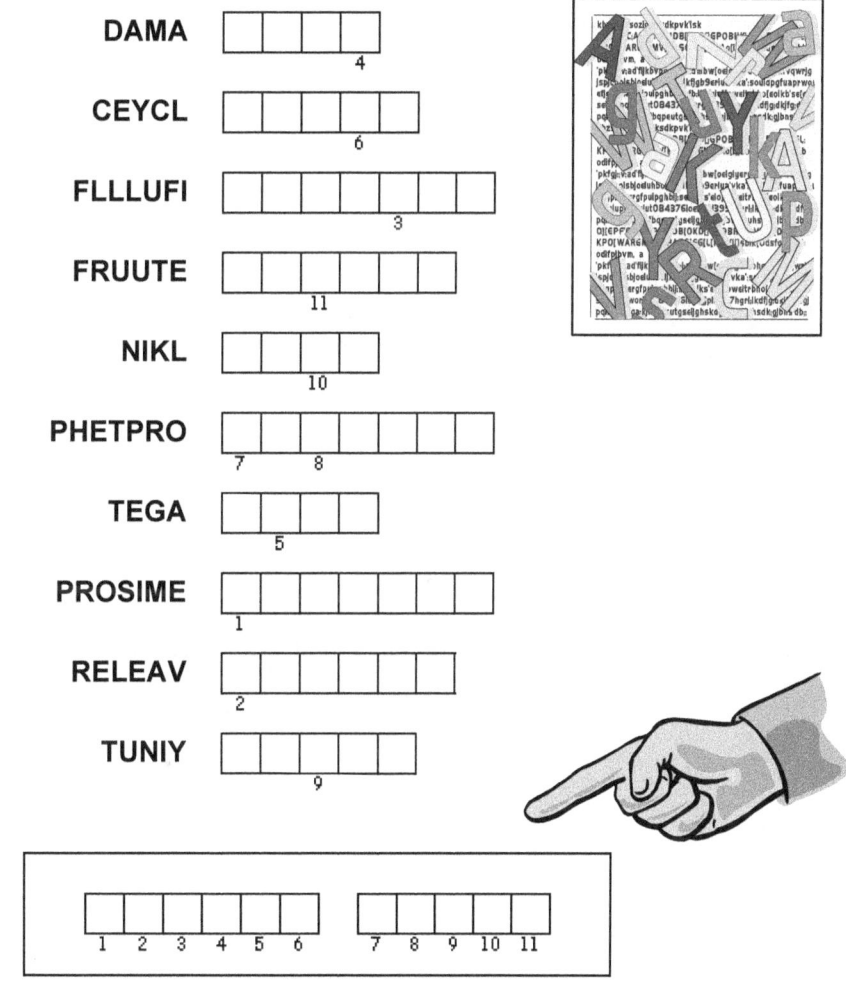

If you need a hint, turn this page upside down.

One of the titles of the Báb.

Bahá'í Children's Classes and Retreats: Theme 3, p. 113

The Báb – Additional Activities

Puzzle Solutions

Mystery Dates

| 1844 | = Declaration of the Báb |
| 1850 | = Martyrdom of the Báb |

Cryptogram

"Is there any remover of difficulties save God?"

Number Puzzle

9	1	2	7
1	9	7	2
2	7	9	1
7	2	1	9

9	6	3	1
6	9	1	3
1	3	9	6
3	1	6	9

9	4	1	5
4	9	5	1
1	5	9	4
5	1	4	9

Word Search

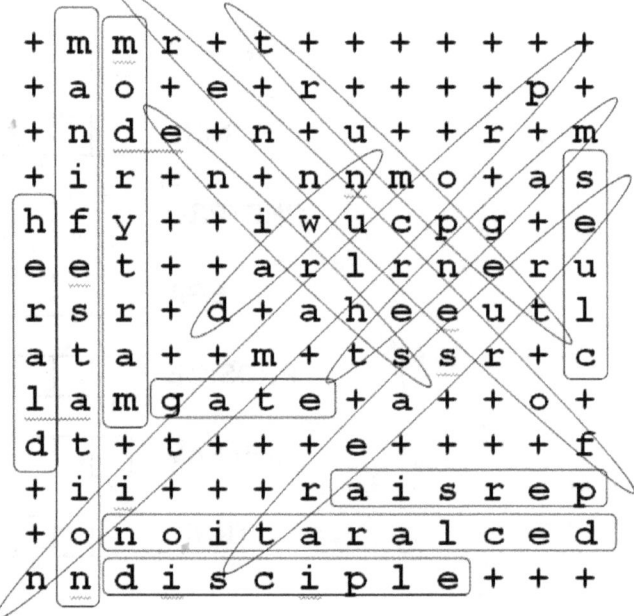

Word Scramble

Ada**m**	p**r**ophet
cyc**l**e	g**a**te
fulf**i**ll	**p**romise
fu**t**ure	r**e**veal
li**n**k	un**i**ty

Primal Point

Bahá'í Children's Classes and Retreats: Theme 3, p. 114

The Báb – Additional Activities

ILLUMINATED PRAYER

> Craft activities are designed to reinforce the material presented during class. The children will be decorating prayers of the Báb. When they have completed their project and cleaned up their work area, they may assist others who need help. Remind them to label all projects with their names. Quiet music can be played in the background if desired.

The illumination* of sacred manuscripts is a classic art form that is still popular in many parts of the world. Along with calligraphy, it is one of the most famous arts of Iran. In Muslim tradition, passages from the Qur'án were written in flowing calligraphy and embellished with beautiful hand-painted designs.

When illuminating a passage, the text is usually written first, with blank spaces left for decoration. The intent is to frame the Word of God like a jewel in a specially-designed setting. The passage might begin with a large initial capital letter, and be surrounded by elaborate scrollwork, miniature illustrations, ornamental borders and geometric designs. Traditional illuminated manuscripts from the European Middle Ages were often decorated with paint made from real gold or silver. For our purposes however, construction paper and glitter will suffice.

> * To see some illuminated pages, visit: < www.google.com > click on "Images" in the top left corner, then type "calligraphy illumination" in the search box. For some striking examples from the Báb's native land, type "Persian calligraphy illumination." For a brief history, visit: < www.wikipedia.org > and type "illuminated manuscript" in the search box.

Materials

- ❑ Construction paper in a variety of colors
- ❑ Prayers of the Báb (one per child)
- ❑ Rulers and pencils
- ❑ Scissors
- ❑ Markers
- ❑ Glue sticks
- ❑ Decorations → stickers, notary seals, glitter, felt, sequins, ribbon, fabric scraps, sandpaper, craft foam

Is there any Remover of difficulties save God? Say: Praised be God! He is God! All are His servants and all abide by His bidding!
— The Báb

Instructions

1. Select one prayer (English or Spanish) from the following page.
2. Cut out the prayer and glue it to a piece of construction paper. (The prayer can also be hand-lettered directly onto the paper after lightly drawing some guide lines using the ruler and pencil.)
3. Add stickers, drawings or other decorations to beautify the prayer.

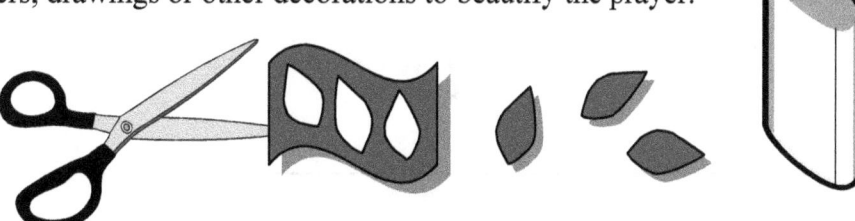

Bahá'í Children's Classes and Retreats: Theme 3, p. 115

*Is there any Remover
of difficulties save God?
Say: Praised be God!
He is God!
All are His servants
and all abide by His bidding!*

The Báb

*¿Quién puede librarnos
de las dificultades salvo Dios?
Di: ¡Alabado sea Dios!
¡Él es Dios!
Todos somos sus siervos
y todos nos atenemos
a su mandato.*

El Báb

The Báb – Additional Activities

Online Slide Show

As a follow-up to Lesson #2, the children might enjoy watching the following seven-minute slide show commemorating the Declaration of the Báb. The show includes pictures of the Báb's declaration chamber and other historical photos. The music is by Smith and Dragoman and the text is adapted from *The Dawn-breakers*.

www.nybahai.org/declaration/index.html

Coloring Pages

The coloring book pages can be found in the handouts section of this teacher's guide. They are designed to illustrate *Stories from the Life of the Báb*. The coloring pages can be incorporated with the relevant lessons or used as an alternative craft activity for younger children. The pages can also be downloaded from < **www.UnityWorksStore.com** >. Click on Children's Classes > The Báb > student handouts.

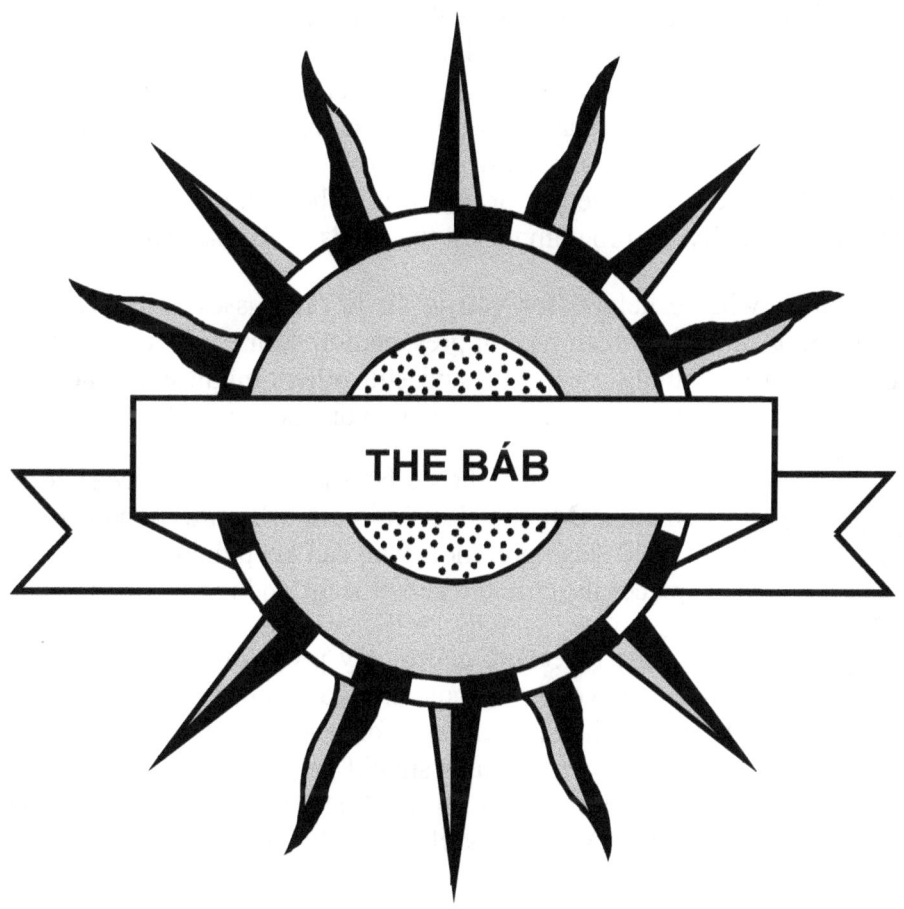

Children's Performance

The Báb: Gate to Bahá'u'lláh

CHILDREN'S PERFORMANCE*

To the Coordinator

The children's performance provides students with an opportunity to demonstrate and reinforce what they have learned. This is often the highlight for children and adults. The fact that children will be performing in front of a live audience serves as excellent motivation for them to learn the material presented in class. The program includes prayers, songs, memorized passages, short talks, demonstrations, a showing of crafts and a dramatic presentation. The following pages include a detailed agenda for the event, rehearsal instructions, scripts and other materials. Feel free to modify the program to suit the needs of the participants.

As the coordinator, it will be helpful for you to sit in on classes and take notes on which children might be best suited for which type of presentation. Some will memorize quotes easily, others may be good at explaining a concept, and still others might enjoy acting or saying a prayer. Assign parts or ask for volunteers. Be sure everyone is included.

One or two children should be asked to serve as Master or Mistress of Ceremonies (MC). Select children who are responsible, with strong voices and stage presence, who can keep the program moving forward. This places the children center stage and in charge of the presentation.

Before the rehearsal, gather any props and costumes, and remind the adult and youth volunteers that you will need their assistance. Determine their preferences for rehearsal groups. A copy of the agenda and the rehearsal groups should be given to each volunteer. Copies of the appropriate script or reading should be given to the adults and children who will be working on that part of the program.

Rehearsal for the Show

During rehearsal time, the coordinator's tasks include:

- ❏ Meet together with all the participants to explain the nature of the program.
- ❏ Talk about program order, where to sit, use of strong voices so the audience can hear, eye contact, learning the parts rather than reading them, and how to use a microphone if needed.
- ❏ Assign adults and youth to work with each rehearsal group.
- ❏ Assign parts to each child depending on interest and ability.
- ❏ Distribute costumes and props as appropriate.
- ❏ Inform groups when the rehearsal time is almost over.
- ❏ Collect all props and set them out for the show.

> * Note: While the children's performance has typically been scheduled for the evening, the program could be held at any time. During a weekend retreat, Saturday evening is often the most convenient time for inviting neighbors and friends. This means that activities from the fourth class on Sunday morning will not be included in the presentation. If using a weekly format, however, these activities can easily be added to the final program.

The Báb – Children's Performance

MATERIALS NEEDED

Note: Items in italics are included with this section.

- *Agenda*
- *Rehearsal groups* and *Rehearsal notes*
- Welcome sign (if desired)
- *Sample program* (for distributing to the audience)
- Background music (to be played as people are arriving)
- Microphone and sound system (if needed)
- Art exhibit (children's art can be hung from a clothesline or displayed on a table)
- Song sheets for all (including audience) and music (for song leader)
- Felt board and easel (if doing the Primal Point lesson)
- Map of Persia on an easel
- *Opening prayer* ("Say God sufficeth…")
- Memory quotes
- Soil of the Heart (reading from handout packet, props)
- *Soil demonstration* (instructions and props)
- Six stories about the life of the Báb (handout packet, any props)
- *Treasure in Shiraz* (scripts, instruments, costumes and props for readers' theater)
- *Quiz on the Báb* and *quiz answers* (bells or other sound makers)
- *The Primal Point* (felt lesson script and pieces)
- Story about the Martyrdom of the Báb (reading, bullets, costumes if desired)
- Large photograph of the Shrine of the Báb (if available)
- Craft samples
    __ Gate of God (wood or paper model)
    __ Primal Point poster
    __ Candle holder
    __ Shrine of the Báb coloring page
- Refreshments

Note: The Primal Point felt lesson and craft from Lesson #4 have been included in the children's performance, but these can be omitted if time is short or if the topic hasn't been covered yet. The play, "Treasure in Shiraz," is also included to show where it fits in the program, but if there is not enough time to rehearse or to gather all of the materials needed, the play should be omitted.

The Báb – Children's Performance

 SAMPLE AGENDA FOR MC _____ (90 min.)

(1) **Welcome guests** to our program on **"THE BÁB: GATE TO BAHÁ'U'LLÁH"** (cell phones off)

(2) **Opening Music** _____

(3) **Intro** *(don't read):* At the last children's retreat, we learned about God, the creator of the universe, and how He sends Divine Teachers or Manifestations to bring us His Word. This weekend, we have been studying about one of God's Manifestations, known as the Báb, and tonight we are pleased to present what we have learned. We'll begin with a prayer revealed by the Báb.

(4) **Prayer** ("Say God sufficeth...") _____

(5) **Introduce** each section and each presenter and thank them afterwards.

THE BÁB'S BIRTH, EARLY LIFE and STATION (30 min.)

- ☐ Song: Hoy Es el Día, 1st verse only (ALL)
- ☐ Reading: Soil of the Heart _____ _____
- ☐ Demonstration: Preparing the Soil _____ _____
- ☐ Six stories about the life of the Báb ⟶
- ☐ Memory quote: "Good news! Good news!" _____
- ☐ Song: The Báb Blew His Trumpet (ALL)

1. The Promise _____
2. 19th Century Persia _____
3. Birth & Early Life _____
4. School Days _____
5. Honest Merchant _____
6. Wife & Child _____

DECLARATION OF THE BÁB (25 min.)

- ☐ *Say: This is when the Báb first announced that He was a Messenger of God.*
- ☐ "Treasure in Shiraz" (a readers' theater on the Declaration of the Báb)
- ☐ Craft: Gate of God _____ _____ _____
- ☐ Memory quote: "Awake, awake..." _____
- ☐ Song: 1844 (ALL)

QUIZ SHOW and PRIMAL POINT (20 min.)

- ☐ Quiz show on the life of the Báb ⟶
- ☐ Felt lesson: The Primal Point _____ _____
- ☐ Craft: The Primal Point _____ _____ _____

1. _____
2. _____
3. _____
4. _____
5. _____

MARTYRDOM OF THE BÁB (15 min.)

- ☐ Memory quote: "Remover of difficulties" _____
- ☐ Song: Remover of difficulties (ALL)
- ☐ Story: Martyrdom of the Báb _____ _____
- ☐ Song: Say God Sufficeth (ALL)
- ☐ Craft: A Candle for the Báb _____ _____ _____
- ☐ Craft: Shrine of the Báb coloring page _____ _____
- ☐ Song: Queen of Carmel (ALL + invite audience to stand and sing)

- ☐ *Say: We hope you liked our program. Please join us for refreshments!*

The Báb – Children's Performance

REHEARSAL GROUPS

Scripts and instructions are included on the following pages.

PROGRAM COORDINATOR: _____ MC: _____

- ❑ Select and orient 1 or 2 MCs. Provide a clipboard, pencil and copy of the agenda.
- ❑ Divide children into 3 groups and assign volunteers to each group (6-8 volunteers total).
- ❑ Make sure each child has at least one part in addition to the group songs.
- ❑ Practice the play all together after the three small group rehearsals.
- ❑ Songs can be practiced together after rehearsing the play and again after dinner.
- ❑ Invite several children to talk about their craft projects (see below).
- ❑ One or two children can be asked to perform a short musical selection to begin the program.

Rehearse each part below with the children. The order will be different during the show.

GROUP #1: Memory Quotes *(2 adults + 2-4 children)*

- ❑ Quote #10: "Say, God sufficeth" _____ (opening prayer)
- ❑ Quote #16: "Good News!" _____ (show trumpet)
- ❑ Quote #7: "Awake, awake" _____
- ❑ Quote #9: "Remover of difficulties" _____

(easier parts)

GROUP #2: Storytelling *(2-3 adults + 3-6 children)*

See rehearsal notes. Children will retell these stories in their own words.

- ❑ 1. The Promise _____
- ❑ 2. 19th Century Persia _____
- ❑ 3. Birth & Early Life _____
- ❑ 4. School Days _____
- ❑ 5. Honest Merchant _____
- ❑ 6. Wife & Child _____

(medium parts)

GROUP #3: Readings, Demos and Quiz *(2-3 adults + 6 or more children)*

See rehearsal notes. If necessary, use children from the other groups after they have finished.

- ❑ Soil of the Heart (reading and demo) _____ _____
- ❑ Martyrdom of the Báb (story) _____ _____
- ❑ Primal Point (felt lesson) _____ _____ _____ _____
- ❑ Quiz show host _____ and panelists _____ _____ _____ _____

(harder parts)

CRAFT PROJECTS *(1 adult + 4 or more children)*

- ❑ Show each craft, explain how we made it and what it means (1-3 children each):

    The Gate of God _____ _____ _____
    A Candle for the Báb _____ _____ _____
    Shrine of the Báb coloring page _____ _____ _____
    Primal Point poster _____ _____ _____

The Báb – Children's Performance

REHEARSAL NOTES

Storytelling *(3-6 children)*

<u>Materials</u>: Children should review "Stories from the Life of the Báb" (see Lesson #1)

1. If rehearsal or performance time is limited, you might select only a few stories to share.
2. If desired, divide into 2-3 groups to practice, with one adult for each group.
3. Have each child re-read the story, then retell it in his/her own words.
4. Encourage children to speak naturally rather than reading.
5. They can make a sketch or write a few key words on a card as a memory aid.
6. Have them practice in pairs until they can tell their story smoothly in 1-2 minutes.
7. Use props if desired (e.g., mirror, veil, large map, green turban, Holy Book, bag of coins)

1. The Promise _____
2. 19th Century Persia _____
3. Birth & Early Life _____
4. School Days _____
5. Honest Merchant _____
6. Wife & Child _____

Soil of the Heart *(reading and demo with 2 children)* _____ _____

<u>Materials</u>: Reading from handout packet, props (see end of Lesson #1), map of Persia

1. Have two students practice reading the story out loud, alternating paragraphs.
2. They can hold up various items as they are mentioned (weeds, stones, seeds, etc.).
3. Have them point to the map of Persia when that land is indicated.
4. After the reading, students should present the soil demonstration (below).

The Báb – Children's Performance

SOIL DEMONSTRATION

1. Each student has some large seeds and a planter pot filled with hard-packed dirt.
2. One of the students "plows" the soil in his/her pot to loosen the dirt (carefully so it doesn't spill) and adds some "fertilizer" to the pot.
3. Then both students sprinkle seeds on the dirt in their own pots.
4. The first student should also mix the seeds into the soil.
5. One student can then ask the other, or explain to the audience:

   - What happens to the seeds if the hard soil is not prepared?
     (They stay on top and won't grow.)

   - What will happen if the wind blows?
     (The seeds that stayed on the surface may blow away.)

   - What can this teach us about the role of a Forerunner or Herald who prepares us for the next Messenger of God? *(It's like a plow, digging up the soil of human hearts, preparing us to accept new ideas, and to recognize the Manifestation when He comes.)*

Martyrdom of the Báb *(story with 2 children)* _____ _____

<u>Materials</u>: Reading from handout packet, bullets, costumes if desired

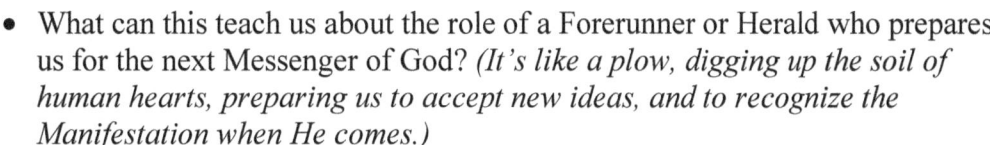

1. Have children read the story, then re-tell it in their own words.
2. They can divide it however they wish (alternating, or with one telling the first half and one the second half, for example)
3. Encourage them to speak naturally rather than reading.
4. They can make a sketch or write a few key words on a card as a memory aid.
5. Have them practice until they can tell the story smoothly in under 5 minutes.
6. They should hold up the "bullets" when appropriate.

Primal Point *(felt lesson with 2-4 children)* _____ _____

<u>Materials</u>: Script, felt pieces, felt board with easel (from Lesson #4)

1. Have students present the felt lesson (script on next page).
2. Use 1 or 2 alternating narrators, and 1 or 2 demonstrators.

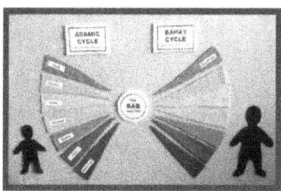

Bahá'í Children's Classes and Retreats: Theme 3, p. 125

The Báb – Children's Performance

Script for Felt Lesson

"The Primal Point"

	NARRATION	ACTION
1	Throughout the ages, God has sent many divine Teachers to the world. It all started with Adam who taught us there was only one God, and who showed us the difference between right and wrong.	Place felt pointer for Adam at an angle on left side of board.
2	Each Prophet brought the teachings of God to His own people. (Do you remember some of their names? That's right.) And each Prophet told us of a great Teacher who would come in the future, to unite all the religions and bring peace to the world.	Add pointers for the remaining Prophets, except Bahá'u'lláh. (See layout on next page.)
3	The One promised by all of these Manifestations is Bahá'u'lláh. Bahá'u'lláh said that we are all part of one human family and that all the great religions come from the same God.	Place pointer for Bahá'u'lláh on top right, leaving a space in the middle.
4	The Báb is <u>also</u> a Messenger of God. He came before Bahá'u'lláh to prepare the people for the Promised One. The Báb is the Gate to Bahá'u'lláh, who showed people the way.	Add circle for the Báb.
5	The Báb is called the **Primal Point**. He pointed people towards the Promised One. He is the link between the old and the new. The Báb is the connecting point between the Adamic Cycle (which began with Adam), and the Bahá'í Cycle, which we live in today.	Add signs for Adamic and Bahá'í cycles. **Adamic** **Bahá'í**
6	The Adamic Cycle lasted for 6,000 years. The Adamic Cycle is called the Age of Prophecy because during that time, God's Messengers told us about things that would happen in the future.	Point to the left side of the chart.
7	The Bahá'í Cycle is called the Age of Fulfillment because now it is time for God's promises from the past to come true.	Point to the right side of the chart.
8	During the Bahá'í Cycle, many more Prophets will come under the shadow of Bahá'u'lláh. The Bahá'í Cycle will last 500 thousand years. **That's a long time!**	Add remaining pointers on right.
9	The left side also represents mankind's childhood. The right side represents its maturity—when the human race will grow up, and all people will learn to live in unity and peace.	Add child to left of pointers. Add adult to right of pointers.

Bahá'í Children's Classes and Retreats: Theme 3, p. 126

The Báb – Children's Performance

Quiz Show *(5 children)*

Materials: Quiz on the Life of the Báb, quiz answers

One host _____ and four panelists _____ _____ _____ _____

1. Line children up (standing or sitting) as if facing an audience.
2. Have the host ask the quiz questions in order (below).
3. Panelists can take turns answering, ring a bell, or make another sound if they wish to be called on. (Practice and make it fun!)
4. During the program, they can confer among themselves or ask an audience member for help if needed.

Quiz on the Life of the Báb

1. Who was Siyyid 'Alí-Muhammad?
2. What does "the Báb" mean?
3. Why was He called a Siyyid?
4. When and where was He born?
5. Describe the city of Shiraz.
6. Why was the Báb raised by His uncle?
7. When His uncle sent the Báb to school, why did the teacher send Him home?
8. Where did the Báb's knowledge come from?
9. What work did the Báb do after leaving school?
10. Did the Báb ever have His own family?
11. What did the Báb look like?
12. Why did He wear a green turban on His head?
13. What kind of person was He?
14. What is Persia called today, and what was it like at the time of the Báb?
15. Was the Báb a Manifestation of God?
16. Were most people expecting Him when He came?
17. What is the name of the Báb's religion and Holy Book?
18. Why is the Báb also called a Herald?
19. What was His main message?

The Báb – Children's Performance

Answers to Quiz on the Life of the Báb

Note: If one panelist is answering most of the questions, the host should call on others as well.

1. Who was Siyyid 'Alí-Muhammad? *(The Báb)*
2. What does "the Báb" mean? *(Gate or door)*
3. Why was He called a Siyyid?
   (Descendent of the Prophet Muhammad)
4. When and where was He born? *(The city of Shiraz in Persia, October 20, 1819)*
5. Describe the city of Shiraz. *(Roses, poets, gardens, trees, flowers, nightingales)*
6. Why was the Báb raised by his uncle? *(Father died)*
7. When His uncle sent the Báb to school, why did the teacher send Him home?
   (Knew more than the teacher; had innate knowledge)
8. Where did the Báb's knowledge come from? *(From God)*
9. What work did the Báb do after leaving school? *(Cloth merchant with uncle)*
10. Did the Báb ever have His own family? *(Wife; baby son died at birth)*
11. What did the Báb look like? *(Handsome, slender, dark hair, dark eyes, light skin)*
12. Why did He wear a green turban on his head?
    (As a symbol, to show He was descended from the Prophet Muhammad)
13. What kind of person was He? *(Courteous, gentle, honest, trustworthy, prayerful)*
14. What is Persia called today, and what was it like at the time of the Báb?
    (Iran; a lot of ignorance, prejudice, fighting, dishonesty, violence)
15. Was the Báb a Manifestation of God? *(Yes)*
16. Were most people expecting Him when He came?
    (No; some awaiting their own Promised One)
17. What is the name of the Báb's religion and Holy Book? *(Bábí Faith, the Bayán)*
18. Why is the Báb also called a Herald?
    (Announced the coming of another Manifestation)
19. What was His main message?
    (Prepare your hearts for the coming of Bahá'u'lláh)

The Báb – Children's Performance

"Treasure in Shiraz"

Readers' Theater Presentation on the Declaration of the Báb

— 15-Minute Dramatic Re-enactment with Music and Sound Effects —

*Adapted by R. Gottlieb from Dawn-breakers, chap. 1-3;
The Báb, Balyuzi, p. 15-23; Release the Sun, Sears, p. 3-17*

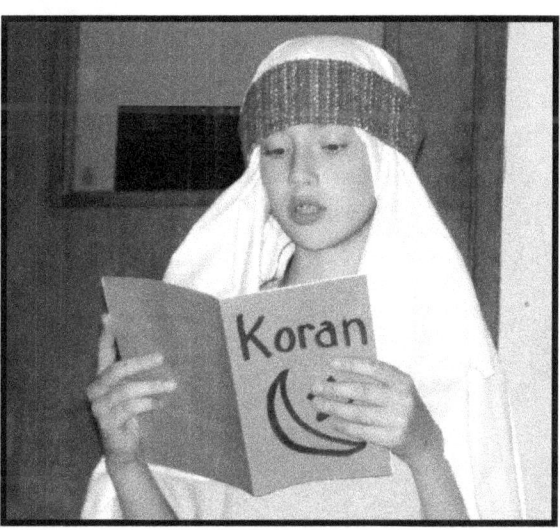

Dramatizing Historic Episodes of the Faith

"As to your question concerning the advisability of dramatizing Bahá'í historic episodes; the Guardian would certainly approve, and even encourage that the friends should engage in such literary pursuits which, no doubt, can be of an immense teaching value. What He wishes the believers to avoid is to dramatize the personages of the Báb, Bahá'u'lláh and 'Abdu'l-Bahá, that is to say to treat them as dramatic figures, as characters appearing on the stage. This, as already pointed out, he feels would be quite disrespectful. The mere fact that they appear on the scene constitutes an act of discourtesy which can in no way be reconciled with Their highly exalted station. Their Message, or actual Words, should be preferably reported and conveyed by Their disciples appearing on the stage."

On behalf of Shoghi Effendi to an individual, July 25, 1936, Lights of Guidance, p. 99

The Báb – Children's Performance

"Treasure in Shiraz"

To the Director

Pre-Production

1. Read through the script, production notes and list of materials beforehand.

2. Recruit assistants as needed to help with music, props, costumes, set decoration and casting. Give each assistant a copy of the full script.

3. Make or obtain all of the props and costumes. While these are not essential to the production, they add flavor and charm, and should be included if possible. Most of the items can be found around the house (e.g. brooms, pillows, teapot), or can be purchased inexpensively from secondhand and discount stores.

4. Obtain musical instruments or audio recordings for the sound effects.

5. Arrange space for the rehearsal and final performance. This should include a staging area (where actors prepare for the next scene), a prop table, costume rack and full-length mirror if available.

6. Set up microphones (if needed), audio player and any other equipment.

7. Decorate the set (Shiraz city gate with trees and roses, the Báb's room).

8. Hold an orientation meeting with your assistants to review their responsibilities and to answer any questions. The children will be divided into three groups—speaking parts, silent parts, and music and sound effects. Assign two adults to work with each group.

Production Notes

1. Gather the children, introduce your assistants, and explain the nature of the play. We will be presenting a dramatic re-enactment of the Declaration of the Báb. There are nine speaking parts (reading from a script), nine silent parts (carrying posters, swords, etc.), and eight parts for music and sound effects. Costumes are available for most roles. Some of the children may play more than one part. The narrator and Mulla Husayn have the two largest roles.

2. Assign key roles to children with good reading ability, strong voices and some stage presence. (If desired, these roles can be cast through an audition process.) Select children for the remaining roles or ask for volunteers.

3. Distribute scripts (or relevant portions of the script) and read through the entire play together, with each child performing his/her part. A highlighter pen can be used to mark the parts if desired. Encourage the children to speak slowly using a loud, clear voice. Music and sound effects can be practiced separately and incorporated later.

Portion of script	Who gets copies
Full script	Assistants, musicians, narrator, Mulla Husayn
Jewish prayer	Jewish reader
Christian prayer	Christian reader
Muslim prayer	Muslim reader
Section #6-9	Three students (don't separate sections)
Section #10-11	Siyyid Kázim

4. Distribute the props and rehearse again. This time, practice on stage and "block" each scene—showing the children where to enter and exit, walk or stand. The script notes contain basic stage directions, but the director may need to improvise to ensure that the movements and positions appear natural, fit the dialog, and allow the actors to be easily seen by the audience. Children should hold their scripts at chest height so their faces are visible.

5. Briefly rehearse the musicians. This is not a professional performance. Rather, music and sound effects are symbolic (see next page) and are integrated throughout the text to enhance the theme. Allow children to improvise as appropriate.

6. Bring everyone together and distribute the costumes for a final dress rehearsal. Make sure all of the actors pause for the sound effects. The narrator should practice with a microphone if one will be used during the performance.

7. Collect scripts, costumes, props and instruments, and set them out neatly in the staging area to prepare for the show.

The Báb – Children's Performance

Assign children to the following parts

Speaking Parts

	Role	Costumes	Props	Actor
1	Narrator			
2	Mulla Husayn			
3	Jewish prayer		Book (Torah)	
4	Christian prayer		Book (Bible)	
5	Muslim prayer		Book (Qur'án)	
6	Siyyid Kázim		Clues poster, pointer	
7	Student #1			
8	Student #2			
9	Student #3			

Silent Parts (If necessary, one child could play several parts.)

	Role	Costumes	Props	Actor
1	3-4 children with stars		Large stars on sticks	
2	Sign carrier		"The End is Near" sign	
3	Chart carrier		Bible chart	
4	Ascension robe seller		Robe with "On Sale" tag	
5	Horse rider		Two broom horses	
6	Shaykh Ahmad		Scroll tied with ribbon	
7	Poster carrier		"1260 = 1844" poster	
8	Mulla Husayn's brother		Sword	
9	Mulla Husayn's nephew		Sword	

Musicians (If necessary, one or two people could play all of the parts. Bring a music stand if needed.)

Code	Instrument	Significance	Musician
T	Trumpet [1]	Announcement	
S	Santur [2]	Search	
Ch	Chimes	Time (start, flashback, pause)	
D	Drum or tambourine	Calamities	
G	Guitar	Promised One is near	
C	Coconut shell clappers	Horses' hoof beats	
R	Rain stick or rattle	Shooting stars	
P	Persian chant	Prayer	

1. See music page below for sample trumpet selections. For additional ideas, visit: < www.sounddogs.com > and enter "trumpet fanfare" in the search box. Then scroll down to the fanfares and click on the "MP3" button to hear a preview. You can also check: < www.google.com > and click on "Images" in the top left menu. Enter "trumpet fanfare sheet music" in the search box. You can also use the "trumpet voice" on an electronic keyboard, or an audio recording such as the World Congress CD, track 2, available from: < www.BahaiBookstore.com > enter product code: MWCCD.

2. You can also play a recording such as the World Congress CD–track 3, or use a different instrument.

The Báb – Children's Performance

"Treasure in Shiraz"

Materials

- 6-8 paper stars on sticks or dowels[1]
- Large sign: The end is near!*
- Bible math poster: 2300 – 456 = 1844*
- Ascension robe[2]
- 2 horses[3]
- 3 holy books (Torah, Bible, Qur'án)[4]
- Scroll tied with ribbon
- 2 plastic or cardboard swords
- Poster with clues to the Prophet (see Lesson #2)
- Easel
- Pointer
- Poster: 1260 = 1844*
- Musical instruments (see previous page)
- Audio recording (or a real voice) of Persian chanting
- Audio player
- Costumes[5]
- Shiraz city gate bordered by artificial trees[6]
- The Báb's room
    - Low table covered with silk cloth
    - Green turban on pillow[7]
    - Small rug
    - Large pillows for Mulla Husayn to sit on
    - Teapot with glass cups on tray
    - Decorative cloth as a backdrop on the wall
- Prop box, table, costume rack and mirror for staging area
- Extra copies of the script
- Don't forget the camera!

* Enlarge signs if desired. Then clip to poster board and attach to a yardstick with duct tape.

---

1. We used a 10-pack of large silver stars from the Dollar Store, taped to bamboo plant stakes.

2. A white bathrobe tied with a rope belt works well.

3. Use a toy hobby horse or a broom and some imagination.

4. Fold a sheet of construction paper in half lengthwise, write the book title in large letters on the front, and add the appropriate religious symbol. Use a different color for each book, and tape the relevant reading inside in the middle near the top.

 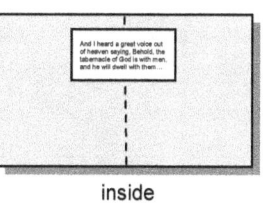

5. Simple costumes can be created from old sheets, bathrobes, belts, vests and scarves.

6. The actors can enter through a garden trellis or rebar arch decorated with artificial roses.

7. Green cloth can be formed into a turban and placed on the table to represent the Báb.

The Báb – Children's Performance

"Treasure in Shiraz"

Setting the Stage
(one possible arrangement)

Seat children near or behind the stage in three groups according to their roles (speaking, silent, musical), along with the adult in charge of each group.

If a suitable "gate" is not available, one can easily be created from stacked cardboard boxes taped together in back and decorated with a few flowers.

A Few Stage Directions
(Looking at the audience from the actor's viewpoint)

STAGE LEFT	Left side of the stage
STAGE RIGHT	Right side of the stage
UPSTAGE	Going towards the audience
DOWNSTAGE	Going away from the audience towards the back of the stage

Bahá'í Children's Classes and Retreats: Theme 3, p. 134

The Báb – Children's Performance

"Treasure in Shiraz"
Script for Readers' Theater on the Declaration of the Báb

Adapted by R. Gottlieb from Dawnbreakers, chap. 1-3;
Balyuzi, The Báb, p. 15-23; Sears, Release the Sun, p. 3-17

Children should enter from stage right. Readers should pause during visual and sound effects. Children carrying signs and stars should walk across the stage and back, holding their props high.

	Role	Dialogue + Sound Effects	Audio	Action
1	Narrator	**(T)(Ch)** The year was 1844, and many Christians believed it was time for the second coming of Christ. Comets and <u>shooting stars</u> filled the night skies, **(R)** and people said the <u>end of the world</u> was at hand. **(D)** Based on Bible prophecy, Christian scholars calculated that Jesus would return in <u>1844</u>.	See music page for trumpet parts	Narrator enters Stars, "end" sign & Bible math poster are carried across stage
2	Narrator	In America, some believers gave away all their possessions, and some stores even sold <u>special robes</u> **(G)** for the coming event. A rich woman from England bought <u>two horses</u> **(C)** —one for herself and one for Jesus when He would return. It was 1844, and around the world, people of other religions were also waiting and praying—for their own Promised One to appear.		Carry robe across Ride one horse and carry the other across
3	Three readers	*(Read Jewish, Christian and Muslim prayers.)* *(Each steps forward to read, then steps back in line.)*		3 readers walk on and off together
4	Narrator	Yes, all over the world, people were waiting and praying. But in Persia, the excitement over the coming of God's Messiah was greater than in any other land. In fact, many people believed the Promised One was already here, and they were searching for Him. **(S)** One man, <u>Shaykh Ahmad</u>, traveled to the Persian city of Shiraz, in search of the Promised One. Shaykh Ahmad became a great teacher and told his followers that the Promised One would soon appear. **(G)** Just before Shaykh Ahmad passed away, he asked his favorite student, <u>Siyyid Kázim</u>, to lead his followers in this spiritual quest.	**(G)** Improvise a few notes, or play one loud slow strum on A7; hear each note	Shaykh A. enters through gate with scroll Siyyid K. enters and takes scroll Shaykh A. leaves

The Báb – Children's Performance

5	Narrator	Siyyid Kázim taught that the coming of the Promised One would be like a trumpet blast…(T)… a trumpet blast to awaken the sleeping peoples of the world. After Siyyid Kázim died, his young follower, <u>Mulla Husayn</u>, continued the search for the Promised One. Mulla Husayn invited the others to join him, but most of them refused.	See music page	Siyyid steps back with head down and leaves, as Mulla H. enters and takes scroll
6	Mulla Husayn	Come friends! Let us go in search of the Promised One!		3 students enter
7	Student #1	No! We must remain and protect the honor of our departed leader! **(D)**	Drum	#1 leaves
8	Student #2	No! Our enemies are dangerous and powerful! **(D)**	Drum	#2 leaves
9	Student #3	No! We must stay and take care of the children! **(D)**	Drum	#3 leaves
10	Narrator	So Mulla Husayn set out with only his <u>brother</u> and his <u>nephew</u> for companions. He vowed never to stop until he found the Promised One. The words of his teacher, Siyyid Kázim, were still ringing in his ears… **(Ch)**		Brother and nephew enter—all 3 arm-in-arm
11	Siyyid Kázim	The Promised One will be of noble lineage... A descendant of the Prophet Muhammad. In His name, "Ali" will come before the name of the Prophet. He will be young (between the ages of 20 and 30), of medium height, and will not smoke. He will possess innate knowledge. In the year 1260 His Cause shall be revealed. **(Ch)**		Siyyid K. enters, puts poster on easel and reads using pointer Siyyid exits
12	Narrator	It was now the year <u>1260</u> (1844 on the Christian calendar). Mulla Husayn's heart was filled with excitement, and he was drawn like a magnet to the city of <u>Shiraz</u>. **(S)** After walking for many days, the three young men arrived, hot and tired, at the gate of the city. Mulla Husayn told the others to find lodging for the night, then go to the mosque and wait for his return.		1260=1844 poster is carried across Brother and nephew exit
13	Mulla Husayn	Something draws my heart into the city, but I shall meet you at the mosque tonight for evening prayers. **(P)**	Persian chanting off stage	

14	Narrator	As Mulla Husayn walked alone near the gate of the city, praying with all his heart that God would lead him to the Promised One, a Young Man approached. **(G)** He wore a <u>green turban</u> (a symbol that he was descended from the Prophet Muhammad), and on his face was a smile of loving welcome. The stranger embraced Mulla Husayn as though they were old friends, and invited him to his home to rest after the long journey.	**(G) A7 chord (one strum)**	**Narrator points to turban**
15	Mulla Husayn	I explained that my two companions were waiting for me. "God will surely watch over them," He replied.		**Speaking to audience**
16	Narrator	When they arrived at the house, the Young Man gave Mulla Husayn some tea. They prayed together and Mulla Husayn again begged God to help him find the Promised One.		**Enter home, drink tea**
17	Mulla Husayn	"O my God! I have striven with all my soul, and until now have failed to find thy Promised Messenger." **(S)**		**Praying, palms up**
18	Narrator	Then the Youth asked Mulla Husayn about his search, and how he would recognize the Promised One.		
19	Mulla Husayn	"He will be descended from the Prophet Muhammad, between the ages of 20 and 30, of medium height, not a smoker, and in his name, 'Ali' will come before the name of the Prophet."		**Speaking to narrator**
20	Narrator	There was a silence...**(Ch)**...the pause that precedes the breaking of the dawn. Then his Host replied with a vibrant voice, "Behold! All these signs are manifest in Me!" **(G)** Mulla Husayn was so shocked, that at first he could not believe it. But as the Báb continued speaking, Mulla Husayn realized that this noble Youth was the One he had been searching for. **(G)**		**Speaking to audience** **Mulla H. looks surprised**
21	Mulla Husayn	His name was 'Ali-Muhammad. In His name, "Ali" came before that of the Prophet. He was 25 years old. He was announcing Himself now in the year 1260. Wasn't that all foretold by Siyyid Kázim?		**Pointing to poster**
22	Narrator	The Báb explained that He was a Messenger of God and also the Herald of a second Manifestation with a mission even greater than His own.		

The Báb – Children's Performance

23	Mulla Husayn	I still remember his words: "O thou who art the first to believe in me. Verily, I am the Báb, the Gate of God." (T)	See music page	Speaking to audience
24	Narrator	Mulla Husayn's long search was over. (S) *(Invite the full cast to join you on stage for a bow.)*		Mulla exits

Prayers for Script Section #3

JEWISH: From the Torah

I wait for the Lord, my soul doth wait, and in his word do I hope...
And it shall come to pass in that day, that the great trumpet
shall be blown...And the Lord shall be king over all the earth...
Blessed be the Lord God, the God of Israel. Amen. Amen.

(Psalms 130:5, Isaiah 27:13, Zechariah 14:9, Psalm 41:13)

CHRISTIAN: From the Bible

Thy kingdom come. Thy will be done on earth, as it is in heaven...
...And they shall see the Son of man coming in the clouds
of heaven with power and great glory. And he shall send
his angels with a great sound of a trumpet. Amen.

(Matthew 6: 9-10, Matthew 24:30-31)

MUSLIM: From the Qur'án

And for thy Lord, wait thou patiently.
For when there shall be a trump on the trumpet...
On that day we will roll up the heavens...
And...as to "the Hour" there is no doubt of its coming.

(Qur'án Sura 74:7-8, 21:104, 18:20)

The Báb – Children's Performance

"Treasure in Shiraz"

Trumpet Music for Readers' Theater

Script item #1: Introduction to the play (for trumpet in C)

Script item #5: "…like a trumpet blast" (for trumpet in C)

Script item #23: "I am the Báb, the Gate of God." (for trumpet in Bb)

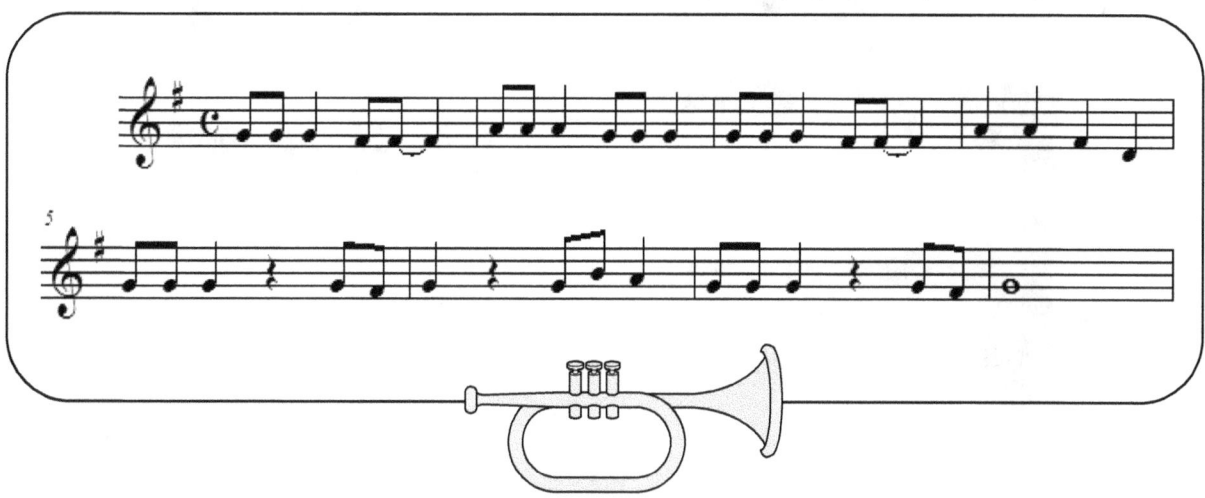

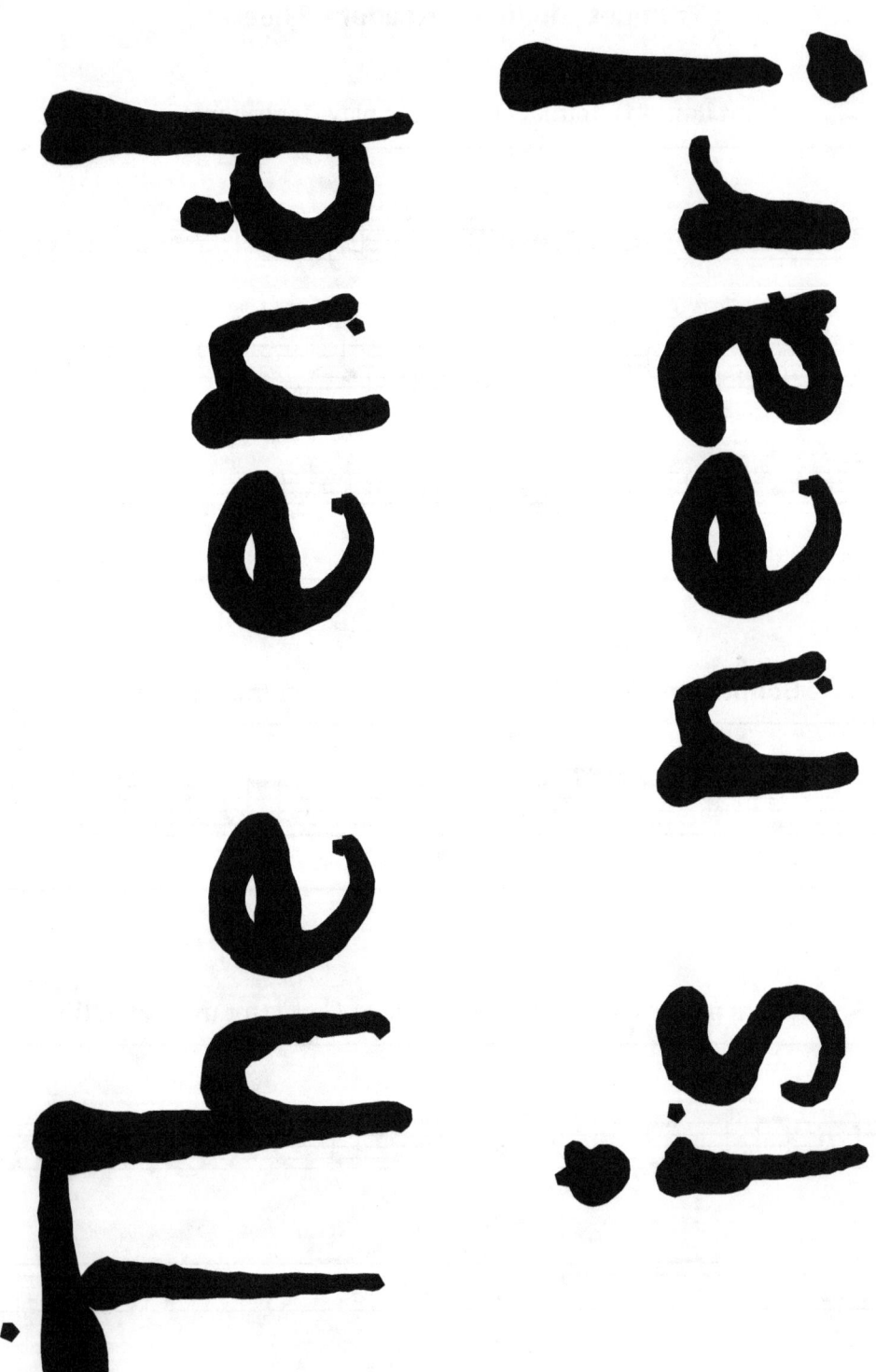

The Báb – Children's Performance, Baháʼí Children's Classes and Retreats: Theme 3, p. 140

$$2300 - 456 = 1844$$

1260 = 1844

The Báb – Children's Performance, Bahá'í Children's Classes and Retreats: Theme 3, p. 142

The Báb – Children's Performance

A few photos from the play

Opening Prayer

Say:
God sufficeth all things
above all things,
and nothing in the heavens
or in the earth
but God sufficeth.

Verily,
He is in Himself
the Knower,
the Sustainer,
the Omnipotent.

– the Báb

Bahá'í Children's Class Performance

The Báb: Gate to Bahá'u'lláh

*"It is my hope that your hearts may become
as ready ground, carefully tilled and prepared...
Then will the garden of your hearts bring forth its flowers..."*

From the Bahá'í Writings

Welcome

Opening music and prayers

The Báb: His Birth, Early Life and Station
- Hoy Es el Día (song)
- Soil of the Heart (reading and demonstration)
- Six stories about the life of the Báb
- Memory quote
- The Báb Blew His Trumpet (song)

Declaration of The Báb
- Treasure in Shiraz (readers' theater)
- Gate of God (craft)
- Memory quote
- In 1844 (song)

Quiz Show and Primal Point
- Quiz show on the life of the Báb
- The Primal Point (felt lesson)
- The Primal Point (craft)

Martyrdom of the Báb
- Memory quote
- Remover of Difficulties (song)
- Martyrdom of the Báb (story)
- Say God Sufficeth (song)
- A Candle for the Báb (craft)
- Shrine of the Báb (craft)
- Queen of Carmel (song)

Refreshments

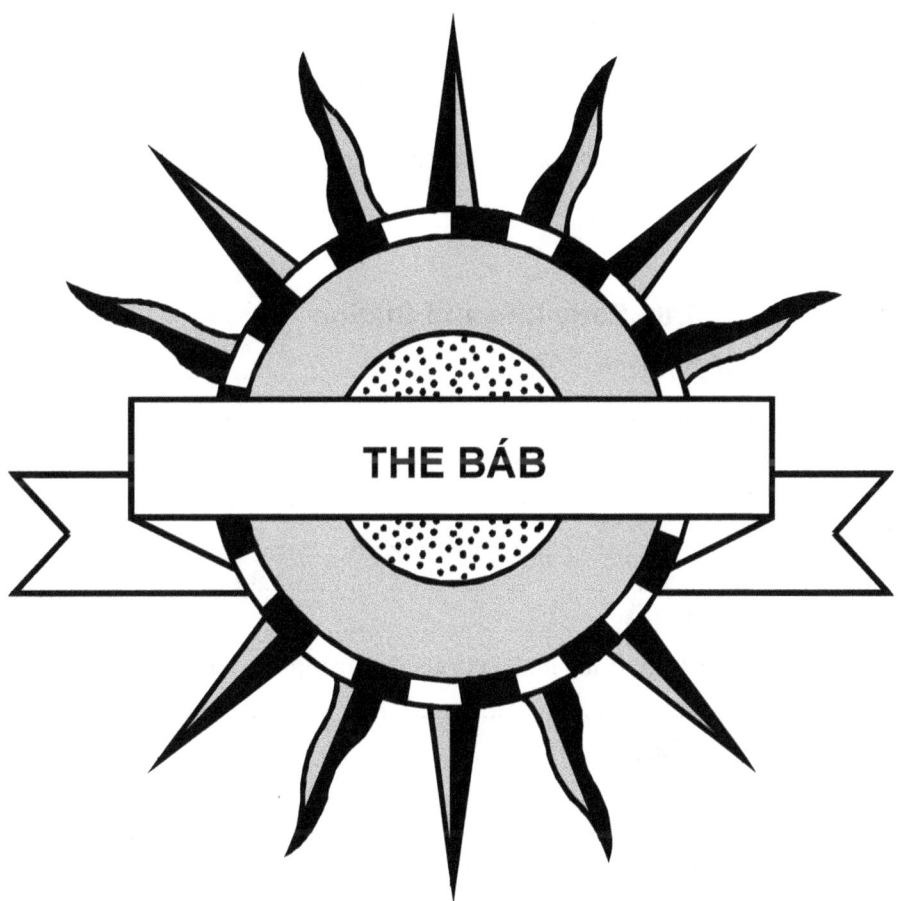

Handouts

The student handouts from all of the lessons are included in this section for ease of photocopying. These handouts can also be downloaded from: www.UnityWorksStore.com. Click on Children's Classes > The Báb > student handouts.

The Báb: Gate to Bahá'u'lláh

HANDOUTS

Orientation and All Lessons

Song Sheet	149
Quotations	151
Stories from the Life of the Báb (packet of readings)	153
Coloring Pages	169

LESSON #1: His Birth, Early Life and Station

Preparing the Soil of the Heart	155
The Promise	156
19th Century Persia	157
Birth and Early Life	158
School Days	159
An Honest Merchant	160
Wife and Child of the Báb	161
Stories from the Life of the Báb (instructions for group leaders)	27
Map of the Middle East	162
Quiz on the Life of the Báb	167

LESSON #2: Declaration of the Báb

Spiritual Treasure Hunt	163

LESSON #3: Martyrdom of the Báb

Imprisonment and Martyrdom of the Báb	165
Martyrdom of the Báb (instructions for group leaders)	61
Shrine of the Báb (coloring page)	177

LESSON #4: The Primal Point

The Primal Point (worksheet)	84

The Báb: Gate to Bahá'u'lláh

Name _____

SONG SHEET

Most of these songs are copyrighted and used with permission. See music section for details.

Hoy Es el Dia
(by Greg Shaw)

Hoy es el día de la Puerta de la Gloria,
Hoy es el día de **Alí el Báb**. (2x)

> Hoy es el día, hoy es el día,
> Hoy es el día de … (2x)

Hoy es el día de la Gloria de Dios,
Hoy es el día de **Bahá'u'lláh**. (2x)

Hoy es el día del Siervo del la Gloria,
Hoy es el día de **'Abdu'l-Bahá**. (2x)

Hoy es el día de la unidad del mundo,
Hoy es el día de **la Fe Bahá'í**. (2x)

O God, my God
(Words of the Báb)

O God, my God,
My Beloved,
My heart's Desire.

Remover of Difficulties
(Words of the Báb)

Is there any Remover of
difficulties save God?
Say: Praised be God!
He is God! All are His servants
and all abide by His bidding!

Say God Sufficeth
(Words of the Báb)

Say: God sufficeth
all things above all things,
and nothing in the heavens
or the earth but God sufficeth.
Verily, He is in Himself
the Knower, Sustainer,
the Omnipotent.

Song of the Prophets
(by Marvin Dryer)

Krishna, Buddha, Zoroaster,
Abraham, Moses, Christ,
Muhammad, the Báb, Bahá'u'lláh,
The spirit's the same.
Bahá'u'lláh teaches for today,
Tells us to look to the spirit,
Not to worship the name.

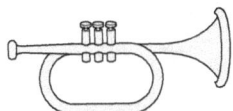

The Báb Blew His Trumpet
(Traditional gospel song; lyrics by R. Gottlieb)

Well, the Báb blew his trumpet,
Announcing to the world the time had come.
Yes, you all know the date,
When He opened the Gate,
The Gate to the Promised One.

Oh-o-o-o-o-o-o-o
We are flowers in God's garden.
The Báb was sent,
To cultivate our hearts,
So that the seed (so that the seed)
Of faith could grow there,
And now we only have to do our part.

When the Báb was a child,
His teacher sent Him home from school,
'Cause he knew that the Báb,
Got his knowledge from God,
But his uncle said to follow the rules.

(chorus)

Well, the Báb was the Herald,
Herald of the promised Day,
The Day that would come,
When the earth would be one,
And everything would be okay.

(chorus)

Bahá'í Children's Classes and Retreats: Theme 3, p. 149

The Báb: Gate to Bahá'u'lláh

1844
(by Tom Shreck)

From many hands and many lands
The prophecy has come
That one great day the Lord would say,
The earth must now be one;
And light must flow to man below
Through God's great Gate or Door,
And all this came to pass as last
In eighteen-forty-four.

**In eighteen-forty-four Lord,
In eighteen-forty-four,
Oh the world passed away
On the twenty-third of May
In eighteen-forty-four.**

Old Samuel Morse sat by his set,
A thinking what to say
Within the first sent telegraph
That was to wing its way;
Across the plains and mountaintops
The word went out once more:
"What hath God wrought?"
Well, He wrought a lot…in 1844.

Krishna said in India, centuries ago
That when the Cause of God was lost,
His Spirit would bestow
Again the force of righteousness
On earth as was before;
And Krishna's Spirit
Came to earth…in 1844.

The Bible says Christ will return
When Daniel is fulfilled,
And 23 long centuries see Israel rebuilt;
Well, 23 in the 4th B.C.,
Though my math's pretty poor,
Results in Christ's returning date…in 1844.

Jesus said, O people,
I have something yet to say,
But you just couldn't bear it yet,
You'll have to wait the day
When I return to you again
In the Glory of the Lord;
Like a Thief in the Night,
He slipped into sight…in 1844.

The Moslem scriptures talk about
The coming of the end,
And when the 12th Imam would visit
All the world again;
Well, all these prophecies came true
With the dawning of the Cause,
When Ali-Muhammad became the Báb
In the garden of Shiraz.

'Abdu'l-Bahá went 'round the world
In 1912 to say:
Listen now, my children,
The world was changed that day;
That day of God's great Glory,
That day *we've waited for*,*
That day of May, the 23rd, in 1844.

    * modified from original

Queen of Carmel
(Melody by Jeannie Rebstock, lyrics arranged from the Bahá'í Writings by Sharon Babbit)

Standing on the mountain,
Looking across the bay.
The Queen of Carmel reigns,
She reigns majestically.

**Cry out, O Zion!
Cry out to your Lord.
Cry out, O Zion!
Circle 'round in adoration,
Circle 'round your Lord.**

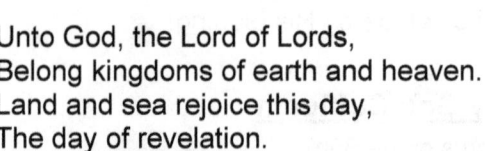

Unto God, the Lord of Lords,
Belong kingdoms of earth and heaven.
Land and sea rejoice this day,
The day of revelation.
    (chorus)

Robed in white and crowned in gold,
She stands for unity.
God will sail His Ark on thee,
As mentioned in the Book of Names.
    (chorus)

The Báb: Gate to Bahá'u'lláh   Name: _____

Quotations from the Bahá'í Writings

WORDS OF THE BÁB

SHORTER

(1) O God, my God, my Beloved, my heart's Desire. *(DB, p.30)*

(2) …The dawn hath indeed broken; "Is not the rising of the Morn…near at hand?"
(Quoting from the Qur'án, SWB, p.50)

(3) Arise in His name, put your trust wholly in Him, and be assured of ultimate victory.
(To the Letters of the Living, DB, p. 94)

(4) O Thou who art the first to believe in Me! Verily I say, I am the Báb, the Gate of God. *(To Mulla Husayn, DB, p.63)*

(5) Heed not your weaknesses and frailty; fix your gaze upon the invincible power of the Lord… *(DB, p. 94)*

(6) O LORD! Enable all the peoples of the earth to gain admittance into the Paradise of Thy Faith. *(SWB, p. 191)*

LONGER

(7) Awake, awake, for, lo! the Gate of God is open and the morning light is shedding its radiance upon all mankind. *(To Mulla Husayn,* DB, *p.85)*

(8) How often the most insignificant of men have acknowledged the truth, while the most learned have remained wrapt in veils. *(SWB, p. 91)*

(9) Is there any Remover of difficulties save God? Say: Praised be God! He is God! All are His servants and all abide by His bidding! *(SWB, p. 217)*

(10) Say: God sufficeth all things above all things, and nothing in the heavens or in the earth but God sufficeth. Verily, He is in Himself the Knower, the Sustainer, the Omnipotent. *(Bahá'í Prayers, p. 29)*

Bahá'í Children's Classes and Retreats: Theme 3, p. 151

The Báb: Gate to Bahá'u'lláh

LONGEST

(11) I am the Primal Point from which have been generated all created things. I am the Countenance of God Whose splendour can never be obscured, the Light of God Whose radiance can never fade. *(SWB, p. 12)*

(12) O My beloved friends! You are the bearers of the name of God in this Day… Scatter throughout the length and breadth of this land, and, with steadfast feet and sanctified hearts, prepare the way for His coming. *(To the Letters of the Living, DB, p.94)*

(13) O peoples of the earth! Verily the resplendent Light of God hath appeared in your midst, invested with this unerring Book, that ye may be guided aright to the ways of peace and, by the leave of God, step out of the darkness into the light… *(SWB, p. 60)*

(14) I am the Lamp which the Finger of God hath lit within its niche and caused to shine with deathless splendour. I am the Flame of that supernal Light that glowed upon Sinai in the gladsome Spot, and lay concealed in the midst of the Burning Bush. *(SWB, p. 74)*

(15) I am…I am, I am, the promised One! I am the One whose name you have for a thousand years invoked, at whose mention you have risen, whose advent you have longed to witness, and the hour of whose Revelation you have prayed God to hasten.
(In response to the mullas who interrogated Him, asking who He claimed to be and what message He brought., DB, p. 315-316)

(16) GOOD NEWS! GOOD NEWS! The Sun of Truth is rising!
GOOD NEWS! GOOD NEWS! Heavenly food is being sent from above!
GOOD NEWS! GOOD NEWS! The Trumpet is sounding!

…O Ye that sleep, Awake!   …Be Happy! Be full of Joy!
This is the day of the Proclamation of the Báb! *('Abdu'l-Bahá in London, p. 126-127)*

(17) Of all the tributes I have paid to Him Who is to come after Me, the greatest is this, My written confession, that no words of Mine can adequately describe Him, nor can any reference to Him in My Book, the Bayan, do justice to His Cause.
(Quoted in Gleanings from the Writings of Bahá'u'lláh, p. 10)

References

DB   The Dawn-breakers
SWB Selections from the Writings of the Báb

Stories from the Life of the Báb

Name: _____

The Báb: Gate to Bahá'u'lláh

These stories, along with full-page color pictures designed to accompany the stories, are available for download from: **www.UnityWorksStore.com**. Click on Children's Classes > The Báb > student handouts. Illustrations can be posted on the wall during classes as an aid for visual learners and to help bring the lessons and readings to life.

Note: The images on the following pages are intended to help children remember events from the life of the Báb. It would not be appropriate to represent the Manifestation of God in any human form, "whether pictorially, in sculpture or in dramatic representation..." (On behalf of The Universal House of Justice, Lights of Guidance, p. 99)

Bahá'í Children's Classes and Retreats: Theme 3, p. 154

Preparing the Soil of the Heart

In early spring, when it is still cold outside, farmers work to prepare the soil so plants will be able to grow. They pull out weeds and remove stones. They spread fertilizer, and they plow[1] the earth so it is ready to receive the seeds.

Then, when the sun warms the earth and the spring rains come once again, it is time to plant and the seeds are put into the ground. They grow strong because the farmers have prepared the soil.

The same thing happens when a new Age[2] begins. First, God sends a Herald[3] or Forerunner[4] to tell people that a Messenger of God is about to appear. The Herald prepares people's hearts so they can recognize God's Manifestation when He comes.

Before Jesus came, God sent John the Baptist to tell people that soon someone much greater would appear. This also happened when God sent Bahá'u'lláh to the world. First, the Báb appeared in the land of Persia.

The Báb announced that He was a Messenger from God whose main mission was to prepare the way for Bahá'u'lláh. God sent Him to warn the people that the Promised One of all religions was coming soon.

The Báb's religion was called the Bábí Faith and his Holy Book is the Bayán. In the Bayán, the Báb told His followers to have good conduct, not to smoke or drink, to show respect for women, and to always take care of the poor.

His laws and teachings were very strict in order to show that the new Faith was a sharp break from the old ways. The Báb's Message was like a plow, digging up the soil of human hearts, or a trumpet blast waking them from a long sleep. It was time to get ready for the new Age.

Thousands and thousands of people heard about the Báb and believed His message. He had prepared them for the coming of Bahá'u'lláh.

1. **plow:** To break up the soil in preparation for planting
2. **Age:** A very long period of time, the start of a new era in history. In religious terms, a new cycle marked by the coming of a new Manifestation of God bringing new teachings and laws.
3. **herald:** Forerunner, messenger, bringer of important news, one who announces that something is going to happen
4. **forerunner:** One who comes before another to prepare the way

1 The Promise

Long before the Báb was born, long before there were cars and phones and computers, back since the beginning of time, God has sent His Prophets or Messengers to the world. We call them Manifestations[1] of God. They are like perfect mirrors, chosen by our Creator to reflect His Light to humankind. Whenever people forget God's teachings and the world is again filled with darkness, He sends another Manifestation to show us the way.

These Manifestations also brought a special Promise from God—that in the future, a great universal Teacher would come and there would be peace throughout the world. Jesus promised his followers that He would come back, so Christians are expecting the Return of Christ. Jews are waiting for the Messiah, and Muslims are looking for the Qá'im. All the great religions are awaiting a Promised One.

In the early 19th century, a great religious revival[2] was taking place around the world. Many people felt certain that it was time for their Promised One to appear. Some had calculated the exact year as 1844.

Right around that time, strange things began to occur. One night, thousands of meteors[3] flashed across the sky. Some people were scared, but others believed it was a sign from God. All kinds of new machines were invented. Before, the fastest a person could travel was by horse; now they could go by train. Before, messages had to be carried by hand; now they could be sent instantly through a wire. Something miraculous was happening.

There was growing excitement as 1844 drew near. In Germany, some people left their homes and sailed to Palestine (in the Holy Land) to search for the Promised One. In the United States, thousands of people gathered outside to wait because they thought He would come down from the sky. In Persia (now called Iran), many people traveled throughout the land to search for Him.

1. **manifest:** To show, reveal or make known
2. **revival:** A re-awakening, a new start, a rebirth of hope
3. **meteor:** A rock from space that burns up after entering the Earth's atmosphere, creating a brief streak of light

Study Questions

1. What is a Manifestation of God?
2. When does God send a Manifestation?
3. What special Promise did all the Manifestations bring? Give some examples.
4. In the early 19th century, what were many religious people expecting?
5. What unusual things were happening at that time?

2 19th Century Persia

In the early 19th century, just before the Báb appeared in Persia (now called Iran), most of the people there were Muslims.[1] Sadly, they had forgotten much of what Muhammad had taught them. The country was in a terrible state of corruption[2] and ignorance.

People were lazy and dishonest. Their hearts were filled with hatred, prejudice[3] and greed. Even the king thought only of his own comfort. Hardly anyone cared for the poor. There was violent fighting among different religious groups and people were often killed.

The condition of women was especially bad. Men believed that girls should not go to school. They should not learn to read or write. They should not learn a profession or find out about events happening in the world.

Women were only allowed to take care of the house and the children. They could not have a paying job. When they did go out, they had to cover their faces with a veil[4] so no one could see them. Women were prisoners of the household and the houses did not even have windows opening on the outside world.

In addition, the citizens of Persia had no rights. The highest law was the decision of the king. If someone went against the king, he or she would be punished in cruel and inhuman ways. Criminals were sometimes shot from cannons or chopped up into little pieces or buried alive. It was a savage[5] time.

1. **Muslim:** A follower of Muhammad (the Founder of Islam)
2. **corrupt:** Lying or being dishonest in return for money or personal gain
3. **prejudice:** A dislike for certain people before you even get to know them
4. **veil:** A piece of cloth worn by a woman to cover her head and face
5. **savage:** Vicious, brutal, cruel, violent, barbaric, wild, out of control

Study Questions

1. Find Persia on the map.
2. What were many people like in 19th century Persia?
3. Why weren't they following the laws of their Prophet Muhammad?
4. How did the different religious groups treat each other?
5. Describe the condition of women and girls.
6. Who made all the laws and what happened to people who broke them?

The Báb: Gate to Bahá'u'lláh

3 Birth and Early Life of the Báb

The Báb was born in Persia on October 20, 1819 (about 200 years ago), in the city of Shiraz. Known as the "city of roses," Shiraz is famous for its poets, beautiful gardens, green shade trees and abundant[1] flowers. In the springtime, a stream of crystal clear water flows through the town and the air is perfumed with the scent of roses. The enchanting song of the nightingale[2] can be heard all night long, and is especially loudest at the hour of dawn.

The Báb was born into a family of respected merchants.[3] His parents named their infant son 'Alí-Muhammad. He was also given the title of *Siyyid*:

- *Muhammad* (after the Prophet of their religion—Islam)
- *Alí* (for Muhammad's son-in-law, the first Imám or leader of Islam after Muhammad)
- *Siyyid* (which means descendant[4] of the Prophet Muhammad)

Siyyid 'Alí-Muhammad had a very special name! He is now known as the Báb, which means "Gate" or "Door," because He opened the way to Bahá'u'lláh. (That story comes later.)

The Báb was a remarkable child. Everyone who met Him was amazed by the sweetness of His character, His polite manners, His honesty, gentleness and courtesy. He also had unusual knowledge and wisdom for a small boy. The Báb didn't care much for children's games, but instead preferred to pray, meditate and talk about spiritual matters. He often chanted His prayers in a melodious[5] voice.

Physically, the Báb was handsome and slender, with dark hair, dark eyes and light skin. He wore a green turban[6] on His head to show that He was descended from the Prophet.

When the Báb was still a small child, His father died, so His uncle took care of Him and raised Him as his own son.

1. **abundant:** Plentiful, a lot of something
2. **nightingale:** A small songbird that sings sweetly, especially at night
3. **merchant:** One who buys and sells items that people need
4. **descendant:** A person related to someone who lived in the past
5. **melodious:** Musical, harmonious, pleasant-sounding, sweet
6. **turban:** A man's headdress made of a long piece of wrapped fabric

Study Questions

1. When and where was the Báb born? Find Persia (now Iran) on the map.
2. Describe the city of Shiraz.
3. What name was the Báb given by His parents, and its significance?
4. What was the Báb like as a child?
5. What did the Báb look like?
6. Why did He wear a green turban on His head?
7. Why was He raised by His uncle?

4 School Days

When He was about six years old, the Báb was sent to school. The teacher immediately noticed the excellent character of his new student and the extraordinary knowledge that He showed.

One day the teacher asked the Báb to recite[1] the first words of the Muslim Holy Book, the Qur'án. The Book begins: "In the Name of God, the Compassionate, the Merciful." The Báb said He would not recite the words until the teacher explained what they meant. (You see, the Qur'án is written in Arabic but all the students spoke the Persian language.)

The teacher pretended not to know the meaning, so the Báb Himself began to explain. The teacher was astonished by the beauty and power of His words. He saw that the Báb was no ordinary child, and he brought Him back to His uncle saying, "I commit Him to your protection…for He, verily,[2] stands in no need of teachers such as I."[3]

The Báb's uncle was not happy and he scolded the young child. He told the Báb to return to school, to remain silent and to listen carefully to every word spoken by the teacher.

The Báb promised to follow His uncle's instructions, but He could not keep His great knowledge to Himself. "Day after day," recalled the teacher, "He continued to manifest[4] such remarkable evidences of superhuman wisdom as I am powerless to recount."[3] This knowledge was not learned from books and teachers. It came directly from God.

The teacher finally convinced the Báb's uncle to take Him home and teach Him the family business. The Báb became a cloth merchant[5] and worked for a time in His uncle's store. In later years, both the uncle and the teacher became followers of the Báb.

1. **recite:** To speak out loud
2. **verily:** Really, truly
3. **Ref:** Shoghi Effendi, The Dawn-Breakers, p. 75, 76
4. **manifest:** To show, reveal, make known
5. **merchant:** One who buys and sells items that people need

Study Questions

1. What did the teacher notice when the Báb first started school?
2. What happened when the teacher asked the Báb to recite from the Qur'án?
3. Why did the teacher bring the Báb home to His uncle?
4. Why was the uncle upset and what happened when he took the Báb back to school?
5. Where did the Báb's knowledge come from?
6. What did the Báb do after His uncle brought Him home again?

5 | An Honest Merchant

When the Báb was fifteen, He went to work for his uncles as a merchant.[1] He regularly gave large sums of money to the poor and spent many hours in prayer. He was also well-respected as a businessman. He was known for his honesty and humility, and was always completely fair.

One day, a man gave the Báb a valuable item to sell for him and told the Báb what the selling price should be. Sometime later, the man received his money from the Báb, but it was far more than he had asked for. When the man wrote to ask why, the Báb replied:

> "What I have sent you is entirely your due. There is not a single farthing[2] in excess of what is your right. There was a time when the trust[3] you had delivered to Me had attained[4] this value. Failing to sell it at that price, I now feel it My duty to offer you the whole of that sum."[5]

The man was surprised and begged the Báb to take back the extra money, but the Báb refused. He knew it would have been worth more had He sold it sooner, so He decided to give the man the full amount. Not everyone would be so honorable.[6]

1. **merchant:** One who buys and sells items that people need
2. **farthing:** The lowest value or smallest amount; a former British coin worth less than a penny
3. **trust:** Money or property being held for someone else
4. **attained:** Reached
5. **Ref:** Shoghi Effendi, The Dawn-Breakers, p. 79-80
6. **honorable:** Guided by strong moral principles

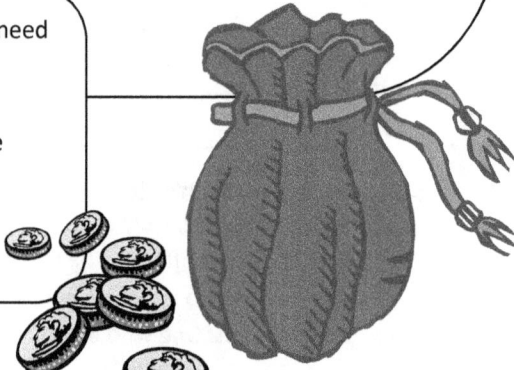

Study Questions

1. How old was the Báb when He went to work for His uncles and what was His job?
2. How did He spend His time when He wasn't working?
3. What kind of reputation did He have as a businessman?
4. What happened when a man asked the Báb to sell a valuable item for him?
5. Why did the Báb pay the man more than He Himself had received for that item?
6. Why do you think the man was surprised?

6 Wife and Child of the Báb

When the Báb was 22, His mother felt it was time for Him to take a wife, and as was the custom, she helped to arrange a marriage for her son.

A short time later, the Báb and Khadíjih-Bagum, a sweet and gentle young woman, were married. They lived together happily for a brief while, but soon after the wedding, Khadíjih-Bagum had a frightening dream.

In her dream, there was a ferocious lion in the courtyard[1] of their home. Her arms were wrapped around the neck of the lion, and it dragged her around the courtyard 2½ times. She woke up feeling very scared and told the Báb about her dream. He said it meant their happy life together would not last more than 2½ years. Khadíjih-Bagum was greatly worried and upset by this, but the Báb comforted her and prepared her to accept the difficulties that lay ahead.

The following year (1843), a baby boy was born to Khadíjih-Bagum. It was a difficult birth and both her own life and the life of the child were in great danger. Sadly, the infant died at birth. They called him Ahmad, and the Báb and His young wife mourned[2] together in their great loss.

The Báb wrote a beautiful letter to comfort His wife, and told her that Ahmad was now in Heaven. He revealed a special prayer in honor of their tiny son, and He also prayed that someday, He might also give His own life in the path of God.

"O my God, my only Desire! Grant that the sacrifice of My son, My only son, may be acceptable unto Thee. Grant that it be a prelude[3] to the sacrifice of My own, My entire self, in the path of Thy good pleasure."[4]

1. **courtyard:** An inside patio surrounded by the walls of the house
2. **mourn:** Weep for, grieve, cry over the loss of a loved one
3. **prelude:** An event that introduces or comes before something else
4. **Ref:** Shoghi Effendi, The Dawn-Breakers, p. 77

Study Questions

1. What happened when the Báb was 22 years old?
2. What happened in Khadíjih-Bagum's dream and what did it mean?
3. What happened to their only child?
4. How did the Báb comfort His wife at the loss of their son?
5. When His son died, what did the Báb ask of God?

The Báb: Gate to Bahá'u'lláh

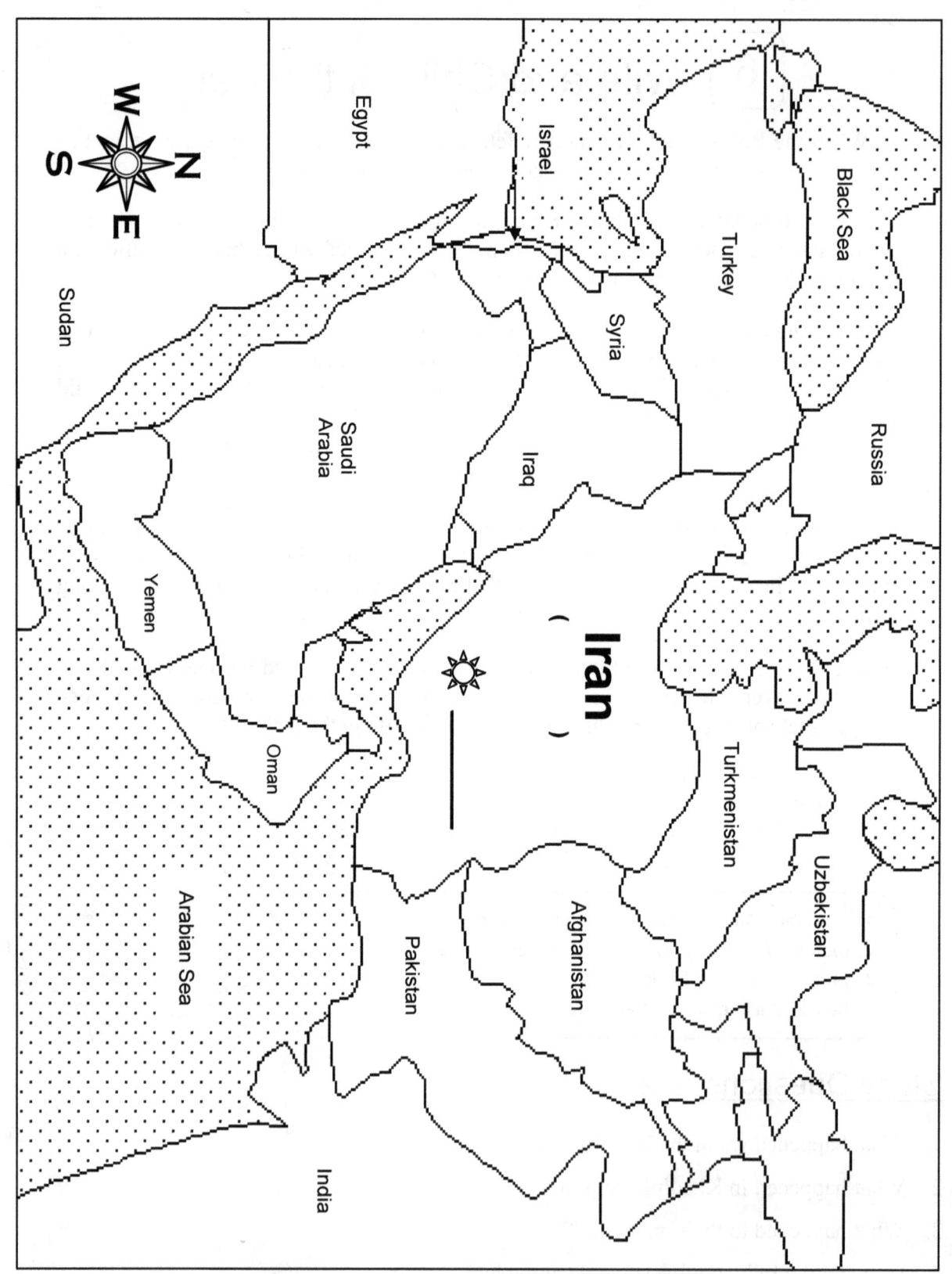

Bahá'í Children's Classes and Retreats: Theme 3, p. 162

Spiritual Treasure Hunt
Mulla Husayn and the Search for the Báb

It was springtime in Persia in 1844, just before the coming of the Báb. Many people had heard about the Qá'im[1], a Divine Teacher like Jesus or Muhammad, who had been promised by God in the Muslim holy book, the Qur'án.

Many people thought that the Promised Qá'im would not come for a very long time. Others felt certain He was coming soon, while a few believed that He was already living in the world.

Whenever God sends a new Messenger, only a few people recognize Him at first. Some might see Him on the street or hear Him talk, but do not realize that He is a Manifestation because their hearts have not been prepared.

Others may be too busy thinking about their own problems, and still others just don't want to listen. But there are always some whose hearts are ready, and they are expecting Him.

One very brave and pure-hearted man, Mulla Husayn, was expecting the Qá'im and wanted to go search for Him. He decided to leave his home and family and travel throughout the land of Persia.[2]

Mulla Husayn could only find two people to go with him—his brother and his nephew. In order to prepare their hearts for this "holy adventure," the three young men went to a quiet place for 40 days to pray.

When they started out on their journey to find the Promised One, they didn't know who to look for or where to search, but Mulla Husayn felt drawn **"like a magnet"** to the city of Shiraz.

The three men traveled on foot across the desert for many days. Finally they reached Shiraz with its fragrant flower gardens and beautiful green trees. They were tired and thirsty after their long walk under the hot sun.

Mulla Husayn told his companions to go to the mosque[3] and he would meet them there later for evening prayers.

As Mulla Husayn walked alone near the gate of the city, praying with all his heart that God would lead him to the Promised One, a Young Man approached. He wore a green turban and on His face was a smile of loving welcome.

Mulla Husayn did not know that this was the One he had been searching for. The stranger put His arms around Mulla Husayn as if they were old friends, and invited him to His home to rest after such a long journey. But Mulla Husayn explained that his traveling companions were waiting for him.

"Commit them to the care of God," said the Young Man. "He will surely protect and watch over them."[4]

He was so kind and confident that Mulla Husayn felt unable to refuse the invitation, and he followed the Báb into the city. He thought perhaps this kind stranger could help him find the promised Qá'im.

---

1. **Qá'im:** "He Who arises" – the Promised One of Islam (Shoghi Effendi, God Passes By, p. 57)
2. **Ref:** For the story of Mulla Husayn's search, see The Dawn-breakers, p. 50-65
3. **mosque:** A Muslim house of worship
4. **Ref:** The Dawn-breakers, p. 52

The Báb: Gate to Bahá'u'lláh

When they arrived at the Báb's house, the Báb poured water over Mulla Husayn's hands to wash away the dust of travel, and served him tea. They prayed together and Mulla Husayn again begged God to help him find the Promised One. He still did not know who the Báb was. →

Finally, the Báb asked about Mulla Husayn's quest,[5] and how he would recognize the Promised Qá'im. Mulla Husayn replied that his teacher had given him specific clues to look for.

The Promised One would be...

- Descended from the Prophet Muhammad.
- Between 20 and 30 years old.
- Of medium height.
- A non-smoker.
- In His name, "Ali" will come before the name of the Prophet.
- He will have innate knowledge that comes from God.
- He will reveal His Mission in the year 1260 (1844 on our calendar).

"The Báb paused for a while and then with a vibrant[6] voice declared: 'Behold, all these signs are manifest in Me!'"[7]

Mulla Husayn was so shocked that at first he could not believe it. But as the Báb continued speaking, Mulla Husayn realized that this was the One he had been searching for.

The Báb explained that He was a Messenger of God and also the Herald of a second Manifestation with a mission even greater than His own.

The Báb's declaration took place on the eve of May 23, 1844. He was only 25 years old.

This was the first time that the Báb had told anyone who He was. Mulla Husayn was the first* to believe in Him, but the Báb asked him not to tell anyone yet.

He said that 17 more pure-hearted souls would have to find Him on their own, searching by themselves, just as Mulla Husayn had done. He said that God would guide their steps.

Then, when all 18 had discovered the Báb, He would send them out across the land to tell people that the Promised Qá'im had come, and to prepare them for the coming of Bahá'u'lláh. It was the dawn of a new Day.

---

5. **quest:** Special mission, or search for something of great importance
6. **vibrant:** Lively, dynamic, energetic, full of life
7. **Ref:** The Dawn-breakers, p. 57

---

* Earlier, the wife of the Báb had recognized that He was a Holy Person but she did not know He was the Promised Qá'im. (Hour of Dawn, p. 27; Adib Taherzadeh, The Revelation of Baha'u'llah vol. 2, p. 382, 385)

Imprisonment and Martyrdom of the Báb

After the Báb declared to His first follower, Mulla Husayn, He waited for other disciples[1] to discover Him as well. Soon 18 pure souls, including Mulla Husayn, had recognized Him. The Báb sent these first believers throughout Persia to teach the new Faith and to prepare people for the coming of Bahá'u'lláh.

The Báb's Message spread quickly. Before long, He had thousands of enthusiastic followers. This made the religious and government leaders jealous. They were afraid of losing their own power, just like the authorities during the time of Jesus.

The Prime Minister[2] thought he could destroy the Báb's influence by sending Him far away. Although the Báb hadn't done anything wrong, He was arrested and sent to the prison of Mah-Ku, a stone castle in the remote[3] mountains of northern Persia. The Prime Minister thought that now everyone would forget about the Báb.

It was so cold in the prison, that when the Báb washed His face, the water would freeze to ice on His skin. There was no light in the prison either, not even a lamp, so the Báb spent every night in complete darkness. Can you imagine how cold and dark it was, all alone in that faraway place?

But the people of Mah-Ku found out about their innocent prisoner and soon came to love the Báb. Those who lived nearby would go to the prison every morning on the way to work, and ask for the Báb's blessing. Even the prison guards became His friends. They let the Báb's followers visit Him in prison, too.

Before long, all the people were talking about the great Light that was shining out of that dark prison. Do you know what they meant? Yes, they were talking about the Báb.

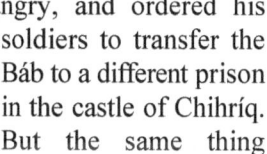

When the Prime Minister heard about this, he became very angry, and ordered his soldiers to transfer the Báb to a different prison in the castle of Chihríq. But the same thing happened again. The guards learned to love their gentle prisoner, and many people came to visit Him.

This time, when the news reached the Prime Minister, he demanded that the Báb be brought to the city of Tabriz immediately. He wanted to find a way to get rid of the Báb once and for all. The king's soldiers put chains on the Báb's hands and feet and around His neck, and brought Him to Tabriz.

As soon as He reached the city, the Báb was arrested and put on trial, but He was not afraid. He boldly told the religious leaders that He was a Messenger of God and that they should follow Him.

This made them even angrier. They took Him outside to be whipped and beaten with a stick across His bare feet. Then they took Him back to prison and sentenced Him to be killed the next day.

That night, in His prison cell, the Báb's face seemed to glow with a special radiance[4] and joy. He knew that He would soon be in Heaven with God.

1. **disciple:** Follower, believer, supporter
2. **Prime Minister:** Head of the government, chief officer appointed by the king
3. **remote:** Far away, distant, isolated, hard to find, difficult to get to
4. **radiance:** Brightness, glow, sparkle, happiness, joy, warmth

The Báb: Gate to Bahá'u'lláh

Early the next morning, a guard came and took the Báb out to be shot by a firing squad.[5] The Báb was giving final instructions to His secretary and asked the guard to wait, but the guard refused. The Báb told him that nothing on earth could stop Him from finishing His conversation, but the guard still said no.

The Báb was brought before a group of soldiers. Ten thousand people had climbed onto the rooftops to watch the execution. Many were laughing. Some were shouting insults and throwing garbage at the Báb.

Sam Khan, the captain of the soldiers, had been ordered to shoot the Báb. But Sam Khan didn't want to kill an innocent man. He was afraid that God would be angry with him, and he told the Báb how troubled he was. The Báb told Sam Khan not to worry, and to follow his instructions. If he were sincere, God would help him.

The soldiers tied a rope around the Báb's arms and over a nail in the wall, suspending[6] Him above the ground. **Seven hundred and fifty** soldiers lined up in three rows and pointed their rifles at the Báb.

Then Sam Khan shouted, **"Fire! Fire! Fire!"** one row at a time. Can you imagine the loud noise and all of the smoke from **750** rifles? With all those bullets, can you imagine what happened to the Báb?

But when the smoke cleared, everyone gasped in astonishment. The bullets had cut the ropes, and the Báb had disappeared!

The soldiers rushed all around looking for Him. They found Him back in His cell talking with His secretary again. "I have finished My conversation...," He said calmly. "Now you may proceed to fulfill your intention."[7] But Sam Khan and his soldiers knew that a miracle had occurred. God had saved them from killing the Báb, and they refused to shoot at Him again.

Another **750** soldiers were brought in and the Báb was suspended once more. When the soldiers raised their guns to fire, the Báb spoke His last words to the crowd: "The day will come when you will have recognized Me; that day I shall no longer be with you."[8] The people became very quiet.

This time, the soldiers succeeded in killing the Báb. It was noon on July 9th, 1850. The Báb was only 30 years old.

The moment the shots were fired, a great storm suddenly broke over the city. A strange wind blew through the streets. Thick dust blocked out the sunlight and blinded the eyes of those who were watching. The entire city was in darkness. The crowd became frightened and stood in complete silence.

The Báb's friends took His body, and hid it from His enemies for many years. Finally, they carried Him to the Holy Land,[9] where He is buried on Mount Carmel in a beautiful shrine with a golden dome. Today, the Shrine of the Báb is a holy place visited by people from all over the world.

---

5. **firing squad:** A group of soldiers who carry out an execution by gunfire
6. **suspend:** To hang something from above
7. **meaning:** Now you may carry out your plan (Ref: Shoghi Effendi, God Passes By, p. 53)
8. **Ref:** Shoghi Effendi, The Dawn-Breakers, p. 514
9. **Holy Land:** Refers to present-day Israel

The Báb: Gate to Bahá'u'lláh

Quiz on the Life of the Báb

1. Who was Siyyid 'Alí-Muhammad? _____
2. What does "the Báb" mean? _____
3. Why was He called a Siyyid? _____
4. When and where was He born? _____
5. Describe the city of Shiraz. _____
   _____
6. Why was the Báb raised by His uncle? _____
7. When His uncle sent the Báb to school, why did the teacher send Him home?
   _____
8. Where did the Báb's knowledge come from? _____
9. What work did the Báb do after leaving school? _____
10. Did the Báb ever have His own family? _____
11. What did the Báb look like? _____
12. Why did He wear a green turban on His head? _____
13. What kind of person was He? _____
14. What is Persia called today, and what was it like at the time of the Báb?_____
    _____
15. Was the Báb a Manifestation of God? _____
16. Were most people expecting Him when He came? _____
17. What is the name of the Báb's religion and Holy Book? _____
18. Why is the Báb also called a Herald? _____
19. What was His main message? _____

References for Stories of the Báb

The Báb: The Herald of the Day of Days. H.M. Balyuzi. George Ronald Publishers: Oxford, England, 1973.

The Dawn-Breakers: Nabil's Narrative of the Early Days of the Bahá'í Revelation. Translated and Edited by Shoghi Effendi. Bahá'í Publishing Trust: Wilmette, Illinois, 1932, 1996 edition. (See especially pages xxiii - xxxi for a description of 19th-century Persia.)

From Mountain to Mountain. Hitjo Garst. George Ronald Publishers: Oxford, England, 1983.

God and His Messengers. David Hofman. George Ronald Publishers: Oxford, England, 1973; 1978 edition.

The Hour of Dawn. Mary Perkins. George Ronald Publishers: Oxford, England, 1976.

Nine Holy Days. Jackie Mehrabi. Bahá'í Publishing Trust: London, 1975.

Promulgation of Universal Peace. 'Abdu'l-Bahá. Bahá'í Publishing Trust: Wilmette, Illinois, 1982 edition.

The Prophets of God. Mahnaz Afshin. Hemkunt Press: New Delhi, India, 1987.

The Báb: Gate to Bahá'u'lláh

Stories from the Life of the Báb

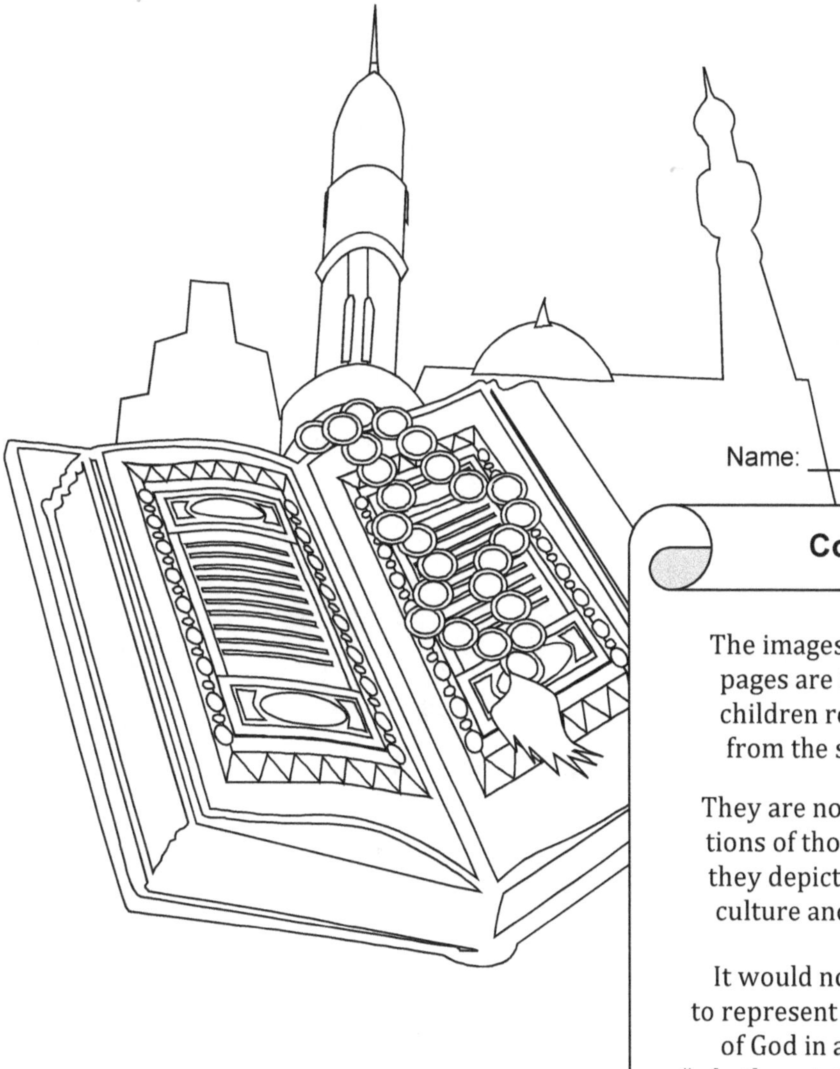

Name: _____

Coloring Book

The images on the following pages are intended to help children remember events from the story of the Báb.

They are not accurate illustrations of those events. Rather, they depict something of the culture and type of activity.

It would not be appropriate to represent the Manifestations of God in any human form, "whether pictorially, in sculpture or in dramatic representation…"

– On behalf of The Universal House of Justice, Lights of Guidance, p. 99

© UnityWorks. Available from www.UnityWorksStore.com

Bahá'í Children's Classes and Retreats: Theme 3, p. 169

The Báb: Gate to Bahá'u'lláh

There was violent fighting among different groups and people were often killed. It was a savage time.

Bahá'í Children's Classes and Retreats: Theme 3, p. 170

The Báb: Gate to Bahá'u'lláh

Women were prisoners of the household. When they did go out, they had to cover their faces with a veil so no one could see them.

Bahá'í Children's Classes and Retreats: Theme 3, p. 171

The Báb: Gate to Bahá'u'lláh

The Báb was born in Persia in the city of Shiraz. Famous for its poets and beautiful gardens, the air is perfumed with the scent of roses. The enchanting song of the nightingale can be heard all night long.

The Báb: Gate to Bahá'u'lláh

Soon after the wedding, Khadíjih-Bagum had a frightening dream about a ferocious lion in the courtyard of their home.

Bahá'í Children's Classes and Retreats: Theme 3, p. 173

The Báb: Gate to Bahá'u'lláh

Mulla Husayn could only find two people to go with him—his brother and his nephew. To prepare their hearts for this "holy adventure," they went to a quiet place for 40 days to pray.

Bahá'í Children's Classes and Retreats: Theme 3, p. 174

The Báb: Gate to Bahá'u'lláh

The stranger was so kind and confident that Mulla Husayn felt unable to refuse the invitation, and he followed the Báb into the city.

Bahá'í Children's Classes and Retreats: Theme 3, p. 175

The Báb: Gate to Bahá'u'lláh

Early the next morning, a guard came and took the Báb out to be shot by a firing squad.

Bahá'í Children's Classes and Retreats: Theme 3, p. 176

The Báb: Gate to Bahá'u'lláh

**The Báb is buried on Mount Carmel
in a beautiful shrine with a golden dome.**

Bahá'í Children's Classes and Retreats: Theme 3, p. 177

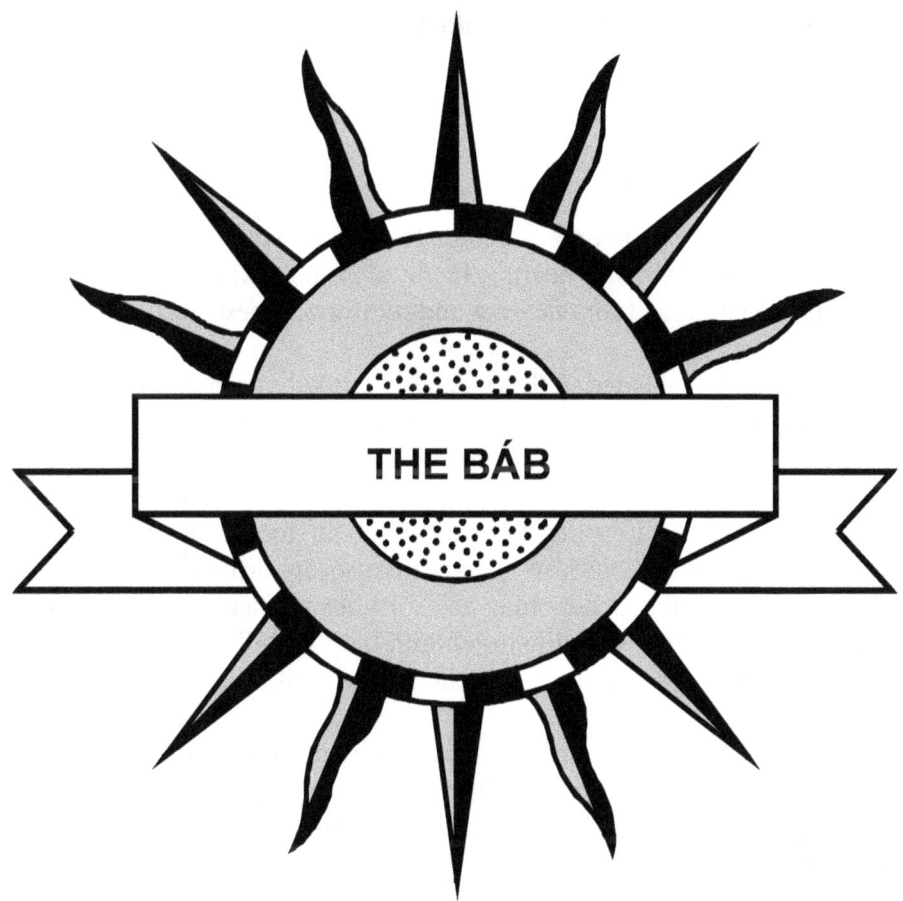

Music

"The art of music is divine and effective. It is the food of the soul and spirit. Through the power and charm of music the spirit of man is uplifted. It has wonderful sway and effect in the hearts of children, for their hearts are pure, and melodies have great influence in them."

'Abdu'l-Bahá, The Promulgation of Universal Peace, p. 52

The Báb: Gate to Bahá'u'lláh

Music Program

*"We, verily, have made music as a ladder for your souls,
a means whereby they may be lifted up unto the realm on high..."*

(Baha'u'llah, Kitáb-i-Aqdas, p. 38)

To the Music Coordinator

Singing brings people together for an enjoyable activity. It uplifts the souls and connects the hearts. It is also an excellent tool for memorizing information and for teaching and reinforcing new ideas.

The songs included in this teacher's guide have been selected to help children learn about the Báb. The students should have song sheets in their folders. As the music coordinator, your job is to help them learn some of these songs.

If the children's classes are held during a weekend retreat format, a morning sing-a-long has been scheduled each day for this purpose. There are also opportunities for singing after lunch and in the evenings. Classroom teachers may ask for your assistance with music that is part of their class. In addition, the music coordinator should help with the children's performance and the rehearsal. Check with the organizers for a schedule with the exact times.

As the song leader, you should be enthusiastic, confident and encouraging. Be patient with children who are shy or who don't catch on right away. When teaching a song for the first time, you will need to sing slowly, with a lot of repetition. If you play an instrument, you can bring it with you to accompany the singing and to keep the beat.

Be sure to learn the songs and the correct meaning and pronunciation of all the words beforehand, and arrive early so your session starts on time. Bring a music stand if available.

A song sheet and musical scores are included on the following pages. Some of the selections have been simplified and shortened for group singing with children. If you know a different melody for a particular song, use the version you feel most comfortable with. Songs in other languages have been included and may be used if desired.

To start a sing-a-long session:

- Ask the children to take out their song sheets and find the first song.
- Ask them what they think the song is about, and explain if necessary.
- Pronounce and define any difficult words.
- Play the song through once, encouraging those who know it to sing with you.
- If necessary, have children repeat each line in a speaking voice before trying to sing.
- Give the starting note and play or clap out the rhythm while everyone sings.
- Practice several times before going on to the next song.

The Báb: Gate to Bahá'u'lláh

Transposing a Song

Idea from Dick Grover

If the notes of a song are too high or too low to sing comfortably, you can easily change the song to a new key – called *transposing*. On a guitar, the easiest way to change the key is by using a capo. You can also follow the steps below.

1. Start by determining the original key (usually the first chord on the sheet music). Play that chord and sing a few lines of the song. If it is too high or too low, you will need to find a more comfortable key.

2. Play a different chord and try singing the song in that key. If it feels comfortable, you have found the right key. If not, play another chord and sing a few lines until you have found a comfortable key to sing in. You will transpose the song to that key. For example, if the song is too low in the original key of D but feels just right in the key of G, you will transpose the entire song to the key of G.

3. Using the chart and moving clockwise, count the number of steps from the original chord to the transposed chord. For example, there are five steps from D to G.

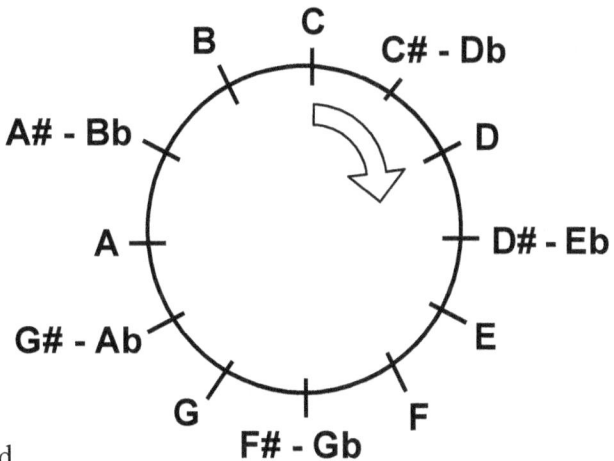

4. Then go through the entire song, changing all the chords by the same number of steps. Based on our example, you would raise all the D chords to G. All the E chords would change to A. An A7 would become a D7, etc. Write the new chord directly over the syllable you will be singing with that chord, or you will be out of rhythm when you play the song.

means "sharp" (It raises that note by a half step.)

b means "flat" (It lowers that note by a half step.)

C# and Db are the same note and count together as one step.
This is also true for D# and Eb, F# and Gb, G# and Ab, A# and Bb.

Bahá'í Children's Classes and Retreats: Theme 3, p. 181

The Báb: Gate to Bahá'u'lláh   Name _____

SONG SHEET

Most of these songs are copyrighted and used with permission. See music section for details.

Hoy Es el Dia
(by Greg Shaw)

Hoy es el día de la Puerta de la Gloria,
Hoy es el día de **Alí el Báb**. (2x)

> **Hoy es el día, hoy es el día,
> Hoy es el día de …** (2x)

Hoy es el día de la Gloria de Dios,
Hoy es el día de **Bahá'u'lláh**. (2x)

Hoy es el día del Siervo del la Gloria,
Hoy es el día de **'Abdu'l-Bahá**. (2x)

Hoy es el día de la unidad del mundo,
Hoy es el día de **la Fe Bahá'í**. (2x)

O God, my God
(Words of the Báb)

O God, my God,
My Beloved,
My heart's Desire.

Remover of Difficulties
(Words of the Báb)

Is there any Remover of
difficulties save God?
Say: Praised be God!
He is God! All are His servants
and all abide by His bidding!

Say God Sufficeth
(Words of the Báb)

Say: God sufficeth
all things above all things,
and nothing in the heavens
or the earth but God sufficeth.
Verily, He is in Himself
the Knower, Sustainer,
the Omnipotent.

Song of the Prophets
(by Marvin Dryer)

Krishna, Buddha, Zoroaster,
Abraham, Moses, Christ,
Muhammad, the Báb, Bahá'u'lláh,
The spirit's the same.
Bahá'u'lláh teaches for today,
Tells us to look to the spirit,
Not to worship the name.

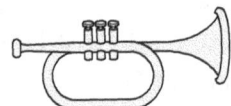

The Báb Blew His Trumpet
(Traditional gospel song; lyrics by R. Gottlieb)

Well, the Báb blew his trumpet,
Announcing to the world the time had come.
Yes, you all know the date,
When He opened the Gate,
The Gate to the Promised One.

**Oh-o-o-o-o-o-o-o
We are flowers in God's garden.
The Báb was sent,
To cultivate our hearts,
So that the seed (so that the seed)
Of faith could grow there,
And now we only have to do our part.**

When the Báb was a child,
His teacher sent Him home from school,
'Cause he knew that the Báb,
Got his knowledge from God,
But his uncle said to follow the rules.

   (chorus)

Well, the Báb was the Herald,
Herald of the promised Day,
The Day that would come,
When the earth would be one,
And everything would be okay.

   (chorus)

The Báb: Gate to Bahá'u'lláh

1844
(by Tom Shreck)

From many hands and many lands
The prophecy has come
That one great day the Lord would say,
The earth must now be one;
And light must flow to man below
Through God's great Gate or Door,
And all this came to pass as last
In eighteen-forty-four.

**In eighteen-forty-four Lord,
In eighteen-forty-four,
Oh the world passed away
On the twenty-third of May
In eighteen-forty-four.**

Old Samuel Morse sat by his set,
A thinking what to say
Within the first sent telegraph
That was to wing its way;
Across the plains and mountaintops
The word went out once more:
"What hath God wrought?"
Well, He wrought a lot…in 1844.

Krishna said in India, centuries ago
That when the Cause of God was lost,
His Spirit would bestow
Again the force of righteousness
On earth as was before;
And Krishna's Spirit
Came to earth…in 1844.

The Bible says Christ will return
When Daniel is fulfilled,
And 23 long centuries see Israel rebuilt;
Well, 23 in the 4th B.C.,
Though my math's pretty poor,
Results in Christ's returning date…in 1844.

Jesus said, O people,
I have something yet to say,
But you just couldn't bear it yet,
You'll have to wait the day
When I return to you again
In the Glory of the Lord;
Like a Thief in the Night,
He slipped into sight…in 1844.

The Moslem scriptures talk about
The coming of the end,
And when the 12th Imam would visit
All the world again;
Well, all these prophecies came true
With the dawning of the Cause,
When Ali-Muhammad became the Báb
In the garden of Shiraz.

'Abdu'l-Bahá went 'round the world
In 1912 to say:
Listen now, my children,
The world was changed that day;
That day of God's great Glory,
That day *we've waited for,**
That day of May, the 23rd, in 1844.

* modified from original

Queen of Carmel
(Melody by Jeannie Rebstock, lyrics arranged from the Bahá'í Writings by Sharon Babbit)

Standing on the mountain,
Looking across the bay.
The Queen of Carmel reigns,
She reigns majestically.

**Cry out, O Zion!
Cry out to your Lord.
Cry out, O Zion!
Circle 'round in adoration,
Circle 'round your Lord.**

Unto God, the Lord of Lords,
Belong kingdoms of earth and heaven.
Land and sea rejoice this day,
The day of revelation.

   (chorus)

Robed in white and crowned in gold,
She stands for unity.
God will sail His Ark on thee,
As mentioned in the Book of Names.

   (chorus)

The Báb: Gate to Bahá'u'lláh

SONGS ABOUT THE BÁB

1. 1844 185
2. Hoy Es el Día 186
3. O God, my God 187
4. Queen of Carmel 188
5. Remover of Difficulties 189
6. Say God Sufficeth 190
7. Song of the Prophets 191
8. The Báb Blew His Trumpet 192

Acknowledgements

Our deepest gratitude goes to the composers for permission to include their songs in this book. Some of the songs have been simplified and shortened for the purpose of group singing with children.

"1844" by Tom Shreck has been a children's favorite at our Bahá'í winter and summer schools for years. We would be grateful to anyone who can help us locate the composer. Marvin Dryer's popular "Song of the Prophets" was originally titled "Bahá'í Talking Blues" and has many more verses. Another favorite, "Hoy Es el Día" by Gregory Shaw, can be heard online in various languages at: < http:// tindeck.com/users/goodspirit >.

The much-loved "Queen of Carmel" was inspired by the *Tablet of Carmel* revealed by Bahá'u'lláh. The beautiful melody was created by Jeannie Rebstock, a 16-year-old seeker at the time in 1969. The lyrics were arranged by her Bahá'í friend Sharon Babbitt. Sharon writes that "the song was never copyrighted. It was our gift to the world." The song can be heard on the *Music of the Bahá'í World Congress* CD, available from: < www.bahaibookstore.com >.

"The Báb Blew His Trumpet" is based on "We are Soldiers in God's Army," a Bahá'í song that was popular in the 1970's. We have changed the title and created new verses to fit the theme, keeping the same rousing gospel tune—which is now in the public domain. For the older Bahá'í version with Van Gilmer and the Voices of Bahá, visit: < www.youtube.com/watch?v=eVn-3rhKn9k >.

Three of the songs, "O God, my God," "Remover of Difficulties," and "Say God Sufficeth," feature words of the Báb set to music. The melodies included here have passed into the realm of Bahá'í folk songs and their origins have been lost. We would be pleased to hear from any artists we have been unable to locate and acknowledge.

Bahá'í Children's Classes and Retreats: Theme 3, p. 184

Baha'i Children's Classes and Retreats: Theme 3, p. 185

Hoy Es el Dia

by Greg Shaw
Used with permission

Baha'i Children's Classes and Retreats: Theme 3, p. 186

O God, My God

Words of the Bab
Composer unknown

O God, my God, my Be - lo - ved - my heart's De - si - re.

Can be sung *a cappella* and repeated several times.

Remover of Difficulties

Words of the Bab
Composer unknown*

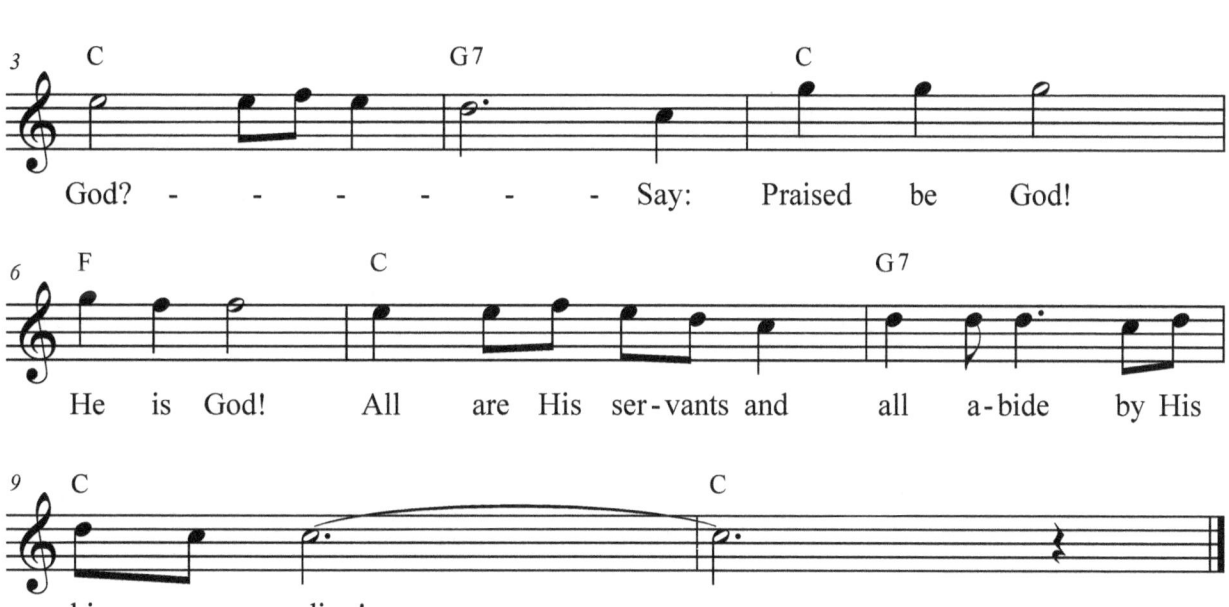

* Music transcribed by Dick Grover

Say God Sufficeth

Words of the Bab
Composer unknown*

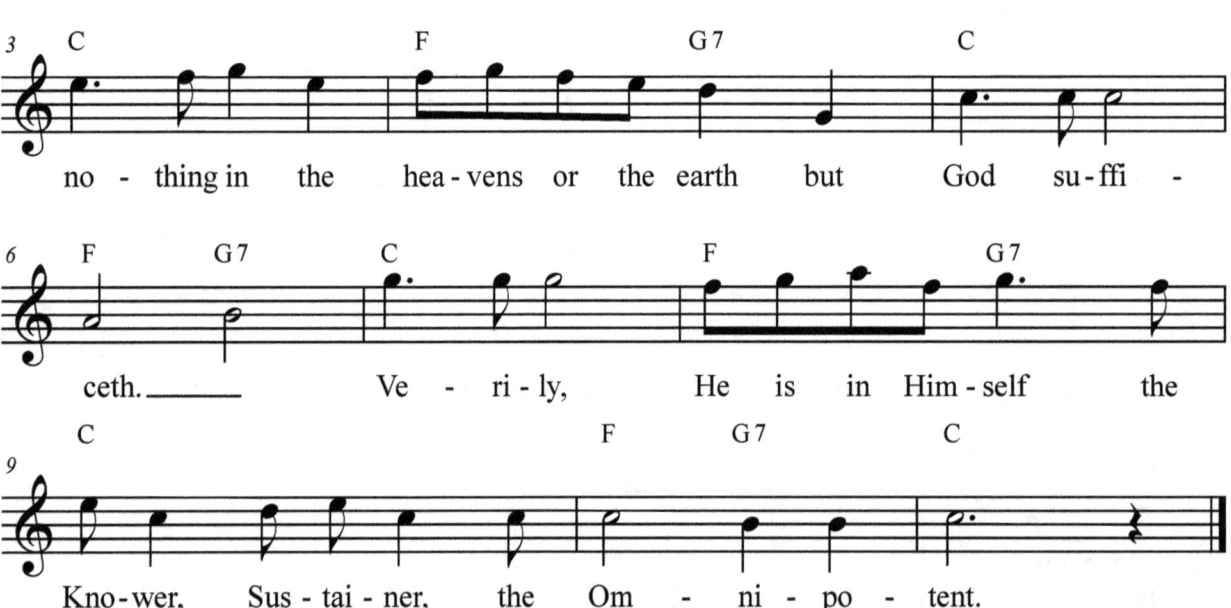

* Music transcribed by Dick Grover

Song of the Prophets

(c) Marvin Dryer
Used with permission

The Bab Blew His Trumpet

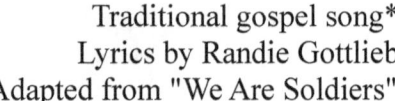

Traditional gospel song*
Lyrics by Randie Gottlieb
Adapted from "We Are Soldiers"

Well, the Bab blew his trum-pet, _____ a-noun-cing
When the Bab was a chi-ld, _____ His
Well, the Bab was the He-rald, _____

to the world the ti-me had come. ___ Yes, you all know the date, when He
teacher sent Him ho-me from school, 'Cause he knew that the Bab, got his
Herald of the pro-mised Day, ___ the Day that would come, when the

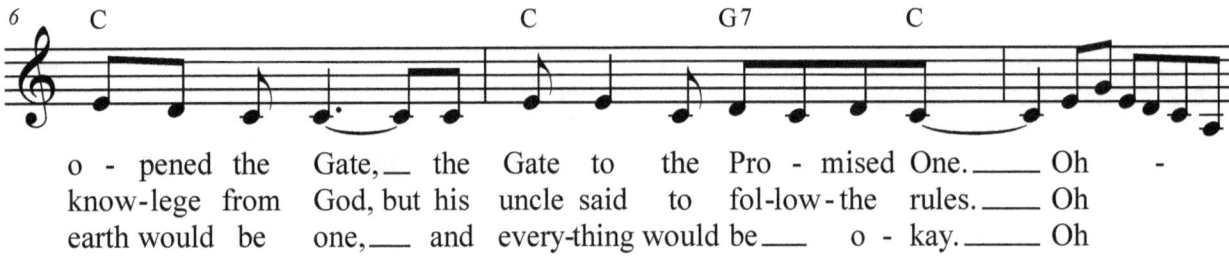

o-pened the Gate, __ the Gate to the Pro-mised One. ___ Oh -
know-lege from God, but his uncle said to fol-low- the rules. ___ Oh
earth would be one, __ and every-thing would be ___ o-kay. ___ Oh

We are flo-wers in God's gar-den.   The Bab was sent to cul-ti-vate our hearts, so that the

seed, so that the seed of faith could grow there, And now we on-ly have to do our part.

* Transcribed by Jonathan Gottlieb

Baha'i Children's Classes and Retreats: Theme 3, p. 192

The Báb: Gate to Bahá'u'lláh

CLOSING ACTIVITIES

At the end of the retreat or after the final class session on this theme, the organizers may wish to plan some closing activities for the participants. We have found the following schedule to be very effective. After the cleanup, call everyone together for a celebration of their achievements.

1. **Opening:** Begin with singing and prayers.

2. **Memory quotes:** Ask for volunteers to recite any individual memory quotes learned. Then recite the main quotes together as a group, for example:

3. **Evaluation:** Conduct a short oral evaluation of the activities. Go around the room and ask each child, youth and adult to share brief thoughts on the three items to the right, which should be written on the board. Anyone may skip his or her turn. Suggestions can be considered in planning for the next class or retreat. An adult should take notes.

   ➢ I liked…
   ➢ I learned…
   ➢ I suggest…

4. **Appreciations:** The organizers can then share any closing comments regarding the importance of teachers (see sample quotes below) and present small gifts of appreciation to the teachers, youth volunteers, musicians, cooks and other helpers. Ask capable children to read the quotes. (The second quote usually gets a good laugh!)

> "Among the greatest of all services that can possibly be rendered by man to Almighty God is the education and training of children…It is, however, very difficult to undertake this service, even harder to succeed in it." (Selections from the Writings of 'Abdu'l-Bahá, p. 133)
>
> "If, in this momentous task, a mighty effort be exerted, the world of humanity will shine out with other adornings…The very demons will change to angels…the wild-dog pack to gazelles…and ravening beasts to peaceful herds…" (Selections from the Writings of 'Abdu'l-Bahá, p. 130)
>
> "It followeth that whatever soul shall offer his aid to bring this about will assuredly be accepted at the heavenly Threshold, and extolled by the Company on high." (Selections from the Writings of 'Abdu'l-Bahá, p. 134)
>
> "If one should, in the right way, teach and train the children, he will be performing a service than which none is greater at the Sacred Threshold." ('Abdu'l-Bahá, Bahá'í Education, p. 32)

5. **Follow-up:** Any follow-up suggestions and messages from the sponsoring Institution can be shared at this time (see next page for ideas).

6. **Graduation:** A simple ceremony (see Retreat Manual) can be held to recognize children who will be "graduating" to the Junior Youth Spiritual Empowerment Program.

7. **Announcements:** Share logistical information (lost-and-found items, rides home, etc.).

8. **Song:** Close with a sing-along, for example, "Hoy Es el Día" or "1844."

9. **Group photo:** Be sure everyone is included!

10. **Dessert:** We have a well-loved tradition of serve-yourself ice cream sundaes.

Ideas for Thank-you Gifts

As part of the closing activities, you may wish to present small thank-you gifts to the volunteers. The page with quotes from Bahá'u'lláh and 'Abdu'l-Bahá about the soil of the heart (see end of this section) makes a nice gift when photocopied onto parchment or rainbow-print paper. It is also available in color as part of the online download packet for this teacher's guide: < **www.UnityWorksStore.com** >. Additional ideas are offered below:

- The Bahá'í Media Bank offers beautiful photographs of the Shrine of the Báb. Visit **http://media.bahai.org** and click on Buildings & Places > Haifa > Shrine. The images can be downloaded and printed on cardstock or laminated.

- Special Ideas sells several items that would make nice gifts, including a booklet of *Prayers from the Báb* (code BK-1048), *Prayers of the Báb Postcard* in English or Spanish (PC-A2), *Selections from the Writings of the Báb* (BK-SFWBS), a set of twelve full-color posters of the Shrine of the Báb and the Terraces (PR-BAB), and bookmarks with a photo of the Shrine (BKMK-22). Visit **www.bahairesources.com** and enter the product code in the "Advanced search" box.

- UnityWorks has produced a colorful PowerPoint fireside on "The Three Central Figures of the Bahá'í Faith," including a section on the life, declaration and martyrdom of the Báb. Visit **www.UnityWorksStore.com** and click on Power-Point Firesides to download the slide show.

The Báb: Gate to Bahá'u'lláh

FOLLOW-UP ACTIVITIES

Teachers and sponsoring institutions can help children apply their new knowledge and skills by providing a variety of opportunities for practice. Some examples are listed below:

- Ask the children to share during Feast what they have learned.

- Encourage them to recite memorized passages during a devotional meeting.

- Invite them to visit a class for younger children and to share one of the stories about the life of the Báb.

- Ask them to talk about the role and station of the Báb during a home visit.

- Encourage them to teach their friends and invite them to children's classes.

- Organize a children's fireside on "The Báb: Gate to Bahá'u'lláh" including the *Soil of the Heart* demonstration and the *Primal Point* felt lesson. Have children invite their families, friends and neighbors.

- Finished craft projects can be used as teaching tools.

- Skits, demonstrations and songs from the lessons can be performed during Holy Days, Unit Convention or cluster reflection meetings.

- Teachers can write a brief report on the children's class activities and submit this with photos to the local paper.

The Báb: Gate to Bahá'u'lláh

The Soil of the Heart

"Consider now,
were the parched and barren soil
of these hearts to remain unchanged,
how could they ever
become the Recipients
of the revelation
of the mysteries of God...?"

Bahá'u'lláh, Kitáb-i-Iqán, p. 46

"It is my hope
that your hearts
may become
as ready ground,
carefully tilled and prepared...
Then will the garden
of your hearts
bring forth its flowers..."

'Abdu'l-Bahá,
Promulgation of Universal Peace, p. 24

Bahá'í Children's Classes and Retreats: Theme 3, p. 196

The Báb
Gate to Bahá'u'lláh

References for Teachers

The Báb: Gate to Bahá'u'lláh

References for Teachers

LESSON #1: His Birth, Early Life and Station
Nineteenth Century Persia 199
Soil of the Heart 199
Khadíjih-Bagum, Wife of the Báb 200

LESSON #2: Declaration of the Báb
Sounding of the Trumpet 201
Declaration of the Báb 202
To Mullá Husayn 202

LESSON #3: Martyrdom of the Báb
Martyrdom of the Báb 204
Tribute to the Followers of the Báb 205
Shrine of the Báb 206

LESSON #4: The Primal Point
Primal Point 207
Creative Energies Released 208
Inaugurator of a New Cycle 208
Prophecies Fulfilled 208

ADDITIONAL REFERENCES
Two-fold Station of the Báb 210
I Am All the Prophets 210
Relationship Between the Báb and Bahá'u'lláh 210
Bahá'u'lláh Accepts the Cause of the Báb 211
The Sun at Morn and Midday 212
The Báb Extols Bahá'u'lláh 212
Bahá'u'lláh Pays Tribute to the Báb 213
The Báb's Final Gift to Bahá'u'lláh 213
Táhirih 214
Letters of the Living 214
Additional References and Websites 216

LESSON #1

His Birth, Early Life and Station

Teachers may wish to study the following references in order to gain a deeper understanding of the material presented in each lesson.

Nineteenth Century Persia

In the early part of the nineteenth century the horizon of Persia was shrouded in great darkness and ignorance. The people of that country were in a condition of barbarism. Hatred and bigotry prevailed among the various religions; bloodshed and hostility were frequent among sects and denominations of belief. There were no evidences of affiliation and unity; violent prejudice and antagonism ruled the hearts of men.

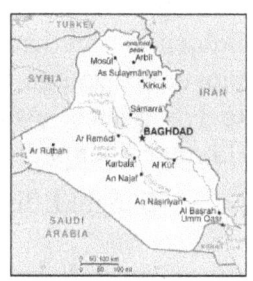

('Abdu'l-Bahá, *Promulgation of Universal Peace*, p. 341)

The status of woman in former times was exceedingly deplorable, for it was the belief of the Orient that it was best for woman to be ignorant. It was considered preferable that she should not know reading or writing in order that she might not be informed of events in the world. Woman was considered to be created for rearing children and attending to the duties of the household. If she pursued educational courses, it was deemed contrary to chastity; hence women were made prisoners of the household. The houses did not even have windows opening upon the outside world.

('Abdu'l-Bahá, *Promulgation of Universal Peace*, p. 166)

The people among whom He appeared were the most decadent race in the civilized world, grossly ignorant, savage, cruel, steeped in prejudice, servile in their submission to an almost deified hierarchy…

(Shoghi Effendi, *God Passes By*, p. 4)

Soil of the Heart

"…were the parched and barren soil of these hearts to remain unchanged, how could they ever become the Recipients of the revelation of the mysteries of God…?"

(Bahá'u'lláh, *Kitáb-i-Iqán*, p. 46)

"It is my hope that your hearts may become as ready ground, carefully tilled and prepared… Then will the garden of your hearts bring forth its flowers…"

('Abdu'l-Bahá, *Promulgation of Universal Peace*, p. 24)

Khadíjih-Bagum, Wife of the Báb

The wife of the Báb, unlike His mother, perceived at the earliest dawn of His Revelation the glory and uniqueness of His Mission and felt from the very beginning the intensity of its force. No one except Táhirih, among the women of her generation, surpassed her in the spontaneous character of her devotion nor excelled the fervor of her faith. To her the Báb confided the secret of His future sufferings, and unfolded to her eyes the significance of the events that were to transpire in His Day. He bade her not to divulge this secret to His mother and counselled her to be patient and resigned to the will of God. He entrusted her with a special prayer, revealed and written by Himself, the reading of which, He assured her, would remove her difficulties and lighten the burden of her woes. "In the hour of your perplexity," He directed her, "recite this prayer ere you go to sleep. I Myself will appear to you and will banish your anxiety." Faithful to His advice, every time she turned to Him in prayer, the light of His unfailing guidance illumined her path and resolved her problems.

(Shoghi Effendi, trans., *The Dawn-Breakers*, p. 191-192)

LESSON #2

Declaration of the Báb

Teachers may wish to study the following references in order to gain a deeper understanding of the material presented in each lesson.

Sounding of the Trumpet

The Blast hath been blown on the Trumpet of the Bayán as decreed by the Lord, the Merciful, and all that are in the heavens and on the earth have swooned away except such as have detached themselves from the world, cleaving fast unto the Cord of God, the Lord of mankind.

(Bahá'u'lláh, *Tablets of Bahá'u'lláh*, p. 244)

Once more hath the eternal Spirit breathed into the mystic trumpet, and caused the dead to speed out of their sepulchres of heedlessness and error unto the realm of guidance and grace. And yet, that expectant community still crieth out: When shall these things be?

(Bahá'u'lláh, *The Kitáb-i-Iqán*, p. 26-27)

Say: By God! The blast hath been blown on the trumpet, and lo, mankind hath swooned away before us! The Herald hath cried out, and the Summoner raised His voice saying: "The Kingdom is God's, the Most Powerful, the Help in Peril, the Self-Subsisting."

(Bahá'u'lláh, *Gleanings from the Writings of Bahá'u'lláh*, p. 43-44)

Táhirih, with her face unveiled, stepped from her garden, advancing to the pavilion of Bahá'u'lláh; and as she came, she shouted aloud these words: "The Trumpet is sounding! The great Trump is blown! The universal Advent is now proclaimed!"

('Abdu'l-Bahá, *Memorials of the Faithful*, p. 202)

A little over four years had elapsed since the birth of the Báb's Revelation when the trumpet-blast announcing the formal extinction of the old, and the inauguration of the new Dispensation was sounded. No pomp, no pageantry marked so great a turning-point in the world's religious history. Nor was its modest setting commensurate with such a sudden, startling, complete emancipation from the dark and embattled forces of fanaticism, of priestcraft, of religious orthodoxy and superstition. The assembled host consisted of no more than a single woman and a handful of men, mostly recruited from the very ranks they were attacking, and devoid, with few exceptions, of wealth, prestige and power. The Captain of the host was Himself an absentee, a captive in the grip of His foes. The arena was a tiny hamlet in the plain of Badasht on the border of Mázindarán. The trumpeter was a lone woman, the noblest of her sex in that Dispensation, whom even some of her co-religionists pronounced a heretic. The call she sounded was the death-knell of the twelve hundred year old law of Islám.

(Shoghi Effendi, *God Passes By*, p. 33-34)

Declaration of the Báb

I am the Mystic Fane which the Hand of Omnipotence hath reared. I am the Lamp which the Finger of God hath lit within its niche and caused to shine with deathless splendour. I am the Flame of that supernal Light that glowed upon Sinai in the gladsome Spot, and lay concealed in the midst of the Burning Bush.

(The Báb, *Selections from the Writings of the Báb*, p. 74)

The circumstances attending the examination of the Báb, as a result of so precipitate an act, may well rank as one of the chief landmarks of His dramatic career. The avowed purpose of that convocation was to arraign the Prisoner, and deliberate on the steps to be taken for the extirpation of His so-called heresy. It instead afforded Him the supreme opportunity of His mission to assert in public, formally and without any reservation, the claims inherent in His Revelation. In the official residence, and in the presence, of the governor of Ádhirbáyján, Násiri'd-Dín Mírzá, the heir to the throne; under the presidency of Hájí Mullá Mahmúd, the Nizámu'l-'Ulamá, the Prince's tutor; before the assembled ecclesiastical dignitaries of Tabríz, the leaders of the Shaykhi community, the Shaykhu'l-Islám, and the Imám-Jum'ih, the Báb, having seated Himself in the chief place which had been reserved for the Valí-'Ahd (the heir to the throne), gave, in ringing tones, His celebrated answer to the question put to Him by the President of that assembly. *"I am,"* He exclaimed, *"I am, I am the Promised One! I am the One Whose name you have for a thousand years invoked, at Whose mention you have risen, Whose advent you have longed to witness, and the hour of Whose Revelation you have prayed God to hasten. Verily, I say, it is incumbent upon the peoples of both the East and the West to obey My word, and to pledge allegiance to My person."*

(Shoghi Effendi, *God Passes By*, p. 21)

To Mulla Husayn

He then addressed me in these words: "O thou who art the first to believe in Me! Verily I say, I am the Báb, the Gate of God, and thou art the Bábu'l-Báb, the gate of that Gate. Eighteen souls must, in the beginning, spontaneously and of their own accord, accept Me and recognize the truth of My Revelation. Unwarned and uninvited, each of these must seek independently to find Me. And when their number is complete, one of them must needs be chosen to accompany Me on My pilgrimage to Mecca and Medina. There I shall deliver the Message of God to the Sharíf of Mecca. I then shall return to Kúfih, where again, in the Masjid of that holy city, I shall manifest His Cause. It is incumbent upon you not to divulge, either to your companions or to any other soul, that which you have seen and heard…"

(Shoghi Effendi, trans., *The Dawn-Breakers*, p. 63)

"I sat spellbound by His utterance, oblivious of time and of those who awaited me," he himself has testified, after describing the nature of the questions he had put to his Host and the conclusive replies he had received from Him, replies which had established beyond the shadow of a doubt the validity of His claim to be the promised Qá'im. "Suddenly the call of the Mu'adhdhin, summoning the faithful to their morning prayer, awakened me from the state of ecstasy into which I seemed to have fallen. All the delights, all the ineffable glories, which the Almighty has recounted in His Book as the priceless possessions of the people of Paradise— these I seemed to be experiencing that night. Methinks I was in a place of which it could be truly said: *'Therein no toil shall reach us, and therein no weariness shall touch us;' 'no vain discourse shall they hear therein, nor any falsehood, but only the cry, "Peace! Peace!"'; 'their cry therein shall be, "Glory to Thee, O God!" and their salutation therein, "Peace!"*, and the close of their cry, *"Praise be to God, Lord of all creatures!"'*

(Shoghi Effendi, *God Passes By*, p. 5)

"This Revelation," Mullá Husayn has further testified, "so suddenly and impetuously thrust upon me, came as a thunderbolt which, for a time, seemed to have benumbed my faculties. I was blinded by its dazzling splendor and overwhelmed by its crushing force. Excitement, joy, awe, and wonder stirred the depths of my soul. Predominant among these emotions was a sense of gladness and strength which seemed to have transfigured me. How feeble and impotent, how dejected and timid, I had felt previously! Then I could neither write nor walk, so tremulous were my hands and feet. Now, however, the knowledge of His Revelation had galvanized my being. I felt possessed of such courage and power that were the world, all its peoples and its potentates, to rise against me, I would, alone and undaunted, withstand their onslaught. The universe seemed but a handful of dust in my grasp. I seemed to be the voice of Gabriel personified, calling unto all mankind: 'Awake, for, lo! the morning Light has broken. Arise, for His Cause is made manifest. The portal of His grace is open wide; enter therein, O peoples of the world! For He Who is your promised One is come!'"

(Shoghi Effendi, *God Passes By*, p. 6)

The Báb: Gate to Bahá'u'lláh – References

LESSON #3

Martyrdom of the Báb

Teachers may wish to study the following references in order to gain a deeper understanding of the material presented in each lesson.

Martyrdom of the Báb

Immediately before and soon after this humiliating treatment meted out to the Báb two highly significant incidents occurred, incidents that cast an illuminating light on the mysterious circumstances surrounding the opening phase of His martyrdom. The farrásh-báshí had abruptly interrupted the last conversation which the Báb was confidentially having in one of the rooms of the barracks with His amanuensis…and was drawing the latter aside, and severely rebuking him, when he was thus addressed by his Prisoner: *"Not until I have said to him all those things that I wish to say can any earthly power silence Me. Though all the world be armed against Me, yet shall it be powerless to deter Me from fulfilling, to the last word, My intention."* To the Christian Sám Khán—the colonel of the Armenian regiment ordered to carry out the execution—who, seized with fear lest his act should provoke the wrath of God, had begged to be released from the duty imposed upon him, the Báb gave the following assurance: *"Follow your instructions, and if your intention be sincere, the Almighty is surely able to relieve you of your perplexity."*

Sám Khán accordingly set out to discharge his duty. A spike was driven into a pillar which separated two rooms of the barracks facing the square. Two ropes were fastened to it from which the Báb and one of his disciples, the youthful and devout…Anís, who had previously flung himself at the feet of his Master and implored that under no circumstances he be sent away from Him, were separately suspended. The firing squad ranged itself in three files, each of two hundred and fifty men. Each file in turn opened fire until the whole detachment had discharged its bullets. So dense was the smoke from the seven hundred and fifty rifles that the sky was darkened. As soon as the smoke had cleared away the astounded multitude of about ten thousand souls, who had crowded onto the roof of the barracks, as well as the tops of the adjoining houses, beheld a scene which their eyes could scarcely believe.

The Báb had vanished from their sight! Only his companion remained, alive and unscathed, standing beside the wall on which they had been suspended. The ropes by which they had been hung alone were severed. "The Siyyid-i-Báb has gone from our sight!" cried out the bewildered spectators. A frenzied search immediately ensued. He was found, unhurt and unruffled, in the very room He had occupied the night before, engaged in completing His interrupted conversation with His amanuensis. *"I have finished My conversation…"* were the words with which the Prisoner, so providentially preserved, greeted the appearance of the farrásh-báshí, *"Now you may proceed to fulfill your intention."* Recalling the bold assertion his Prisoner had previously made, and shaken by so stunning a revelation, the farrásh-báshí quitted instantly the scene, and resigned his post.

Bahá'í Children's Classes and Retreats: Theme 3, p. 204

Sám Khán, likewise, remembering, with feelings of awe and wonder, the reassuring words addressed to him by the Báb, ordered his men to leave the barracks immediately, and swore, as he left the courtyard, never again, even at the cost of his life, to repeat that act… (The) colonel of the body-guard, volunteered to replace him. On the same wall and in the same manner the Báb and His companion were again suspended, while the new regiment formed in line and opened fire upon them. This time, however, their breasts were riddled with bullets, and their bodies completely dissected, with the exception of their faces which were but little marred. *"O wayward generation!"* were the last words of the Báb to the gazing multitude, as the regiment prepared to fire its volley, *"Had you believed in Me every one of you would have followed the example of this youth, who stood in rank above most of you, and would have willingly sacrificed himself in My path. The day will come when you will have recognized Me; that day I shall have ceased to be with you."*

(Shoghi Effendi, *God Passes By*, p. 52-53)

Tribute to the Followers of the Báb

I now proceed to relate what befell the remaining companions of the Báb, those who had been privileged to share the horrors of the confinement with Bahá'u'lláh. From His own lips I have often heard the following account: "All those who were struck down by the storm that raged during that memorable year in Tihrán were Our fellow-prisoners in the Síyáh-Chál, where We were confined. We were all huddled together in one cell, our feet in stocks, and around our necks fastened the most galling of chains. The air we breathed was laden with the foulest impurities, while the floor on which we sat was covered with filth and infested with vermin. No ray of light was allowed to penetrate that pestilential dungeon or to warm its icy-coldness. We were placed in two rows, each facing the other. We had taught them to repeat certain verses which, every night, they chanted with extreme fervour. 'God is sufficient unto me; He verily is the All-sufficing!' one row would intone, while the other would reply: 'In Him let the trusting trust.' The chorus of these gladsome voices would continue to peal out until the early hours of the morning. Their reverberation would fill the dungeon, and, piercing its massive walls, would reach the ears of Násiri'd-Dín Sháh, whose palace was not far distant from the place where we were imprisoned. 'What means this sound?' he was reported to have exclaimed. 'It is the anthem the Bábís are intoning in their prison,' they replied. The Sháh made no further remarks, nor did he attempt to restrain the enthusiasm his prisoners, despite the horrors of their confinement, continued to display."

(Shoghi Effendi, trans., *The Dawn-Breakers*, p. 631-632)

Commenting on the character and influence of those heroes and martyrs whom the spirit of the Báb had so magically transformed Bahá'u'lláh reveals the following: *"If these companions be not the true strivers after God, who else could be called by this name?…If these companions, with all their marvelous testimonies and wondrous works, be false, who then is worthy to claim for himself the truth?...Has the world since the days of Adam witnessed such tumult, such violent commotion?...Methinks, patience was revealed only by virtue of their fortitude, and faithfulness itself was begotten only by their deeds."*

(Shoghi Effendi, *World Order of Baha'u'llah*, p. 125)

Shrine of the Báb

"Every stone of that building, every stone of the road leading to it," He ['Abdu'l-Bahá], many a time was heard to remark, *"I have with infinite tears and at tremendous cost, raised and placed in position." "One night,"* He, according to an eye-witness, once observed, *"I was so hemmed in by My anxieties that I had no other recourse than to recite and repeat over and over again a prayer of the Báb which I had in My possession, the recital of which greatly calmed Me. The next morning the owner of the plot himself came to Me, apologized and begged Me to purchase his property."*

...the day of the first Naw-Rúz (1909), which He celebrated after His release from His confinement, Abdu'l-Bahá had the marble sarcophagus transported with great labor to the vault prepared for it, and in the evening, by the light of a single lamp, He laid within it, with His own hands—in the presence of believers from the East and from the West and in circumstances at once solemn and moving—the wooden casket containing the sacred remains of the Báb and His companion.

When all was finished, and the earthly remains of the Martyr-Prophet of Shíráz were, at long last, safely deposited for their everlasting rest in the bosom of God's holy mountain, 'Abdu'l-Bahá, Who had cast aside His turban, removed His shoes and thrown off His cloak, bent low over the still open sarcophagus, His silver hair waving about His head and His face transfigured and luminous, rested His forehead on the border of the wooden casket, and, sobbing aloud, wept with such a weeping that all those who were present wept with Him. That night He could not sleep, so overwhelmed was He with emotion.

"The most joyful tidings is this," He wrote later in a Tablet announcing to His followers the news of this glorious victory, *"that the holy, the luminous body of the Báb...after having for sixty years been transferred from place to place, by reason of the ascendancy of the enemy, and from fear of the malevolent, and having known neither rest nor tranquility has, through the mercy of the Abhá Beauty, been ceremoniously deposited, on the day of Naw-Rúz, within the sacred casket, in the exalted Shrine on Mt. Carmel..."*

(Shoghi Effendi, *God Passes By*, p. 275-276)

LESSON #4

The Primal Point

Teachers may wish to study the following references in order to gain a deeper understanding of the material presented in each lesson.

Primal Point

"I am the Primal Point from which have been generated all created things."

(The Báb, *Selections from the Writings of the Báb*, p. 12)

Do Thou bless, O Lord my God, the Primal Point, through Whom the point of creation hath been made to revolve in both the visible and invisible worlds, Whom Thou hast designated as the One whereunto should return whatsoever must return unto Thee, and as the Revealer of whatsoever may be manifested by Thee.

(Bahá'u'lláh, *Prayers and Meditations*, p. 299)

"I am the Primal Point," the Báb thus addresses Muhammad Sháh from the prison-fortress of Máh-Kú, *"from which have been generated all created things...I am the Countenance of God Whose splendor can never be obscured, the light of God whose radiance can never fade...All the keys of heaven God hath chosen to place on My right hand, and all the keys of hell on My left...I am one of the sustaining pillars of the Primal Word of God. Whosoever hath recognized Me, hath known all that is true and right, and hath attained all that is good and seemly..."*

(Shoghi Effendi, *World Order of Bahá'u'lláh*, p. 126)

He, as affirmed by Himself, *"the Primal Point from which have been generated all created things,"* *"one of the sustaining pillars of the Primal Word of God,"* the *"Mystic Fane,"* the *"Great Announcement,"* the *"Flame of that supernal Light that glowed upon Sinai,"* the *"Remembrance of God"* concerning Whom *"a separate Covenant hath been established with each and every Prophet"* had, through His advent, at once fulfilled the promise of all ages and ushered in the consummation of all Revelations.

(Shoghi Effendi, *God Passes By*, p. 57)

For, just as in the realm of the spirit, the reality of the Báb has been hailed by the Author of the Bahá'í Revelation as "The Point round Whom the realities of the Prophets and Messengers revolve," so, on this visible plane, His sacred remains constitute the heart and center of what may be regarded as nine concentric circles, paralleling thereby, and adding further emphasis to the central position accorded by the Founder of our Faith to One "from Whom God hath caused to proceed the knowledge of all that was and shall be," "the Primal Point from which have been generated all created things."

The outermost circle in this vast system, the visible counterpart of the pivotal position conferred on the Herald of our Faith, is none other than the entire planet. Within the heart of this planet lies the "Most Holy Land," acclaimed by 'Abdu'l-Bahá as "the Nest of the Prophets" and which must be regarded as the center of the world and the Qiblih of the nations. Within this Most Holy Land rises the Mountain of God of immemorial sanctity, the Vineyard of the Lord, the Retreat of Elijah, Whose return the Báb Himself symbolizes…

(Shoghi Effendi, *Citadel of Faith*, p. 95)

Creative Energies Released

The creative energies released at the hour of the birth of His Revelation, endowing mankind with the potentialities of the attainment of maturity are deranging, during the present transitional age, the equilibrium of the entire planet as the inevitable prelude to the consummation in world unity of the coming of age of the human race.

(Shoghi Effendi, *Citadel of Faith*, p. 81)

Inaugurator of a New Cycle

…the Blessed Báb, Prophet and Herald of the Faith of Baha'u'llah, Founder of the Dispensation marking the culmination of the six thousand year old Adamic Cycle, Inaugurator of the five thousand century Bahá'í Cycle.

(Shoghi Effendi, *Citadel of Faith*, p. 80)

The Báb, acclaimed by Bahá'u'lláh as…the *"Point round Whom the realities of the Prophets and Messengers revolve…"* He Who was, in the words of 'Abdu'l-Bahá, the *"Morn of Truth"* and *"Harbinger of the Most Great Light,"* Whose advent at once signalized the termination of the *"Prophetic Cycle"* and the inception of the *"Cycle of Fulfillment,"* had simultaneously through His Revelation banished the shades of night that had descended upon His country, and proclaimed the impending rise of that Incomparable Orb Whose radiance was to envelop the whole of mankind.

(Shoghi Effendi, *God Passes By*, p. 57)

Prophecies Fulfilled

He the "Qá'im" (He Who ariseth) promised to the Shí'ahs, the "Mihdí" (One Who is guided) awaited by the Sunnís, the "Return of John the Baptist" expected by the Christians, the "Úshídar-Máh" referred to in the Zoroastrian scriptures, the "Return of Elijah" anticipated by the Jews, Whose Revelation was to show forth *"the signs and tokens of all the Prophets"*, Who was to *"manifest the perfection of Moses, the radiance of Jesus and the patience of Job"* had appeared, proclaimed His Cause, been mercilessly persecuted and died gloriously.

(Shoghi Effendi, *God Passes By*, p. 57-58)

The *"Second Woe,"* spoken of in the Apocalypse of St. John the Divine, had, at long last, appeared, and the first of the two *"Messengers,"* Whose appearance had been prophesied in the Qur'án, had been sent down. The first *"Trumpet-Blast"*, destined to smite the earth with extermination, announced in the latter Book, had finally been sounded. *"The Inevitable," "The Catastrophe," "The Resurrection," "The Earthquake of the Last Hour,"* foretold by that same Book, had all come to pass. The *"clear tokens"* had been *"sent down,"* and the *"Spirit"* had *"breathed,"* and the *"souls"* had *"waked up,"* and the *"heaven"* had been *"cleft,"* and the *"angels"* had *"ranged in order,"* and the *"stars"* had been *"blotted out,"* and the *"earth"* had *"cast forth her burden,"* and *"Paradise"* had been *"brought near,"* and *"hell"* had been *"made to blaze,"* and the *"Book"* had been *"set,"* and the *"Bridge"* had been *"laid out,"* and the *"Balance"* had been *"set up,"* and the *"mountains scattered in dust."*

(Shoghi Effendi, *God Passes By*, p. 58)

The *"cleansing of the Sanctuary,"* prophesied by Daniel and confirmed by Jesus Christ in His reference to *"the abomination of desolation,"* had been accomplished. The *"day whose length shall be a thousand years,"* foretold by the Apostle of God in His Book, had terminated. The *"forty and two months,"* during which the *"Holy City,"* as predicted by St. John the Divine, would be trodden under foot, had elapsed. The *"time of the end"* had been ushered in, and the first of the *"two Witnesses"* into Whom, *"after three days and a half the Spirit of Life from God"* would enter, had arisen and had *"ascended up to heaven in a cloud."*

(Shoghi Effendi, *God Passes By*, p. 58)

ADDITIONAL REFERENCES ON THE BÁB

All teachers may wish to study the following references.

Two-fold Station of the Báb

There can be no doubt that the claim to the twofold station ordained for the Báb by the Almighty, a claim which He Himself has so boldly advanced, which Bahá'u'lláh has repeatedly affirmed, and to which the Will and Testament of 'Abdu'l-Bahá has finally given the sanction of its testimony, constitutes the most distinctive feature of the Bahá'í Dispensation. It is a further evidence of its uniqueness, a tremendous accession to the strength, to the mysterious power and authority with which this holy cycle has been invested. Indeed the greatness of the Báb consists primarily, not in His being the divinely-appointed Forerunner of so transcendent a Revelation, but rather in His having been invested with the powers inherent in the inaugurator of a separate religious Dispensation, and in His wielding, to a degree unrivaled by the Messengers gone before Him, the scepter of independent Prophethood.

(Shoghi Effendi, *World Order of Baha'u'llah*, p. 123)

I Am All the Prophets

In the time of the First Manifestation the Primal Will appeared in Adam; in the day of Noah It became known in Noah; in the day of Abraham in Him; and so in the day of Moses; the day of Jesus; the day of Muhammad, the Apostle of God; the day of the 'Point of the Bayán'; the day of Him Whom God shall make manifest; and the day of the One Who will appear after Him Whom God shall make manifest. Hence the inner meaning of the words uttered by the Apostle of God, 'I am all the Prophets', inasmuch as what shineth resplendent in each one of Them hath been and will ever remain the one and the same sun.

(The Báb, *Selections from the Writings of the Báb*, p. 126)

Relationship Between the Báb and Bahá'u'lláh

The purpose underlying this Revelation, as well as those that preceded it, has, in like manner, been to announce the advent of the Faith of Him Whom God will make manifest.

(The Báb, *Selections from the Writings of the Báb*, p. 105)

"Well is it with him," is His prophetic announcement, *"who fixeth his gaze upon the Order of Bahá'u'lláh, and rendereth thanks unto his Lord. For He will assuredly be made manifest. God hath indeed irrevocably ordained it in the Bayán."*

(The Báb, quoted in Shoghi Effendi, *God Passes By*, p. 25)

He preceded Me that He might summon the people unto My Kingdom, as it hath been set forth in the Tablets, could ye but perceive it! O would that men of hearing might be found who could hear the voice of His lamentation in the Bayán bewailing that which hath befallen Me at the hands of these heedless souls, bemoaning His separation from Me and giving utterance to His longing to be united with Me, the Mighty, the Peerless.

(Bahá'u'lláh, *Summons of the Lord of Hosts*, p. 52)

The Báb, whose trials and sufferings had preceded, in almost every case, those of Bahá'u'lláh, had offered Himself to ransom His Beloved from the perils that beset that precious Life; whilst Bahá'u'lláh, on His part, unwilling that He who so greatly loved Him should be the sole Sufferer, shared at every turn the cup that had touched His lips. Such love no eye has ever beheld, nor has mortal heart conceived such mutual devotion. If the branches of every tree were turned into pens, and all the seas into ink, and earth and heaven rolled into one parchment, the immensity of that love would still remain unexplored, and the depths of that devotion unfathomed.

(Shoghi Effendi, trans., *The Dawn-Breakers*, p. 372-373)

Bahá'u'lláh Accepts the Cause of the Báb

He it was [Bahá'u'lláh] Who, scarce three months after the [Bábí] Faith was born, received, through the envoy of the Báb, Mullá Husayn, the scroll which bore to Him the first tidings of a newly announced Revelation, Who instantly acclaimed its truth, and arose to champion its cause. It was to His native city and dwelling place that the steps of that envoy were first directed, as the place which enshrined "a Mystery of such transcendent holiness as neither Hijáz nor Shíráz can hope to rival." It was Mullá Husayn's report of the contact thus established which had been received with such exultant joy by the Báb…

(Shoghi Effendi, *God Passes By*, p. 66-67)
(Also see William Sears, *Release the Sun*, p. 151-152)

The story of Bahá'u'lláh's immediate acknowledgement of the truth of the Message of the Báb, when He read a few lines of the Báb's newly-revealed Writings, may lead some to an erroneous conclusion that Bahá'u'lláh had no prior knowledge of the Báb's Revelation and that He was converted through reading a page of that historic scroll. Such a belief is contrary to many statements of the Báb and Bahá'u'lláh themselves. For the Báb has made it very clear in His Writings that every word revealed by Him had originated from 'Him Whom God shall make manifest', Whose station was exalted beyond any description. The spiritual link of divine revelation existed between the two. The only link which needed to be established was a physical one, and this was achieved by the visit of Mulla Husayn. In the Persian Bayán, the Báb states:

"And know thou of a certainty that every letter revealed in the Bayán is solely intended to evoke submission unto Him Whom God shall make manifest, for it is He Who hath revealed the Bayán prior to His Own manifestation."

There are many passages in the Writings of the Báb similar to the above. Bahá'u'lláh also refers to the Revelation of the Báb as 'My Own previous Revelation'. The perusal of the Writings of the Báb will make it abundantly clear that His relationship with Bahá'u'lláh, Whom He designated as 'Him Whom God shall make manifest', was similar to that of Christ with the 'Heavenly Father' Who is reported in the Gospels as the Source of Christ's Revelation.

(Adib Taherzadeh, *The Covenant of Bahá'u'lláh*, p. 37)

The Sun at Morn and Midday

"...The Revelation of the Báb may be likened to the sun, its station corresponding to the first sign of the Zodiac—the sign Aries—which the sun enters at the Vernal Equinox. The station of Bahá'u'lláh's Revelation, on the other hand, is represented by the sign Leo, the sun's mid-summer and highest station. By this is meant that this holy Dispensation is illumined with the light of the Sun of Truth shining from its most exalted station, and in the plenitude of its resplendency, its heat and glory."

"The Báb, the Exalted One," 'Abdu'l-Bahá more specifically affirms in another Tablet, *"is the Morn of Truth, the splendor of Whose light shineth throughout all regions. He is also the Harbinger of the Most Great Light, the Abhá Luminary. The Blessed Beauty is the One promised by the sacred books of the past, the revelation of the Source of light that shone upon Mount Sinai, Whose fire glowed in the midst of the Burning Bush. We are, one and all, servants of their threshold, and stand each as a lowly keeper at their door." "Every proof and prophecy,"* is His still more emphatic warning, *"every manner of evidence, whether based on reason or on the text of the scriptures and traditions, are to be regarded as centered in the persons of Bahá'u'lláh and the Báb. In them is to be found their complete fulfillment."*

(Shoghi Effendi, *World Order of Bahá'u'lláh*, p. 127)

The Báb Extols Bahá'u'lláh

Of all the tributes I have paid to Him Who is to come after Me, the greatest is this, My written confession, that no words of Mine can adequately describe Him, nor can any reference to Him in My Book, the Bayán, do justice to His Cause.

(The Báb, quoted in *Tablets of Bahá'u'lláh*, p. 77)

Better is it for a person to write down but one of His verses than to transcribe the whole of the Bayán and all the books which have been written in the Dispensation of the Bayan.

(The Báb, *Selections from the Writings of the Báb*, p. 91)

O congregation of the Bayán…the Point of the Bayán Himself hath believed in Him Whom God shall make manifest, before all things were created. Therein, verily, do I glory before all who are in the kingdom of heaven and earth. Suffer not yourselves to be shut out as by a veil from God after He hath revealed Himself. For all that hath been exalted in the Bayán is but as a ring upon My hand, and I Myself am, verily, but a ring upon the hand of Him Whom God shall make manifest—glorified be His mention! He turneth it as He pleaseth, for whatsoever He pleaseth, and through whatsoever He pleaseth.

(The Báb, *Selections from the Writings of the Báb*, p. 168)

Bahá'u'lláh Pays Tribute to the Báb

Behold what steadfastness that Beauty of God hath revealed. The whole world rose to hinder Him, yet it utterly failed. The more severe the persecution they inflicted on that Sadrih [Branch] of Blessedness, the more His fervour increased, and the brighter burned the flame of His love. All this is evident, and none disputeth its truth. Finally, He surrendered His soul, and winged His flight unto the realms above.

(Bahá'u'lláh, *Kitáb-i-Iqán*, p. 233-234)

"Knowledge is twenty and seven letters. All that the Prophets have revealed are two letters thereof. No man thus far hath known more than these two letters. But when the Qá'im shall arise, He will cause the remaining twenty and five letters to be made manifest."…Behold from this utterance how great and lofty is His station! His rank excelleth that of all the Prophets, and His Revelation transcendeth the comprehension and understanding of all their chosen ones.

(Bahá'u'lláh quoting a Muslim tradition, *Kitáb-i-Iqán*, p. 243)

We stand, life in hand, wholly resigned to His will; that perchance, through God's loving kindness and His grace, this revealed and manifest Letter [Bahá'u'lláh] may lay down His life as a sacrifice in the path of the Primal Point, the most exalted Word.

(Bahá'u'lláh, *Kitáb-i-Iqán*, p. 252)

The Báb's Final Gift to Bahá'u'lláh

A fast ebbing life, so crowded with the accumulated anxieties, disappointments, treacheries and sorrows of a tragic ministry, now moved swiftly towards its climax.... Indeed, He Himself had already foreshadowed His own approaching death.... Forty days before His final departure from Chihríq He had even collected all the documents in His possession, and placed them, together with His pen-case, His seals and His rings, in the hands of Mullá Báqir, a Letter of the Living, whom He instructed to entrust them to Mullá Abdu'l-Karím-i-Qazvíní, surnamed Mírzá Ahmad, who was to deliver them to Bahá'u'lláh in Tihrán.

(Shoghi Effendi, *God Passes By*, p. 50-51)

It was exclusively to His [Bahá'u'lláh's] care that the documents of the Báb, His pen-case, His seals, and agate rings, together with a scroll on which He had penned, in the form of a pentacle, no less than three hundred and sixty derivatives of the word Bahá, were delivered, in conformity with instructions He Himself had issued prior to His departure from Chihríq. It was solely due to His [Bahá'u'lláh's] initiative, and in strict accordance with His instructions, that the precious remains of the Báb were safely transferred from Tabríz to the capital, and were concealed and safeguarded with the utmost secrecy and care throughout the turbulent years following His martyrdom.

(Shoghi Effendi, *God Passes By*, p. 69)

Táhirih

O Qurratu'l-'Ayn! I recognize in Thee none other except the 'Great Announcement'—the Announcement voiced by the Concourse on high. By this name, I bear witness, they that circle the Throne of Glory have ever known Thee.

(The Báb, *Selections from the Writings of the Báb*, p. 72)

Gradually, spontaneously, some in sleep, others while awake, some through fasting and prayer, others through dreams and visions, they discovered the Object of their quest, and were enlisted under the banner of the new-born Faith. The last, but in rank the first, of these Letters to be inscribed on the Preserved Tablet was the erudite, the twenty-two year old Quddús, a direct descendant of the Imám Hasan and the most esteemed disciple of Siyyid Kázim. Immediately preceding him, a woman, the only one of her sex, who, unlike her fellow-disciples, never attained the presence of the Báb, was invested with the rank of apostleship in the new Dispensation. A poetess, less than thirty years of age, of distinguished birth, of bewitching charm, of captivating eloquence, indomitable in spirit, unorthodox in her views, audacious in her acts, immortalized as Táhirih (the Pure One) by the "Tongue of Glory," and surnamed Qurratu'l-'Ayn (Solace of the Eyes) by Siyyid Kázim, her teacher, she had, in consequence of the appearance of the Báb to her in a dream, received the first intimation of a Cause which was destined to exalt her to the fairest heights of fame, and on which she, through her bold heroism, was to shed such imperishable luster.

(Shoghi Effendi, *God Passes By*, p. 7)

Letters of the Living

These *"first Letters generated from the Primal Point,"* this *"company of angels arrayed before God on the Day of His coming,"* these *"Repositories of His Mystery,"* these *"Springs that have welled out from the Source of His Revelation,"* these first companions who, in the words of the Persian Bayán, *"enjoy nearest access to God,"* these *"Luminaries that have, from everlasting, bowed down, and will everlastingly continue to bow down, before the Celestial Throne,"* and lastly these *"elders"* mentioned in the Book of Revelation as *"sitting before God on their seats,*" "*clothed in white raiment*" and wearing on their heads "*crowns of gold*" —these were, ere their dispersal, summoned to the Báb's presence, Who addressed to them His parting words, entrusted to each a specific task, and assigned to some of them as the proper field of their activities their native provinces. He enjoined them to observe the utmost caution and moderation in their behavior, unveiled the loftiness of their rank, and stressed the magnitude of their responsibilities. He recalled the words addressed by Jesus to His disciples, and emphasized the superlative greatness of the New Day. He warned them lest by turning back they forfeit the Kingdom of God, and assured them that if they did God's bidding, God would make them His heirs and spiritual leaders among men. He hinted at the secret, and announced the approach, of a still mightier Day, and bade them prepare themselves for its advent. He called to remembrance the triumph of Abraham over Nimrod, of Moses over Pharaoh, of Jesus over the Jewish people, and of Muhammad over the tribes of Arabia, and asserted the inevitability and ultimate ascendancy of His own Revelation.

(Shoghi Effendi, *God Passes By*, p. 7)

Galvanized into action by the mandate conferred upon them, launched on their perilous and revolutionizing mission, these lesser luminaries who, together with the Báb, constitute the First Váhid (Unity) of the Dispensation of the Bayán, scattered far and wide through the provinces of their native land, where, with matchless heroism, they resisted the savage and concerted onslaught of the forces arrayed against them, and immortalized their Faith by their own exploits and those of their co-religionists, raising thereby a tumult that convulsed their country and sent its echoes reverberating as far as the capitals of Western Europe.

(Shoghi Effendi, *God Passes By*, p. 8)

We behold, as we survey the episodes of this first act of a sublime drama, the figure of its Master Hero, the Báb, arise meteor-like above the horizon of Shíráz, traverse the sombre sky of Persia from south to north, decline with tragic swiftness, and perish in a blaze of glory. We see His satellites, a galaxy of God-intoxicated heroes, mount above that same horizon, irradiate that same incandescent light, burn themselves out with that self-same swiftness, and impart in their turn an added impetus to the steadily gathering momentum of God's nascent Faith.

…The heroes whose deeds shine upon the record of this fierce spiritual contest, involving at once people, clergy, monarch and government, were the Báb's chosen disciples, the Letters of the Living, and their companions, the trail-breakers of the New Day, who to so much intrigue, ignorance, depravity, cruelty, superstition and cowardice opposed a spirit exalted, unquenchable and awe-inspiring, a knowledge surprisingly profound, an eloquence sweeping in its force, a piety unexcelled in fervor, a courage leonine in its fierceness, a self-abnegation saintly in its purity, a resolve granite-like in its firmness, a vision stupendous in its range, a veneration for the Prophet and His Imáms disconcerting to their adversaries, a power of persuasion alarming to their antagonists, a standard of faith and a code of conduct that challenged and revolutionized the lives of their countrymen.

(Shoghi Effendi, *God Passes By*, p. 3-5)

Additional References and Websites

Persia's State of Decadence in the Middle of the Nineteenth Century
Shoghi Effendi, The Dawn-Breakers, p. xxxvii- xlviii.

The Ministry of the Báb: 1844-1853
See section I of *God Passes By,* by Shoghi Effendi.

Letters of the Living
For a scholarly discussion of the symbolic meaning of the term "Letters of the Living" (Hurúf-i-Hayy), the title given by the Báb to His first eighteen disciples,
visit the following website:
< www.bahai-encyclopedia-project.org > enter "huruf hayy" in the search box.

The Báb, Forerunner of Bahá'u'lláh,
< info.bahai.org > enter "bab forerunner" for this and related articles
posted on the Bahá'í International Community website.

Birth and Childhood of the Báb
by David Merrick
< bahai-library.com > enter "birth bab" in the search box.

Mission of the Báb
by Douglas Martin
< bahaitalks.blogspot.com > enter "misson bab martin" in the search box.

Martyrdom of the Báb
"Recognizing God's Messengers: Why We Bahá'ís Commemorate the Martyrdom of the Báb"
An article by Brent Poirier in the Huffington Post, 7 February 2011.
< www.huffingtonpost.com > enter "martyrdom bab" in the search box.

Martyrdom of the Báb
by David Merrick
< bahai-library.com > enter "martyrdom bab" in the search box.

Additional Links
For links to additional articles about the Báb,
< www.bahai.org > enter "bab" in the search box.

BIBLIOGRAPHY

'Abdu'l-Bahá in London. 'Abdu'l-Bahá. Bahá'í Publishing Trust: London, 1982 edition.

The Báb: The Herald of the Day of Days. H.M. Balyuzi. George Ronald Publishers: Oxford, England, 1973.

Bahá'í Children's Retreats: A Complete Planning Guide. Randie Gottlieb. UnityWorks LLC: Yakima, Washington, 2010.

Bahá'í Education: A Compilation. Compiled by the Research Department of the Universal House of Justice. Bahá'í Publishing Trust: Wilmette, Illinois, 1978.

Bahá'í Prayers: A Selection of Prayers Revealed by Bahá'u'lláh, the Báb and 'Abdu'l-Bahá. Bahá'í Publishing Trust: Wilmette, Illinois, 1954; 1991 edition.

Bahá'u'lláh – The King of Glory. H. M. Balyuzi. George Ronald Publishers: Oxford, England, 1980.

Children's Stories from the Dawn-Breakers. Zoe Meyer. Bahá'í Publishing Trust: Wilmette, Illinois, 1998.

Citadel of Faith: Messages to America, 1947-1957. Shoghi Effendi. Bahá'í Publishing Trust: Wilmette, Illinois, third printing, 1980.

The Covenant of Bahá'u'lláh. Adib Taherzadeh. Bahá'í Publishing Trust: London, 1972.

Dawn Over Mount Hira. Marzieh Gail. George Ronald Publishers: Oxford, England, 1976.

The Dawn-Breakers: Nabíl's Narrative of the Early Days of the Bahá'í Revelation. Translated and edited by Shoghi Effendi. Bahá'í Publishing Trust: Wilmette, Illinois, 1932; 1996 edition.

Eminent Bahá'ís in the Time of Bahá'u'lláh. Hasan Balyuzi. George Ronald Publishers: Oxford, England, 1985.

From Mountain to Mountain. Hitjo Garst. George Ronald Publishers: Oxford, England, 1983.

Gleanings from the Writings of Bahá'u'lláh. Bahá'u'lláh. Translated by Shoghi Effendi. Bahá'í Publishing Trust: Wilmette, Illinois, 1952; 1983 edition.

God and His Messengers. David Hofman. George Ronald Publishers: Oxford, England, 1973; 1978 edition.

God and the Universe: Teacher's Guide. Randie Gottlieb. UnityWorks LLC: Yakima, Washington, 2007.

The Báb: Gate to Bahá'u'lláh

God Passes By. Shoghi Effendi. Bahá'í Publishing Trust: Wilmette, Illinois, 1944; 1974 edition.

The Hour of Dawn. Mary Perkins. George Ronald Publishers: Oxford, England, 1976.

Kitáb-i-Aqdas. Bahá'u'lláh. Bahá'í World Centre: Haifa, Israel, 1992.

Kitáb-i-Iqán. Bahá'u'lláh. Translated by Shoghi Effendi. Bahá'í Publishing Trust: Wilmette, Illinois, 1931; 1983 edition.

Letter to the Continental Boards of Counsellors. International Teaching Centre. Bahá'í World Centre: Haifa, Israel, 5 December 1988.

Lights of Guidance: A Bahá'í Reference File. Compiled by Helen Hornby. Bahá'í Publishing Trust: New Delhi, India, 1983; revised 1994.

The Manifestation of God: Teacher's Guide. Randie Gottlieb. UnityWorks LLC: Yakima, Washington, 2008.

Martyr-Prophet of a World Faith. William Sears. Bahá'í Publishing Committee: Wilmette, Illinois, 1950.

Memorials of the Faithful. 'Abdu'l-Bahá. Translated by Marzieh Gail. Bahá'í Publishing Trust: Wilmette, Illinois, 1971.

Messages to the Bahá'í World – 1950-1957. Shoghi Effendi. Bahá'í Publishing Trust: Wilmette, Illinois, 1971 edition.

Mulla Husayn. Lowell Johnson. National Spiritual Assembly of the Bahá'ís of South and West Africa: Johannesburg, 1982.

Nine Holy Days. Jackie Mehrabi. Bahá'í Publishing Trust: London, 1975.

Ocean: Free Software Library of the World's Religious Literature. Developed by Chad Jones. < www.bahai-education.org/ocean >.

Prayers and Meditations. Bahá'u'lláh. Translated by Shoghi Effendi. Bahá'í Publishing Trust: Wilmette, Illinois, 1938; 1987 edition.

The Promulgation of Universal Peace. Talks by 'Abdu'l-Bahá during His visit to the U.S. and Canada in 1912. Bahá'í Publishing Trust: Wilmette, Illinois, 1982 edition.

The Prophets of God. Mahnaz Afshin. Hemkunt Press: New Delhi, India, 1987.

Quddús. Lowell Johnson. National Spiritual Assembly of the Bahá'ís of South and West Africa: Johannesburg, 1982.

Release the Sun. William Sears. Bahá'í Publishing Trust: Wilmette, Illinois, 1960; 1995 printing.

The Revelation of Bahá'u'lláh, vol. 2. Adib Taherzadeh. George Ronald Publishers: Oxford, England, 1977; 1988 edition.

Ridván 2000 Message to the Bahá'ís of the World. The Universal House of Justice. Bahá'í World Centre: Haifa, Israel, 2000.

Ruhi Book 3: Teaching Children's Classes, Grade 1. Ruhi Institute. Palabra Publications: West Palm Beach, Florida, 1995.

Selections from the Writings of 'Abdu'l-Bahá. Translated by a Committee at the Bahá'í World Centre and Marzieh Gail. Bahá'í World Centre: Haifa, Israel, 1978; 1982 printing.

Selections from the Writings of the Báb. Translated by Habíb Taherzadeh with a Committee at the Bahá'í World Centre. Bahá'í World Centre: Haifa, Israel, 1976; 1978 printing.

Shoghi Effendi – Recollections. Ugo Giachery. George Ronald Publishers: Oxford, England, 1973.

Summons of the Lord of Hosts. Bahá'u'lláh. Bahá'í World Centre: Haifa, Israel, 2002.

Tablets of Bahá'u'lláh Revealed after the Kitáb-i-Aqdas. Translated by Habíb Taherzadeh with a Committee at the Bahá'í World Centre. Bahá'í World Centre: Haifa, Israel, 1978.

Táhirih. Lowell Johnson. National Spiritual Assembly of the Bahá'ís of South and West Africa: Johannesburg, 1982.

Táhirih the Pure. Martha Root. Kalimát Press: Los Angeles, 2000.

Thief in the Night: The Case of the Missing Millennium. William Sears. George Ronald Publishers: Oxford, England, 18th reprint, 1992.

Unfolding Destiny of the British Bahá'í Community. Shoghi Effendi. Bahá'í Publishing Trust: London, 1981 edition.

The World Order of Bahá'u'lláh. Selected letters of Shoghi Effendi. Bahá'í Publishing Trust: Wilmette, Illinois, 1938; 1974 rev. ed.; 1982 printing.

WORKS BY THE SAME AUTHOR

www.UnityWorksStore.com

Some books also available from: www.BahaiBookStore.com, (800) 999-9019
and Special Ideas: www.bahairesources.com, (800) 326-1197

Check our website for high-quality, low-cost, easy-to-use Bahá'í resources. Download PowerPoint firesides, Five Year Plan study guides, children's class materials, Bahá'í mini ads, and much more!

Activity Books for Bahá'í Children's Classes

This series of easy-to-use teacher's guides is filled with fun, hands-on, kid-tested learning activities designed for ages 8-12. A useful resource for Bahá'í summer and winter schools, Holy Day programs, academic classes and weekend retreats. The activities were developed and tested in the field, in response to the needs of teachers and children, and have been used successfully in multiple settings over many years. Each book includes detailed lessons, copy-ready student handouts, song sheets, craft instructions and more!

"Your curriculum is the best I've seen to teach kids about the Faith. I love it!! They aren't being taught principles, they are investigating, exploring, and owning the principles."
— **Sue Walker, PhD**

Bahá'í Children's Retreats (A Complete Planning Guide)

Want to plan an unforgettable Bahá'í activity for children ages 8-12, but don't know where to begin? This retreat planning guide covers the following topics:

- Sponsorship, Schedules, Forms
- Teachers, Facility, Finances, Publicity
- Registration, Materials, Menus
- Orientation, Children's Performance
- Outdoor Activities and more!

Also included are medical release forms, recipes, a planning checklist and a graduation certificate—everything you need to organize a successful children's retreat. This planning guide is the perfect companion to the activity books on each theme.

"This retreat was life changing. You feel a renewal of passion for educating children!"
— **Lynn Haug, parent**

Bahá'í Public Speaking (Teacher's Guide with Nine Workshops)

This practical, easy-to-use teacher's guide contains nine hands-on workshops on Bahá'í public speaking. It is designed to equip youth, adults and children with the skills and confidence needed to become more effective teachers of the Faith. Participants will learn to speak with clarity and conviction—from the kitchen table to the conference hall. Be prepared for home visits, devotional meetings, fireside talks, direct teaching campaigns and public discourse. Great for junior youth groups, youth workshops and campus clubs!

This training manual can be used in conjunction with Ruhi Book 6.
It comes complete with copy-ready student handouts. Each lesson includes:

- Warm-up activities
- Speaking tips
- Practice exercises
- Homework assignment

"Fabulous! I'm very glad that you're publishing this, and I hope it is widely circulated!"
– **Erica Toussaint**

Once to Every Man and Nation (Stories About Becoming a Bahá'í)

A great gift for seekers, this book brings together 37 heartwarming stories of how people became Bahá'ís. The contributors to *Once to Every Man and Nation* come from all over North America and represent a wide variety of cultural, racial, social and ethnic backgrounds. Young and old, black and white, each with a different experience of life, their very diversity demonstrates the universal appeal of the Bahá'í teachings.

"Will be enjoyed by many believers...thoroughly recommend it."
– **Bahá'í Reviewing Panel of the United Kingdom**

Bahá'í Mini Ads

Thirty small print ads for use with local media campaigns. The series is designed to complement Bahá'í teaching efforts by creating greater awareness and positive interest in the Faith. It includes basic Bahá'í beliefs and principles, short quotations from the Bahá'í Writings, offers of free literature, an invitation to the core activities, and an invitation to join the Bahá'í community. The file is in Microsoft Word format so it is easy to insert local contact information.

"These will surely boost teaching efforts in all communities that use them!"
– **Dale Eng**

PowerPoint Firesides on the Bahá'í Faith

 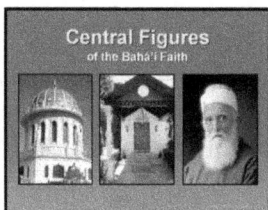 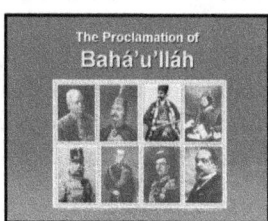 

(1)
**The Bahá'í Faith:
An Introduction***

(2)
**Central Figures
of the Bahá'í Faith**

(3)
**The Proclamation
of Bahá'u'lláh**

(4)
**The Power
of Unity**

These colorful slide shows are designed to introduce the Bahá'í Faith. They offer an overview of the Faith: its Central Figures, purpose, core beliefs and teachings, photographs of its World Center, Houses of Worship, and scenes from Bahá'í community life. The programs have been used to effectively share the Bahá'í teachings in churches, classrooms, public libraries and community firesides.

- Perfect for high school and university students
- Ideal for projecting in large group settings
- Can also be used with a laptop one-on-one

* Also available in Spanish

What People Are Saying

"I don't know if the presentation could have gone any better!...This was one of the most amazing teaching experiences I've ever had!" — **Charisse Johnson, student**

"... a wonderful conclusion to our study of world faiths...it makes for a great end of semester presentation." — **Steve Deligan, high school religion teacher**

"...a fantastic presentation...very understandable...excellent to use for youth."
— **Seth Walker, youth**

"A wonderful trilogy for humans everywhere to learn from." — **Beth Shevin, seeker**

"...a great success tonight in Australia...the Baha'is were very pleased with their professional quality." — **Nancy Watters, traveling teacher**

"...straight-forward...high-quality...a wonderful introduction to the Teachings"
— **Shannon Javid, Regional Bahá'í Council member**

"Very respectful and professional. Job well done!" — **Warren Odess-Gillett**

 **Download from: www.UnityWorksStore.com**

Starting a Bahá'í-Inspired Academic School

This booklet presents basic guidelines and suggestions for those considering the establishment of a Bahá'í-inspired academic school. It provides a useful framework for organizing critical tasks and decisions, utilizing a detailed checklist with hundreds of practical tips.

Escuela de las Naciones (School of the Nations)

Description with color photographs of a Bahá'í-inspired K-6 elementary school established in Puerto Rico in 1991. This monograph provides an overview of the establishment and functioning of the private, non-profit, competency-based school, including the students, facilities, classroom design, curriculum, instructional methods and materials, system of evaluation, schedule, integration of the arts, and service.

Service: Heart of the Curriculum for a Global Civilization

This monograph considers the significance of service to mankind as a central organizing principle for our educational endeavors, and recommends practical strategies for systematically integrating service into the daily life and culture of our schools.

Principles into Practice

Workshop and compilation of Bahá'í Writings on education. This resource is offered as a tool for educators who wish to put Bahá'í principles into practice in their classrooms. Detailed step-by-step instructions for conducting the workshop are presented, and copy-ready student handouts are included. The workshop complements Ruhi Book 3 training and is appropriate for Bahá'ís and friends of the Faith.

Needs Assessment Survey to Determine the Training Requirements of International Bahá'í Traveling Teachers

This doctoral thesis details the training needs of personnel on international service projects. The survey of 200 returned volunteers and Bahá'í Institutions in the 81 countries they visited, was done under the auspices of the U.S. Bahá'í International Goals Committee. The study focuses on cross-cultural communication, critical incidents, training and materials design.

The Báb: Gate to Bahá'u'lláh

List of Activities by Chapter

Opening Activities   **Page**

  1. Unity bingo (ice-breaker) 14
  2. Light dance (ice-breaker) 14
  3. Group singing (instructions, song sheets, musical scores) 149-150, 179-192

Lesson 1: His Birth, Early Life and Station

  1. O God, My God (song) 18
  2. Kingdoms of creation (felt lesson review) 18-19
  3. Preparing the soil of the heart (reading with student questions) 20, 26, 155
  4. Preparing the soil (demonstration) 20
  5. Stories from the life of the Báb (groups read and report) 21-22, 27, 153-161
  6. Peer questions (students ask and answer questions) 22
  7. Birthplace of the Báb (map activity) 23, 28, 162
  8. Quiz on the life of the Báb (quiz) 23, 29, 167
  9. Good news! The Trumpet is sounding! (memory quote) 23-25
  10. The Báb Blew His Trumpet (song) 25

Lesson 2: Declaration of the Báb

  1. Hoy Es el Día (song) 32
  2. Introduction (teacher talk) 32
  3. Spiritual treasure hunt (reading with student questions) 32, 37-38, 163-164
  4. Iran at the time of the Báb (pictures) 33
  5. Feel the force (magnet demonstration) 33-34
  6. Clues to the Báb (group discussion) 34, 39
  7. Awake, awake! (memory quote) 34-35
  8. The Gate of God (craft) 36, 40-50

Lesson 3: Martyrdom of the Báb

  1. Remover of Difficulties (song) 54
  2. Memory quotes (review) 54
  3. Martyrdom of the Báb (reading, questions, bullet demo) 54-55, 59-60, 165-166
  4. Martyrdom of the Báb (small group discussion) 56, 61
  5. Remover of difficulties (memory quote) 56-57
  6. Queen of Carmel (song) 57
  7. A candle for the Báb (play dough craft and coloring page) 57-58, 62-65

Lesson 4: The Primal Point

  1. Song of the Prophets (song) 70

Bahá'í Children's Classes and Retreats: Theme 3, p. 225

2. Memory quotes (review) 70
3. Life of the Báb (review) 70-71
4. The Primal Point (felt lesson) 71, 73-82
5. The Primal Point (worksheet) 71, 83-84
6. 1844 (song) 71
7. The Primal Point (craft) 72, 85-87

Additional Activities

1. Treasure hunt 91-95
2. Outside research project 96-99
3. Jesus and the Báb 100-106
4. Puzzles 107-114
5. Illuminated prayer 115-116
6. Online slide show 117
7. Coloring pages 117, 169-177

Children's Performance

1. Various songs, memory quotes, presentation of crafts 119-145, 149-152
2. Opening prayer (reading) 144
3. Soil of the heart (reading) 26, 155
4. Preparing the soil (demonstration) 124-125
5. Stories about the life and martyrdom of the Báb (short talks) 124, 125, 153-161
6. Treasure in Shiraz (readers' theater) 129-143
7. Quiz show on the life of the Báb (quiz show) 127-128
8. The Primal Point (felt lesson) 125-126
9. Martyrdom of the Báb (story) 125

Music

1. Instructions for group singing 179-181
2. Song sheets 182-183
3. Musical scores 184-192
   A. 1844 185
   B. Hoy Es el Día 186
   C. O God, My God 187
   D. Queen of Carmel 188
   E. Remover of Difficulties 189
   F. Say God Sufficeth 190
   G. Song of the Prophets 191
   H. The Báb Blew His Trumpet 192

Closing and Follow-up Activities 193-196

The Báb: Gate to Bahá'u'lláh – Index

Index of Activities by Category

(Note: Some items are listed in more than one category.)

Arts and Crafts
Page
- A candle for the Báb (play dough sculpting) 57-58, 62-64
- Birthplace of the Báb (map activity) 23, 28, 162
- Coloring pages 117, 169-177
- Illuminated prayer (paper and fabric appliqué) 115-116
- Project presentations (children's performance) 121-123
- Shrine of the Báb (coloring page) 57-58
- The Gate of God (cut and paste) 36, 49-50
- The Gate of God (woodwork) 36, 40-48
- The Primal Point (trace, cut and paste) 72, 85-87

Demonstrations
- Feel the force (magnet demo) 33-34
- Imprisonment and martyrdom of the Báb (750 bullets) 54-55, 59-60, 125, 165-166
- Preparing the soil (*plowing* and *fertilizing* the hearts) 20, 124-125

Dramatizations
- Treasure in Shiraz (readers' theater) 129-143

Felt Lessons
- Kingdoms of creation (review) 18-19
- The Primal Point (role and station of the Báb) 71, 73-82, 125-126

Games and Puzzles
- All puzzles 107-114
  - Cryptogram 112
  - Mazes 107-108
  - Mystery dates 110
  - Number puzzle 111
  - Treasure hunt 91-95
  - Word scramble 113
  - Word search 109
- Puzzle solutions 114

The Báb: Gate to Bahá'u'lláh – Index

Group Discussion, Questions and Answers
Clues to the Báb (group discussion) 34, 39
Imprisonment and martyrdom of the Báb (reading) 54-56, 59-61, 125, 165-166
Jesus and the Báb (comparison) 100-106
Key individuals in the ministry of the Báb (outside research project) 96-99
Peer questions on the life of the Báb (who, what, when…) 22
Preparing the soil of the heart (reading with student questions) 20, 26, 155
Quiz on the life of the Báb (quiz) 23, 29, 127-128, 167
Spiritual treasure hunt (reading with student questions) 32, 37-38, 163-164
Stories from the life of the Báb (reading with questions) 21-22, 27, 124, 153-161

Ice-breakers and Warm-ups
Light dance 14
Unity bingo 14

Memory Quotes and Prayers
All quotations 151-152
    Awake, awake! 34-35
    Good news! The Trumpet is sounding! 23-25
    Remover of difficulties 56-57
Memory quotes (review) 54, 70
Opening prayer (children's performance) 144
Children's performance (recitation) 121-123

Miscellaneous and Audio-Visual
Birthplace of the Báb (map activity) 23, 28, 162
Iran at the time of the Báb (pictures) 33, 51
Online slide show 117

Music
Children's performance 121-123, 129-139, 149-150
Instructions for group singing 179-181
List of songs 184
    1. 1844 .... 71, 185
    2. Hoy Es el Día 32, 186
    3. O God, My God 18, 187
    4. Queen of Carmel 57, 188
    5. Remover of Difficulties 54, 189
    6. Say God Sufficeth 190

Music (continued)

    7. Song of the Prophets 70, 191
    8. The Báb Blew His Trumpet 25, 192
  Musical scores 184-192
  Song sheet 149-150, 182-183

Readings and Stories

  Jesus and the Báb (comparison) 100-106
  Key individuals in the ministry of the Báb (outside research project) 96-99
  Martyrdom of the Báb 54-55, 59-60, 122-125, 165-166
  Preparing the soil of the heart 20, 26, 155
  Spiritual treasure hunt 32, 37-38, 122-124, 163-164
  Stories from the life of the Báb 21-22, 27, 122-124, 153-161
    1. The promise 156
    2. 19th century Persia 157
    3. Birth and early life 158
    4. School days 159
    5. An honest merchant 160
    6. Wife and child 161

Research

  Jesus and the Báb (comparison) 100-106
  Key individuals in the ministry of the Báb (outside research project) 96-99

Review

  Kingdoms of creation (felt lesson) 18-19
  Memory quotes 54, 70
  Nine important facts 71
  Peer questions 71
  Quiz on the life of the Báb 23, 29, 122-123, 127-128, 167
  Three key dates 70
  Who is the Báb? 71

Worksheets

  Birthplace of the Báb (map activity) 23, 28, 162
  Jesus and the Báb (comparison chart) 100-106
  The Primal Point (worksheet) 71, 83-84
  Quiz on the life of the Báb (quiz) 23, 29, 127-128, 167

Music (continued)
    7. Song of the Prophets 70, 191
    8. The Báb Blew His Trumpet 25, 192
  Musical scores 184-192
  Song sheet 149-150, 182-183

Readings and Stories
  Jesus and the Báb (comparison) 100-106
  Key individuals in the ministry of the Báb (outside research project) 96-99
  Martyrdom of the Báb 54-55, 59-60, 122-125, 165-166
  Preparing the soil of the heart 20, 26, 155
  Spiritual treasure hunt 32, 37-38, 122-124, 163-164
  Stories from the life of the Báb 21-22, 27, 122-124, 153-161
    1. The promise 156
    2. 19th century Persia 157
    3. Birth and early life 158
    4. School days 159
    5. An honest merchant 160
    6. Wife and child 161

Research
  Jesus and the Báb (comparison) 100-106
  Key individuals in the ministry of the Báb (outside research project) 96-99

Review
  Kingdoms of creation (felt lesson) 18-19
  Memory quotes 54, 70
  Nine important facts 71
  Peer questions 71
  Quiz on the life of the Báb 23, 29, 122-123, 127-128, 167
  Three key dates 70
  Who is the Báb? 71

Worksheets
  Birthplace of the Báb (map activity) 23, 28, 162
  Jesus and the Báb (comparison chart) 100-106
  The Primal Point (worksheet) 71, 83-84
  Quiz on the life of the Báb (quiz) 23, 29, 127-128, 167

www.ingramcontent.com/pod-product-compliance
Lightning Source LLC
Chambersburg PA
CBHW080538170426

43195CB00016B/2599